Herstories

Ten Autobiographical Narratives
of RLDS Women

Herstories

Ten Autobiographical Narratives
of RLDS Women

Edited by Danny L. Jorgensen and Joni Wilson

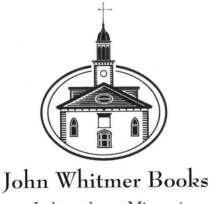

John Whitmer Books

Independence, Missouri

2013

ISBN-13 978-1-934901-33-5

View our complete catalog online at www.JohnWhitmerBooks.com

Learn more about the John Whitmer Historical Association
at www.JWHA.info

PRINTED IN THE UNITED STATES OF AMERICA

Cover, interior design, and typesetting by John C. Hamer
Cover photo: RLDS women in a music club in Independence, Missouri, in 1938.

Dedication &
Acknowledgements

This project was supported in part by grants from the Southern Religion Education Board, Atlanta, Georgia, and the Association for the Sociology of Religion, http://www.sociologyofreligion.com/. The support of the Reorganized Church of Jesus Christ of Latter Day Saints' Women's Ministries and Community of Christ Library–Archives is gratefully acknowledged. In preparing the final manuscript for publication, thanks are owed to Vickie Cleverley Speek for her meticulous efforts editing, to Erin Metcalfe for her careful eye in copy-editing, to John Hamer for his artful skill in design and layout, and to Jan Marshall for overseeing the publication process.

Danny would like to dedicate this work to his mother, Matie F. (Murdock) Jorgensen; his grandmother, Cora May (Jensen) Murdock; and his great-grandmother, (Sylvia) Cordelia "Cordy" (Whiting) Murdock, all of them Reorganized Latter Day Saint women of immense influence in his life.

Contents

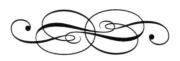

The Challenge of RLDS Herstories:
An Introduction

BY DANNY L. JORGENSEN

A Woman's Prayer

Father, thou hast made us women—
Given us a work to do.
Help us always to be faithful,
Honest, steadfast, ever true.

Help us to uphold the standard
Of thy church and never shirk
Opportunities for service,
But to glorify thy work.

May we oft with gentle fingers
Nurse the sick, caress the child,
Who in faith seeks understanding.
Help us speak in accents mild.

May we deem each task a pleasure
As we strive to serve each day,
And to give thee all honor
As we humbly kneel to pray.

—*Hazel Chambers*

Ten RLDS Women's Narratives

This volume features ten autobiographical narratives presenting the lives and participation of women in the Reorganized Church of Jesus Christ of Latter Day Saints (RLDS) now known as Community of Christ or CofC.[1] Hazel Chamber's prayer, published in the RLDS *Saints' Herald*, is an expression of what it meant to be a woman in 1946.[2] It is but a tiny slice of countless social definitions and images of being a RLDS woman and corresponding *herstories*.[3] This volume is offered as a modest addition to what little is already known about the lives of RLDS women.[4] Their activities, without much recognition or appreciation, have historically sustained this religious organization in a wide variety of ways. It is long past time that the stories of these women–renowned as well as unrecognized–become a part of RLDS history and the story of this new American religion.

These ten oral history interviews and autobiographies are specifically intended to provide renewed opportunities for considering (or reconsidering) the lives of RLDS women, especially the nature and significance of herstories, for scholarly accounts of this religion. It is recommended that attending to these RLDS women's stories commence with the accounts themselves, entailing a very careful reading and—as appropriate—repeated re-readings, looking and listening for how these women frame their experiences and what they tell us about their existence and its meanings. How, for instance, do these RLDS women envision their lives in relationship to religion, family, gender, education, work, and other features of the larger social and cultural world in which they are located existentially? What do they value and regard as meaningful? How and why does this matter for the Latter Day Saint religion, as well as religion in general, in the United States and the world today? Many other questions, aside from these sociologically oriented ones, no doubt will emerge from contemplating the lives and stories of these ten RLDS women and considering what sense and significance is to be made of these materials.

In becoming seriously engaged in these narratives and the innumerably complex issues they raise, the reader is urged to bracket (or suspend), insofar as this is humanly possible, whatever preconceptions she or he may hold for these RLDS women, their lives, their religious participation, and most everything else they discuss. All adequate humanistic studies necessarily begin and proceed from the everyday life experiences and activities of people as defined and enacted by them. For this reason these stories are presented here without much analysis or interpretation, aside from specifying a few theoretical issues and some defining features of the social, cultural, and religious environment in which the lives of these women were located and where they transpired. No special or distinctive claim is being made for these narratives initially, other than that they are authentic accounts by RLDS women about their lives and, as such, deserve our attention and scholarly consideration. Whether or not these cases are common, typical, or representative of the larger population of RLDS women is not an especially relevant issue.

A basic intent of this intellectual exercise—that of vigilantly listening to what these women tell us about their lives and existence—is to use this information, what we may be able to learn from these narratives, as a fresh beginning for contemplating, analyzing, and interpreting the experiences of RLDS women and the history of this religion. Careful reading of these stories is expected to provoke a full range of feelings—from delight, amusement, and joy, to sorrow, anguish, and awe—as well as to promote new ideas, meanings and insights. This project rests on the conviction that while herstories are an indispensable part of the history of this organization of Latter Day Saints and, therefore, also chronicle this new American religion, they have been largely overlooked, neglected, and perhaps even more or less misunderstood. A great deal can surely be said from a variety of intellectual viewpoints—feminist, historical, sociological, psychological, religious or theological, and the like—about the significance of these narratives and those of many other RLDS women. There will be plenty of time and opportunity later, however, after listening to them and fastidiously reflecting about what they are saying to us, to engage in all of the usual human and scholarly meaning-making activities. Those pursuits also necessarily will benefit from recovering and considering many more RLDS herstories.

The Latter Day Saints

The American religion formally organized in April 1830 at Fayette, New York, by Joseph Smith Jr. (1805–44) and a few followers has been a source of creative religious and social change, some of it radical and even revolutionary, from the beginning. It is not widely known that more than a hundred different organizations trace their origins to Joseph Smith and the early Latter Day Saints (1830–44) and, even when this information is available, it is too easily neglected.[5] The majority of these groups are diminutive, many are very small, and some of them no longer exist today. All of these factions are interesting and consequential for comparative purposes and a comprehensive understanding of this religion generally, although only a few of them are relevant to this effort to generate further grounds for an understanding of RLDS women's lives. The Latter Day Saint religion in the United States today is known best by way of its largest organization and, to a much lesser extent, its second-largest organization. Any adequate understanding of the RLDS (and most other manifestations of the Latter Day Saint religion) requires some understanding of how it differs from this religion's principal form.

The largest, most familiar, single organization of this religion is The Church of Jesus Christ of Latter-day Saints (or LDS, known popularly by the nickname "Mormon"). With headquarters at Salt Lake City, Utah, it reported about fourteen million members worldwide in 2010.[6] Utah Mormons comprise about two percent of the United States population. The LDS church is the third-largest form of American Christianity, and one of the five largest US denominations.[7] By the early part of the twentieth century, the Utah Saints had moderated and abandoned many of the more perceptively radical, innovative, and objectionable features of this main variant of the religion. This included theocratic political aspirations, communal economics, and especially polygynous families (involving a man and multiple wives as well as their children), although not its unique salvation theology, grounded in Western esotericism, and associated temple rites.

Community of Christ (formerly the Reorganized Church of Jesus Christ of Latter Day Saints) is the far less recognized and much-smaller, yet second-largest organization deriving from the American prophet Joseph Smith. Headquartered at Independence, Missouri, it has a worldwide membership of about 250,000 people.[8] The Latter Day Saints who formed this collectivity following Joseph Smith's martyrdom in 1844, dissented from many of the more radically innovative features of Mormonism, especially as it developed at Nauvoo, Illinois, in the early 1840s. In 1860, the leadership of this secondary Latter Day Saint organization was accepted and fully embraced by Joseph Smith III, the eldest son of the founding prophet. He directed the Reorganization to a moderate version of the Latter Day Saint religion. Theologically, Smith and the RLDS aimed for a conventional biblical Christianity much like varieties of American Protestantism such as the Methodists.[9]

The Reorganization, for the most part, adamantly opposed multiple wives, and rejected esoteric (secretative) temple rites, theocratic politics, as well as highly concentrated Zionic gatherings and communal economics. It, unlike the LDS, did not prohibit men of color from holding the priesthood, although, the "racial" disposition of the largely white RLDS membership differed little from other Americans.[10] The Reorganization retained the Book of Mormon and other early distinctives of Latter Day Saint restorationism. It, as a dissenting collectivity, placed greater emphasis than the LDS on individualism, congregational autonomy, and the democratic portion of theocratic-democratic governance. The sons and grandson of Joseph Smith III, headed the RLDS until 1996. Breaking with the tradition of a Smith family prophet-president, RLDS leadership was then awarded to W. Grant McMurray (1996–2004) followed by Stephen M. Veazey (2005 to the present).

The historical distinctiveness of the RLDS identity was symbolically constructed around key theological differences with Utah Mormonism, as noted above, reinforced by unique claims to Latter Day Saint legitimacy founded on the special ordination and lineal descent of the prophet-president from Joseph Smith. This collective identity was especially useful for the successful nineteenth-century RLDS strategy of attracting previous members of the early Latter Day Saint movement, particularly those who had not moved west. By the middle of the twentieth century, however, the once highly controversial issues of early Mormon plural marriage, theocratic kingdom building, and communal economics had become little more than vestiges of the previous century. They were reduced mostly to historical talking points and debates among various organizations of the Saints. Not having secretative temple rites, something that had become more sacred than secret anyway, mattered to many RLDS, other Saints, and a few other Americans, although very few of them knew much or cared about Latter Day Saints of any variety. Having a Smith family member as prophet-president was one of a very few historical RLDS distinctives of consequence, and it was more emblematic than critical to the future of the organization, as would be marked by subsequent events.

There is considerable scholarly agreement that the waves of change that would transform the RLDS into the Community of Christ by the beginning of the twentieth-first century peaked in the 1960s following a century of ferment. These changes were accompanied by efforts to appeal to a new audience, principally Americans with no previous exposure to this religion and, especially, Third World peoples, most of whom knew nothing about the Latter Day Saint religion and sometimes little about basic principles of Christianity. They also reflected social and cultural adaptations of the increasingly middle-class, college-educated, professional, urban American membership.

In 1984, the RLDS world conference formally accepted a revelation from Prophet-President Wallace B. Smith—canonized as Doctrine and Covenants section 156—which extended the previously all-male priesthood to women.[11] The extension of priesthood to women might have been, but was not, anchored in historical tradition. A plausible argument can be made that Joseph Smith Jr. awarded priesthood to women at Nauvoo in 1843. Including women in the lay RLDS priesthood, nevertheless, represented a genuinely monumental alteration of traditional gender roles and relationship. Most commentators have seen this transition from the RLDS to CofC as moving in a progressive or liberal direction as postulated by the sociological model whereby "sects" tend to become "denominations." These changes, furthermore, may be seen as a reflection of the modernization of American society, a complex process involving the industrialization, urbanization, rationalization, and individualization of human existence especially in the Western world but also globally.[12]

The ordination of women along with all of the other modifications differentiated the RLDS even further from the early Latter Day Saints and, especially, the Utah Mormon organization. In less than thirty years, RLDS women have achieved substantial equality in the lay priesthood. This transition unquestionably confirms earlier expectations that the church was committed fully to gender equality.[13] Three thousand women had been ordained to the priesthood by 1991.[14] By 1997 there were 5,028 women ministers, which comprised 26 percent of the total priesthood membership of 19,188.[15] There was a slight increase by the next year when 28 percent of active RLDS priesthood members were women; although, only five women, as opposed to 106 men, were full-time paid ministers.[16] Over the twenty-year-period from 1984 to 2004, almost ten thousand women were ordained to the RLDS/CofC priesthood, accounting for more than half of all new clergy.[17]

Women have been ordained to all offices of the priesthood but, most frequently, as priests and elders, much the same as their male counterparts. In 2011, 8,005 women (or about 38 percent) and 12, 633 men (about 61 percent) are serving in the lay Community of Christ priesthood.[18] The proportion of women serving as full-time church appointees in 2004 remained small at only 12 percent of all paid ministers. Many women have served as branch pastors or performed other important leadership roles in local CofC congregations. Community of Christ, nevertheless, still has not addressed the irony of ordaining women to a hierarchical, patriarchal priesthood—as underscored by "patriarchs" being renamed "evangelists"—or the inherent structural limitations of this hierarchy for the larger issues of human equality.[19]

Today women occupy top leadership positions in the Community of Christ's highly centralized and hierarchal world organization at all levels. Becky L. Savage is serving as a counselor to the prophet-president, Stephen M. Veazey, in the supreme three-person leadership group, the First Presidency. By 2010, three female high priests—Linda L. Booth, Susan D. Skoor, and Stassi D. Cramm—were members of the Council of Twelve Apostles, a prime governing and missionary body.[20] Two other women previously served as CofC apostles, Gail E. Mengel (1998–2005) and Mary Jacks Dynes (2002–10). Jane M. Gardner currently is president of the Quorum of High Priests, the highest-ranking body of the hierarchal, lay priesthood.[21] At the present time, or in recent years, additional women have served or are serving in all of the other elite hierarchal leadership entities of the CofC's international headquarters organization, including the presiding bishopric, order of evangelists, presidents of the seventy, and standing high council.

RLDS Herstories

The *herstory* concept derives from feminist critiques during the 1960s of scholarly perspectives that privileged male experiences, activities, roles, and viewpoints over those of females.[22] In a play on words, this difference sometimes contrasts history (his story or his-story) with herstory (her story or her-story). More drastic versions of this argument sometimes held that what people considered "history" was written by men, exclusively from their viewpoints, and only women could correct this oversight and present a uniquely female point of view.[23] Since the 1960s, women increasingly have achieved greater parity with men in most scholarly disciplines, and they have been invaluable in efforts to correct this deficiency in history and many other intellectual pursuits. In most all human studies today, the concern for gender bias is joined with equally significant apprehensions about the exclusion of still other voices and viewpoints, such as those of ethnic minorities and most anyone else who is not part of what the sociologist C. Wright Mills dubbed the "power elite"—the economically and politically dominant white male power structure of America and other Western societies historically.[24]

Herstory, and its variations, is used here purposefully as a captivating means for calling attention to differences in gender perspective. It rejects any contention of male superiority, and it asserts gender equality as a basic human value. This usage of the concept emphasizes the critical importance of attending to multiple views of human existence, especially male and female in this instance, and it cautions against unreflectively privileging one or another voice and viewpoint in all scholarly pursuits concerned with human existence. This usage, however, makes no claim that herstory has been neglected in all cases, or that women and men can not appreciate, empathize, analyze, or interpret the experiences of the other and craft adequate historical interpretations. It thereby represents an unqualified commitment to feminist values devoted to gender equality, indeed human equality in general, to the ultimate benefit of everyone.

Pearl Gardner (1881–1960), a prominent Reorganized Latter Day Saint woman, wrote in 1921 that "The story of this church is history!"[25] Yet, she astutely emphasized: "The history of the church will never be complete until there is written into it the history of its women." Scholarly neglect for women in RLDS history, as Gardner's observations suggest, certainly was not because women lacked consequence or meaning for the story of this organization. Emma Hale Smith Bidamon (1804–79) is an important historical figure in Latter Day Saint history generally and, perhaps, American history too.[26] Controversial, enigmatic, and instrumentally significant for a broad range of events, she was the wife of the founding prophet and the "elect lady" of early Mormonism—mother of the Reorganization's first prophet-president, Joseph Smith III and tremendously influential for the origins, doctrines, and trajectory of the Reorganized church.

The accomplishments of Marietta Hodges Faulconer Walker (1834–1930), although less well-known, also were consummate in RLDS history. "No person," prophet-president Frederick M. Smith observed, "has done more for the development of the work of the Reorganization than has Marietta Walker."[27]

In addition to Emma Smith and Marietta Walker, numerous other highly notable RLDS women—from Eleanor Kearney, Lizzie Ames, Alice Burgess, Gladys Gould, and Alice Edwards, to Kathryn Westwood, Marjorie Troeh, Gail Mengel, Linda Booth, and Becky Savage, for instance—have performed visible and significant roles in the church.[28] Countless other RLDS women, most of them lacking name recognition or celebrity, have made immensely consequential, but much less visible and well known, contributions to the story of this religion. They have supported the priesthood of fathers, husbands, and sons; organized, nurtured, and socialized young people; maintained church budgets, files, and records; visited the elderly, homebound, and sick; directed social activities, authored literature, ministered with music; and performed many other roles vital to the life of the church and its members. While entirely familiar to the membership, these gifts and accomplishments of RLDS/CofC women have been largely taken for granted. Their lives and contributions rarely have been recorded, publicly acknowledged, or esteemed historically.

Nearly forty years after Pearl Gardner's comment about the exclusion of women from the church's history, Paul A. Wellington again found it necessary to note in the foreword to an edited collection of short biographies of RLDS women that "It is to our loss and our shame that we have not done a better job collecting and retaining the information necessary to make a permanent record of the lives of more of our pioneer women."[29] Unfortunately, most of those herstories now have been lost, probably forever.

In June 1993, the RLDS sponsored an "International Conference of Women" in the newly constructed temple at Independence. "About 4,500 women participated," Roger Yarrington, then editor of the publishing division, enthusiastically reported in the church's family magazine, the *Saints' Herald*.[30] "It was an exciting success" he proclaimed, "and has already sent new energy and ideas flowing out to many congregations." Addressing the conference, Grant McMurray of the first presidency acknowledged "that we, the church, have not always treasured you...." And "your stories," he confessed, "have not been known by us." But, he promised: "This day the church receives, embraces, and affirms your story, and the story of all women, past, present, and those yet to come."[31]

Today, however, almost ninety years since Gardner explicitly called it to attention—fifty years since Wellington once again declared it shameful, nearly thirty years since priesthood was extended to women, and approaching twenty years since prophet-president McMurray promised to affirm herstories—there has been far too little progress. The participation and role of women in Community of Christ has changed monumentally, but there still has been precious little effort to tell herstories or write women into the history of the church.[32]

Viewed from the standpoint of the Latter Day Saint religion, generally, the lack of emphasis in the historical literature on RLDS herstories reflects a conundrum. Women are seen as "equal" from the standpoint of the two largest Latter Day Saint organizations. The LDS leadership and priesthood, nevertheless, are exclusively male and hierarchal, thereby raising serious questions about the meaning and practice of genuine equality.[33] The position of the LDS church is that men and women are equal but gender roles are different and separate, a dissimilarity sometimes expressed as "priesthood" and "motherhood." Women may vote and perform a variety of roles in the church—such as preaching, teaching, praying, organizing, and serving as temple workers, as well as missionaries—but men retain ultimate priesthood power and authority politically. Women are encouraged to marry and become homemakers—consistent with an emphasis on family—although, in everyday life, Mormon women do not differ substantially from other Americans. Some Mormon women privately pray to "Mother in Heaven" and quietly continue pressing for extending priesthood offices to women.[34]

While the LDS view of gender explicitly focuses on separate but equal roles, the Community of Christ position seems to be that whatever differences exist between men and women are irrelevant for most gender-role performances. Men and women not only are equal, but the same, when it comes to social roles, other than perhaps those strictly limited by biology such as giving birth. CofC women are not prohibited, in principle, from performing any institutional role, including that of prophet-president. The church takes no position on what other social roles are more or less appropriate for women (or men), and the general view seems to be that women should be encouraged and permitted to do anything men do in the secular society.

Yet, the RLDS/CofC has done little to preserve herstories or write women into the history of the church. The LDS church, on the other hand, has recovered, saved, and encouraged records of women's lives since the 1840s. The newer Mormon history has included LDS women and an emphasis on herstories since at least the 1960s, and there is today an extensive body of high-quality scholarly literature on LDS women's lives.[35]

It also is paradoxical that a substantial amount of RLDS literature is authored by women. They regularly have contributed to church periodicals, including the *Herald* (formerly the *Saints' Herald*, and the *True Latter Day Saints' Herald*, featuring the "Mothers' Home Column" written by and for women), *Zion's Hope, Vision* (previously *Autumn Leaves*), *Stepping Stones, Stride, Daily Bread, Zion's Ensign*, and the *Distaff* (the publication of the women's organization), as well as a wide assortment of other church publications.[36]

Becky Savage provides a useful review of specific portions of this and related church literature devoted to women's lives.[37] Women commonly published in the early *Journal of History* (1908–25), as well as later scholarly oriented sources devoted to the RLDS, including *Courage*, the *John Whitmer Historical Association Journal, Restoration Studies*, and the more general literature on Latter Day Saints. Many other works on RLDS history were authored or edited by women.[38] The most popular RLDS history ever issued is *The Story of the Church* by Inez Smith Davis, published from 1938 to 1985, and reprinted in 1996.[39] Women also authored much of the fiction published by the RLDS church.[40] David Howlett observes that female authors were among the most popular and widely read, and he, therefore, concludes that they were highly influential with the church membership.[41]

The literature directly related to RLDS women's biographies and roles in the church, nevertheless, is modest.[42] RLDS and CofC women have authored theological materials, although much of this literature, until very recently, was produced by men. Theological writings are part of the history of the church, but most of them are not directly relevant to the present concern and emphasis on telling herstories. Much of the published literature by and about RLDS women is intended to be inspirational and faith promoting, rather than critical, analytical, and interpretative, as these activities are ordinarily understood in human studies disciplines. Some of this literature is useful, however, as a part of RLDS women's lives.

Works generally in this genre include: Emma M. Phillips's *33 Women of the Restoration* (Independence, MO: Herald Publishing House, 1960), and *Dedicated to Serve Biographies of 31 Women of the Restoration* (Independence, MO: Herald Publishing House, 1970); Frances Hartman, ed., *Poetic Voices of the Restoration* (Independence, MO: Herald Publishing House, 1961)—predominately, but not exclusively, featuring women's works; Jeannette Nichols, *Her Works Praise Her: A Study Course for Women* (Independence, MO: Herald Publishing House, 1967); Frances Hartman Mulliken's, *First Ladies of the Res-*

toration (Independence, MO: Herald Publishing House, 1985); Naomi Russell's *Profiles* (Independence, MO: Herald Publishing House, 1989), collected from previously published *Herald* interviews—contains almost equal numbers of stories about men and women, along with those of a few couples; and Carol Anderson Anway, ed., *Extending the Call: Testimonies of Ordained Women* (Independence, MO: Herald Publishing House, 1989).

In a similar work, *They Made A Difference* (Independence, MO: Herald Publishing House, 1970), Roy Cheville featured only two women, Emma Smith and Marietta Walker, while presenting twenty-nine RLDS biographies. Stories of two more RLDS women, Velma Ruch and Barbara Higdon, are included in T. Ed Barlow, ed., *Living Saints Witness at Work* (Independence, MO: Herald Publishing House, 1976).

Beatrice Witherspoon: Autobiography of Emma Beatrice Burton (Lamoni, IA: Herald Publishing House, 1915), previously serialized in *Autumn Leaves*, and reprinted in 1970, stands alone in providing a substantial, in-depth, autobiographical telling of the life of an RLDS woman in the published literature. Archival resources on RLDS/CofC women, unlike those on LDS women, are not extensive or substantial. The Community of Christ Library–Archives contains many bits and pieces of information about women's lives, some of it of considerable value for particular purposes, but little extensive autobiographical or biographical information. Highly notable exceptions are two lengthy, richly detailed, and beautifully written autobiographical documents of extraordinary historical importance by Amy E. Burke Robbins (1884–1956), an African American woman, describing her life and participation in the RLDS church, and a set of her poems.[43]

Copies of two of the autobiographies published here, Emma Anderson and Louise Murdock, also are available in the CofC archives.[44] Emma(line) Diamond Christensen's "Things I Remember," also found in the CofC archives, is rare in providing a lengthy, intricate autobiography of an RLDS woman. Beginning in the 1980s, a series of three projects, under the sponsorship of the RLDs Women's Commission, gathered plentiful information about women's lives, the records of which also are in the archives.[45]

The first of these ventures, the RLDS Women's Commission Oral History Project, "Women in the Twentieth Century," aimed to collect the stories of senior women.[46] Local women leaders and other branch members identified prospective candidates who were interviewed by women based on guidelines provided by the women's commission, the principal organization of RLDS women at this time. Few, if any, of the interviewers were trained and some of them exhibited little understanding of the intent of the task. The products, therefore, depended on the interpersonal skills of the person(s) conducting the interview, their understanding of the project, and their ability to convey some sense of its significance, as well as develop rapport with the interviewee when necessary. The results also were influenced by the interviewees' understanding of the task, as well as their opportunity, time, and willingness to participate.

These oral histories, consequently, vary tremendously in quality. Many of them are exceedingly brief and conform too rigidly to the schedule, and most of them generally lack richness and vitality. The corpus of the project fills three loose-leaf binders containing typed transcriptions of about 142 oral interviews. While some of these materials provide useful and valuable information about RLDS women's lives, these oral history interviews were not circulated or published in any form.

The second women's commission project solicited testimonies of women who were among the first to be ordained to the RLDS priesthood (about 1985–86).[47] By 1989, three notebooks containing the testimonies of 204 women had been collected and forwarded to the archives. Fifty-six documents were selected from this project and subsequently published in *Extending the Call*, edited by Carol Anderson Anway (as cited above). These materials are interesting, but their faith-promoting quality and lack of critical attention to a full range of women's experiences severely limits their usefulness for human studies generally.

The third project gathered RLDS women's testimonies pertaining to the revelation (Doctrine and Covenants section 156) which extended priesthood to them.[48] Statements were requested from the membership of the RLDS Women's Ministries Commission, from the period 1972–74, who were asked to seek two additional accounts from other women. The resulting documents, by agreement, were sealed for up to twenty years and not published. Some of them, subsequently, were examined by Lisa Richardson, and the rest were reviewed by Becky Savage who observed that "These 'her stories' need to be shared more widely with their writer's permission, and follow-up stories collected."

Because of the restrictions on this collection it is difficult to know how useful these materials may be for telling, analyzing, and interpreting RLDS herstories. Scholarly works on RLDS women, other than those already cited, include: Judy Ann Gibbs, "A Study of the Status of Mormon and Reorganized Women," senior seminar paper (Graceland College, Independence, MO, May 1973); Nancy Hiles Ishikawa, "Alice Smith Edwards: The Little Princess," *Journal of Mormon History* 6 (1979): 61–74; Harry J. Fielding, "Emma Burton, Spiritual Healer: A Case Study in Cultural Relativity," in *Restoration Studies* 2 (1983): 121–24; L. Madelon Brunson, "Scattered Like Autumn Leaves: Why RLDS Women Organize," *Restoration Studies* 2 (1983): 25–32; Paul M. Edwards, "When Will the Little Woman Come Out of the House?," *John Whitmer Historical Association Journal* 5 (1985): 29–40; Imogene Goodyear's "The Legacy of Early Latter-day Saint Women: A Feminist Critique," *John Whitmer Historical Association Journal* 10 (1990): 21–23; Velma Ruch's "To Magnify Our Calling: A Response to Section 156," in *Restoration Studies* 3 (1986): 97–107; and Patricia Struble's "Mite to the Bishop: RLDS Women's Financial Relationship to the Church," *John Whitmer Historical Association Journal* 6 (1986): 23–32. L. Madelon Brunson's *Bonds of Sisterhood: A History of the RLDS Women's Organization, 1842–1983* (Independence, MO: Herald Publishing House, 1985) is an invaluable scholarly recourse, still without equal.[49] Although they are cited above, it is worth repeating and emphasizing that Rita M. Lester's, "Women in the Reorganized Church of Jesus Christ of Latter-Day Saints," provides an excellent short summary of the scholarly literature on RLDS/CofC women, and Becky Savage's "A Journey Toward the Ordination of Women in the Community of Christ," contributes to the history of priesthood for women.

The two most recent histories of the RLDS church not only reflect professional scholarly standards, they explicitly endeavor to recognize women and value their contributions. Paul M. Edwards mentioned some of the leading women and women's organizations.[50] His history of the church, nevertheless, exhibits a largely traditional approach whereby institutional life is featured, and, as a result, it predominately is a story about prominent men. Richard P. Howard conscientiously included women in both volumes of his history of the RLDS church, devoting one chapter to "expanding the arenas of service for women" and portions of other chapters to honoring women's contributions.[51] In the first volume, Howard spent three chapters examining different philosophies of history. His discussions of history as story, self-understanding, and inclusive vision draw on contemporary images of social history.

In spite of efforts to display the everyday life experiences of RLDS leaders and members, Howard has difficulty integrating them with the story of the institution. The chapter on "some aspects of local church life since 1900," for example, mostly describes formal congregational activities—not the day-to-day lives of the membership. Howard is sensitive to women's issues, but there is no consistent, systematic effort to provide a feminist interpretation of the RLDS tradition.

The Ten Stories

This effort to collect and publish herstories as well as, thereby, to stimulate greater scholarly interest in RLDS women's studies was provoked initially by Louise Minor Murdock, my aunt, who sent me her fascinating autobiography sometime in the late 1980s or early 1990s. Shortly thereafter, while attending the John Whitmer Historical Association (JWHA) meetings at Plano, Illinois, in late September 1991, I responded to a presentation, "The Ethos of Biography," by the noted Mormon historian, Davis Bitton. He stressed the importance of biography for history and especially a need to include the neglected lives and voices of ordinary people. My response sustained Bitton's concerns for studies that included people besides prominent, mostly white men to the exclusion of common folk, especially women, ethic minorities, and other powerless people. I, furthermore, advocated efforts to remediate RLDS history in this way.

During the ensuring group discussion—held in the sanctuary of the historic Plano, Illinois, RLDS meetinghouse—Paul Edwards skeptically questioned whether or not there were sufficient data to successfully pursue such a scholarly enterprise. While attending another professional conference at Kansas City in November 1991, I discussed this matter further with Joni Wilson, a JWHA colleague and friend, and conducted a preliminary search of the RLDS archives for relevant materials. I found the autobiographical account by Emma Diamond Christensen about her turn-of-the-century RLDS missionary life in the South Pacific, but, otherwise, the results were not encouraging. I feared that Edwards's concerns about the availability of appropriate information might be justified.

Even so, I resolved to forge ahead. The *Saints' Herald* ran an advertisement describing my interest in RLDS women's lives and requesting relevant stories. I received a few responses and some potentially useful contacts and materials, but little of special noteworthiness. During the summer of 1992, I was able to research the RLDS archives more extensively and systematically, with the support of two small grants. At Independence, I discussed the project further with Joni Wilson, Paul Edwards, Richard Howard, and various other RLDS officials and friends. Richard Howard, the RLDS church historian, put me into contact with Gail Mengel, the women's ministries commissioner. Among other suggestions, she mentioned an unprocessed collection encompassing three volumes of "Oral Histories of Women Serving the RLDS Church in the Twentieth Century." Gratefully, Commissioner Mengel managed to make these materials available for my review during the middle of the remodeling of her Auditorium office—only two days before the collection was scheduled to be moved to the archives' new temple facility and, therefore, closed for the duration of my Independence research that summer.

The bulk of these approximately 142 oral histories, are skimpy and generally lacking in the kind of in-depth opulence necessary for supplying a thorough portrait of these women's lives. Sixteen of the stories, however, are longer and more adequately descriptive. These accounts sometimes contain religious testimonials, yet all of them describe a wide assortment of everyday life activities. They display a full range of these women's thoughts, feelings, and activities in a wide variety of social situations and settings inside and outside of the RLDS church. There is fitting and representative existential variety in the experiences and activities of these women and their life stories. All of them exhibit a sense of self-worth, some understanding of the merits of the oral history project and history in general, as well as some appreciation for their own story and its location in culture, society, and history. In several cases, these women subsequently edited the oral histories and added new material. Their stories differ in all of these respects from most of this larger set of oral histories.

My attempt to make some of these RLDS herstories more widely available, especially for scholarly review, has been a struggle, and it underscores some of the difficulties with including women in the church's history. In 1993, I submitted a prospectus for the publication of a volume of RLDS women's stories to Roger Yarrington, the Herald House editorial director. The idea is interesting, he wrote in response, but "our experience indicates we would have a hard time recovering our investment on such a book."[52] Yarrington explained that:

> Most of the writers you have chosen are not widely known in the church. I am acquainted with three or four and have the highest regard for them. But the fact remains that we find a limited audience for biographies of even the best-known, historically-important church leaders.

Yarrington's letter did contain an important qualification. "The memoirs you have collected," he observed, "are obviously important to the church and to historical researchers." While there is no disputing that the economic concerns for publishing the volume were legitimate, this experience was exceedingly disappointing and discouraging.

The most valued consultant on this project was my maternal grandmother, Cora Jensen Murdock (1898–1997), who resided during this time at Resthaven (also known as "The Groves," an RLDS retirement facility) in Independence. We talked regularly, interacting almost daily during the summers of 1992 and 1993, while I conducted research in Missouri. She recommended that I add the autobiography of Emma Whiting Anderson—the eldest sister of my great-grandmother (Sylvia) Cordelia Whiting Murdock (1869–1963)—to the collection of RLDS women's stories. Roger Launius had recommended including the autobiographical accounts of Amy E. Robbins, and he provided me with copies of portions of this material. Ultimately, I gathered about twenty especially useful autobiographical accounts of RLDS women: sixteen of the longer oral histories from the Women's Commission Oral History Project; along with the autobiographies of Emma Diamond Christensen, Amy Burke Robbins, Emma Anderson, Louise Murdock, and a few other women.

Joni Wilson collaborated with me from the beginning on this project, talking with other colleagues, brainstorming, speculating, analyzing and interpreting, as well as pondering the importance and possibilities of RLDS women's lives and stories. We eventually picked out ten of the twenty-some stories, and Joni edited and formatted them for publication. Excluded were the autobiographies of Emma Christensen and Amy E. Robbins. The Christensen document is book length and would have required massive editing; and Amy Robbins's story is so unique and significant as to merit a volume of its own.

We included the autobiographies of Emma Anderson and Louise Murdock as two of the most comprehensive documents of appropriate length and content. Then we selected eight of the longer, more-intricate, multifaceted, and richly detailed of the sixteen oral history interviews: The stories of Elsie Townsend, Beatrice Darling, Dorothy Yasaitis, Dorothy Wixom, Enid DeBarthe, Jessie Gamet, Berta Nogel, and Margaret Canham, all came from the RLDS oral history project.[53] This set of ten stories resulted in a manuscript of manageable size and similar, yet appropriately varied content.

Joni and I considered published the stories as part of a book series I edited for Global Publications, while recognizing that this would not place the volume directly before the intended audience. After Global misprinted another volume we edited in 2001, we decided to look elsewhere for a publisher. When the John Whitmer Historical Association started a publication series, we submitted the volume of women's stories described above for consideration, thinking this would be the perfect outlet and audience. JWHA, however, declined interest unless Joni and I were willing to undertake an extensive analysis and interpretation of the stories. I strongly objected, based on the arguments presented in this introduction, for first listening to these women's voices, and the entire project was put aside. We were unable to identify another likely publisher. I figured the project was dead, and dropped it from my research agenda and further publication consideration.

Years later, during the late summer of 2010, Jeanne Murphey contacted me for information about the project and any other information on RLDS women I might be able to supply for the preparation of her presidential address to the JWHA in September. Joni Wilson found an electronic file containing the edited volume of RLDS herstories, and I shared a copy of it with Jeanne, along with a brief overview of the project's history. She expressed tremendous interest in the stories and encouraged John Hamer with John Whitmer Books to consider publication of the volume. The purpose of this account of the difficulties with publishing these stories of RLDS women is not to complain specifically. Instead, it is offered as yet another illustration of some of the obstacles to getting herstories before an appropriate scholarly audience and considered as a part of RLDS history.

All of the RLDS women presented in this book were born in the twentieth century, except for Emma Whiting Anderson (1853–1922), and most lived their lives and died in the twentieth century. Altogether, their lives consequently range chronologically from the earliest days of the Reorganization to the present. Emma's parents, F. Lewis and Ann Janette (Burdick) Whiting, came from families who converted to Mormonism in the early 1830s and resided with the Saints in Ohio, Missouri, and Illinois.[54] Following the martyrdom of Joseph Smith, the Whiting and Burdick families preceded across Iowa with Brigham Young and the largest single body of the Saints. Many of them then joined the schismatic movement headed by Alpheus Cutler.[55]

Emma Whiting Anderson, like most of the Cutlerites and the members of many other schismatic groups remaining in the American Midwest, eventually joined the RLDS.[56] This herstory, consequently, indirectly concerns the first few generations of converts to the Latter Day Saint religion, and, more directly, the first generation of RLDS members. All of the other herstories deal with subsequent generations. Berta Bennett Ruoff Nogel (1920–2010), uncharacteristically, was born into a Utah Mormon family, and she converted as a young woman to the RLDS. Margaret Louise Canham (1922–95), also, was a convert to the Reorganization while the rest of these women were born into RLDS families with at least one parent member.

In addition to Emma Anderson, some of them—like Elsie Andes Doig Townsend (1908–94) and Beatrice Deaver Darling (1910–91)—descended from early converts to the Latter Day Saint religion and formative early Reorganization families. Margaret Canham was Canadian, while all of the other women were born US citizens—a majority of them with Midwestern roots. All of these women were Euro-Americans, although Emma Whiting Anderson, Jessie Marie Carter Gamet (1914–94), and Dorothy Harriet Elkins Wixom (1912–91), all had Native American ancestors.

Eight of these RLDS women were identified by others as important and interesting senior members of local congregations, and the other two, surely, were perceived and regarded in this way, too. Some of these ten women achieved social recognition independently on their own merits, within the larger RLDS community and perhaps the secular society. Elsie Doig Townsend, for instance, was a celebrated RLDS fiction author. Louise Minor Murdock (1916–2009) was party to her parents' Zionic experiment with sheep ranching in the Ozarks, a public schoolteacher, a superintendent of public schools in Washington state, and part of a pioneer family farming operation in Brazil, among many other fascinating activities and occupations. Some of them, like many American women for generations, were known best as wives and mothers, whose gifts and talents supported men and the church. Beatrice Darling, for instance, was a talented musician, as well as the wife of a RLDS church appointee, whom she converted. Descendents of a majority of these RLDS women are active members of Community of Christ today.

The RLDS women featured in this volume, like most people, were not famous, and it is unlikely that they will receive much mention in the history of the institutional church. None of them were ordained to the RLDS priesthood. Their stories tell about mostly ordinary people doing routine, although sometimes quite extraordinary things. With and without social acknowledgement and recognition, all of them were RLDS women of remarkable accomplishments. Most of these women are not typical or average in many ways. As a whole, they probably are not entirely representative of even North American RLDS women. No matter, their stories are authentic accounts of RLDS women—they merit being heard, and these narratives are a rightful part of the history of the church and human existence.

These RLDS herstories, generally, are about people, who, because of their gender, were largely limited to highly traditional and substantially restricted roles in everyday life and church affairs. Mostly, these women performed their proscribed roles without complaint. They mothered and taught the children of the church. They performed music and discovered many other ways to contribute, notwithstanding severe restrictions on what they were permitted to give. They supported the priesthood of fathers, husbands, sons, and other male members. While they did all of these things and more, mostly without complaint, a careful reading of their stories sometimes reveals an underlying dissatisfaction with traditional gender role expectations. They occasionally express disappointment at not being permitted to contribute in other ways, and they inform us—to the extent that we are listening—about the damages to the selves and identities of the sisters that have resulted from these restrictions. Yet, significantly, they tell about the RLDS women's highly creative efforts to transcend these limitations, usually without upsetting or challenging patriarchy.

The Challenge

Making these stories of RLDS women available for consideration is intended to challenge scholars to consider and reconsider the meaning and significance of these lives for the history of this organization, the larger Latter Day Saint religion, as well as religion in North America and the world today. Some of the reasons for this scholarly predicament—of having neglected RLDS herstories—are apparent and informative. In the past, human studies were thought to be mostly about famous people—highly remarkable, major events, featuring men but rarely women, at least in the Western world. This viewpoint was influenced heavily by the Western cultural imagery defining the basic gender institutions for everyone—men and women.[57]

In earliest Euro-American society, women generally were envisioned as the dangerously sinful daughters of Eve—weak, dependent, and, in most all ways, inferior to men, with little to no place outside of their functions of biological reproduction, caring for and raising children, and providing the comforts of home to men.[58] They were responsible for their own salvation but otherwise completely subservient to the social authority of men. This exceedingly negative image of women subsequently was inverted by the Victorian definition of women, characteristic of early Mormonism, as innately pure, good, and moral, as well as especially religious, compliant, dutiful, and nurturing—as captured by the notion of the "cult of true womanhood."[59]

Women's roles in the nineteenth century still were circumscribed by the home and private sphere. While women's participation in public life still was severely limited, American religion increasingly was feminized, and women, thereby, found new opportunity, outside of the private sphere, in religious organizations. Following the American Civil War women agitated more urgently for the right to vote and participate more equitably with men in the public sphere, and by the early portion of the twentieth century their role possibilities had expanded. The Second World War required many more women to work outside of the home in a diversity of occupations, and by the 1960s American women were demanding and acquiring many more equal gender rights and roles.

Reflections of all of these basic American gender institutions, past to present, may be found in contemporary representatives of American religion. Women are being ordained clergy in some denominations, especially those originating in the United States, but this issue remains contested in many denominations—a majority of which prohibit women from being ordained leaders and otherwise limit women's roles in religion and everyday life. The Latter Day Saint religion generally stands somewhere in the middle. LDS gender images and institutions are located toward the conservative—but not ultra-conservative—end. Community of Christ stands toward the more progressive—but hardly radical—end.

The much-larger size and greater resources of the LDS enabled them to invest more in preserving the history of women. The LDS, unlike the RLDS, strongly supported the early Mormon practice of both men and women maintaining diaries and journals. The LDS church sustains a powerful conviction that the Restoration is a monumentally significant historical event and a belief that it is legitimated by religious and secular history. The larger size and greater visibility of the LDS has resulted in correspondingly more interest among scholars of all varieties in Mormon history inclusive of women's lives. This interest has been reinforced by strong public and scholarly concerns for Mormon plural marriage, necessitating a special interest in herstories. All of these factors combined help account for the rather rich and extensive scholarly literature on Mormon women and their lives.

The RLDS/CofC has worked with much more limited resources for preserving and telling herstories. No serious effort was directed to maintaining personal narratives, except perhaps of major male leaders, as opposed to the basic story of the institution. This organization has grown increasingly ambivalent about the uniqueness of Latter Day Saint history for sustaining faith and theology. Community of Christ finally has abandoned all such claims. History therefore has become a sideline rather than a centrally important matter as it is for the LDS. CofC is recreating a Protestant-like theology that requires little to no history, even if it might benefit from an appreciation of historical interpretations. Herstories consequently have gone wanting for attention even while RLDS/CofC women have achieved equality with men organizationally. When Community of Christ has felt a need for herstories, they have been envisioned mostly as faith journeys, not more comprehensive autobiographies, biographies, or other serious scholarly efforts engaged in or encouraged in RLDS women's studies.

Although some of the reasons for the neglect of RLDS herstories are understandable, this situation still is unfortunate. It is especially distressing for those of us who think that RLDS/CofC story necessarily is a part of the history of the Latter Day Saint religion, and American religion. History need not be a central feature of Community of Christ, but it is not irrelevant. It remains significant for the collective identity of the organization and its membership as well as their location in the larger social, cultural, and historical world of human affairs. Some awareness of these matters is a potentially important source of insight into present and further decisions about policies and goals. Human studies are different from religious belief and practice. They are mostly independent enterprises grounded in different methods, issues, and goals; but, they are not incompatible.

In examining the historical features of RLDS women's ordination, Becky Savage identifies a series of issues for further consideration, one of which is developing means appropriate for capturing the histories of women.[60] She observes correctly that: "The women who were pioneers in the change toward a more inclusive church are dying and their history is being lost." Savage recommends a program for training people to conduct oral histories, the development of an interview schedule, transcribing the results, and making them accessible for future use. These are modest suggestions and much more needs to be done.

In addition to collecting the stories of senior members, Community of Christ could encourage the membership to maintain a record of life and its activities. It could make history and human studies a greater priority and devote greater resources to the operations of the church historian and archives. It could encourage and fund these activities at Graceland University and other educational facilities, and it could fund scholarships to support students pursuing appropriate areas of study.

Crafting inclusive histories of the Reorganization will require more than simply adding information about women and their activities to the existing stories of the church. Herstories, like his-stories, reflect distinctive, existentially grounded perspectives whereby the meaning of human experience is symbolically defined. Stories and accounts about women are useful, but necessarily secondary to women's presentations of their lives and experiences. Writing women into their rightful, vital place in the history of the Reorganization, therefore, requires sensitive, empathetic attention to how women have symbolically defined and expressed what their experiences mean to them. Telling women's lives, in other words, involves listening to and hearing women's voices.

To hear their voices is to discover a rich and impressive world of human experience of monumental significance for understanding the past and acting in the present. In reading herstories, I have been astounded, again and again, at the many ways in which women have been required to negotiate, constantly and creatively, with men to achieve an existentially meaningful existence for themselves and others. Herstories remind us that the meanings and values of human existence are emotional and rational. History, understood as narratives of the past, is about the extraordinary and exceptional, but it also about the mundane, routine, and ordinary. The drama of human existence is profoundly social, and intricately interconnected. The drama of our collective existence will remain forever incomplete and incomprehensible unless we listen to and learn what the experiences and lives of women have to teach us about ourselves and all of human existence.

The challenge of this presentation of ten RLDS herstories in short is to: (1) listen carefully to these voices, empathize with their experiences, feel their joys and sorrows, and hear the definitions and meanings they ascribe to their experiences and activities; (2) use the many methodologies and perspectives available in human studies to analyze, critically consider, and interpret these narratives; (3) take what hopefully will be new interpretative insights into these stories as a basis for building a serious program for further studies of RLDS women's lives and writing herstories into the history of the Reorganization, the Latter Day Saint religion, the American religious experience, and the history of humanity generally.

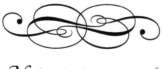

Notes to pages 1–26

1. In April 2001, the Reorganized Church of Jesus Christ of Latter Day Saints changed its given name to Community of Christ. When referring to events transpiring after 2001, the designation Community of Christ will be used while the RLDS name will be retained when referring to previous historical events.
2. Hazel Chambers, "A Woman's Prayer," *Saints' Herald* 93, no. 21 (May 25, 1946), reprinted in Frances Hartman, ed., *Poetic Voices of the Restoration* (Independence, MO: Herald Publishing House, 1961), 89–90.

3. The term *herstory* is sometimes credited to Robin Morgan, ed., *Sisterhood Is Powerful* (New York: Random House, 1970), among other possible sources of origin. In the area of religion, Barbara J. MacHaffie's *Her Story: Women in Christian Tradition* (Philadelphia, PA: Fortress Press, 1986) has been influential.

4. See Rita M. Lester, "Women in the Reorganized Church of Jesus Christ of Latter–Day Saints," in Rosemary Skinner Keller, Rosemary Radford Ruether, and Marie Cantlon, eds., *Encyclopedia of Women and Religion in America* (Bloomington: Indiana University Press, 2006), 728–32, for an excellent summary of the scholarly literature on RLDS/CofC women.

5. Steven L. Shields, *Divergent Paths of the Restoration* (Los Angeles: Restoration Research, 1990).

6. *Church Almanac*, (Salt Lake City: Deseret Morning News, 2010).

7. "Largest Religious Groups in the United States of America," *Adherents.com*, http://www.adherents.com/rel_USA.html#Pew_branches, accessed on December 23, 2010.

8. "Worldwide Membership" under "Our Community," Community of Christ website, http://www.cofchrist.org/news/GeneralInfo.asp, hard copy in possession of author.

9. This probably was not merely coincidental since Young Joseph was raised by his mother, Emma, formerly a Methodist, and ultimately an opponent of plural marriage and its connection to other more radical features of the Nauvoo form of this religion. See Linda King Newell and Valeen Tippetts Avery, *Mormon Enigma: Emma Hale Smith Prophet's Wife, "Elect Lady," Polygamy's Foe, 1804–1879* (Garden City, NY: Doubleday and Company, 1984).

10. Roger D. Launius, *Invisible Saints: A History of Black Americans in the Reorganized Church* (Independence, MO: Herald Publishing House, 1988), especially pp. 111–164.

11. Doctrine and Covenants, RLDS ed. (Independence, MO: Herald Publishing House, 2010).

12. Danny L. Jorgensen, "The Challenge of Modernity for the Reorganized Latter Day Saint Religion Today: An Introduction," ed. Danny L. Jorgensen and Joni Wilson, *Religion and the Challenge of Modernity: The Reorganized Church of Jesus Christ of Latter Day Saints in the United States Today* (Binghamton, NY: Global Publications, 2001), 1–24; and Danny L. Jorgensen, "Modernity and the Reorganization: Prospects for the Future," in Jorgensen and Wilson, *Religion and the Challenge of Modernity*, 135–56.

13. Danny L. Jorgensen, "RLDS Women's Lives: Less Known and Historically Unimportant?" *Restoration Studies* 7 (1998): 63–72.

14. Paul M. Edwards, *Our Legacy of Faith: A Brief History of the Reorganized Church of Jesus Christ of Latter Day Saints* (Independence, MO: Herald Publishing House, 1991).

15. Christina Davis, "Feminism and the 'Cause of Zion'": Becoming a More Inclusive Church," in *Restoration Studies* 8 (2000): 101–108, especially p. 104.

16. George N. Walton, "Statistical Trends in the RLDS Church: 1940–1997," *Restoration Studies* 8 (2000): 26–38, especially p. 37n13, quoting data from *Saints' Herald* 144, no. 5 (May 1997): 209.

17. Becky L. Savage, "A Journey Toward the Ordination of Women in Community of Christ: A Historical Literature Review," (master's thesis, Graceland College, Independence, MO, 2005), 142. During this period, according to Savage, "There were 18,093 ordinations … 52 percent, or 9,909, of these were women, while 48 percent, or 9184, were men."

18. Community of Christ, membership records, January 5, 2011.

19. L. Madelon Brunson, "Stranger in a Strange Land: A Personal Response to the 1984 Document," Restoration Studies 3 (1986): 108–15. Also see Jorgensen, "RLDS Women's Lives," 63; and Davis, "Feminism and the 'Cause of Zion,'" 104.

20. "Councils, Quorums, and Orders," Community of Christ website, http://www.cofchrist.org/directory/councils_quorums_and_orders.asp, accessed December 8, 2010.

21. The Latter Day Saint priesthood is represented by a lesser Aaronic order with offices of deacon, teacher, and priest in rank order, and a greater Melchizedek order of elders and high priests in rank order.

22. See note 3.

23. See Christina Hoff Sommers, *Who Stole Feminism?: How Women Have Betrayed Women* (New York: Touchstone, 1995), for a critique of this line of argument.

24. C. Wright Mills, *The Power Elite and the State: How Policy is Made in America* (New York: Oxford University Press, 1956), coined the term "power elite" in identifying a minute male minority disproportionately controlling the bulk of decision making power (based on wealth and privilege) in the United States and the world, well before this concern for such bias became widespread in scholarly circles.

25. Pearl Gardner, "Women's Department," *Saints' Herald* 68, no. 36 (September 6, 1921): 856. For a brief biography of Gardner, see Emma M. Phillips, *33 Women of the Restoration* (Independence, MO: Herald Publishing House, 1960), 168–72.

26. Newell and Avery, *Mormon Enigma*. Also see Don Compier, "The Faith of Emma Smith," *John Whitmer Historical Association Journal* 6 (1986): 64–72; and Joni Wilson, "Emma's Enduring Compassion: A Personal Reflection," *John Whitmer Historical Association Journal* 19 (1999): 43–62.

27. Phillips, *33 Women of the Restoration*, 38. In spite of this brief biography and considerable material available about the life of Marietta Walker, most of the story of her life remains unpublished.

28. See L. Madelon Brunson, "Precedents Lost: A History of the RLDS Women's Organization, 1842–1974," (master's thesis, University of Missouri–Kansas City, 1981); L. Madelon Brunson, *Bonds of Sisterhood: A History of the RLDS Women's Organization, 1842–1983* (Independence, MO: Herald Publishing House, 1985); Savage, "A Journey toward the Ordination of Women in Community of Christ."

29. Paul A. Wellington, "Foreword," in Phillips, *33 Women of the Restoration*, unnumbered (p. 7).

30. Roger Yarrington, "It's Happening!" *Saints' Herald* 140, no. 9 (September 1993): 3.

31. W. Grant McMurray, "Woven into One," *Saints' Herald* 140, no. 9 (September 1993): 11.

32. Jeanne Murphey, "2010 Address: From Emma to the First Presidency: Women in the Community of Christ History," *John Whitmer Historical Association Journal* 31, no. 1 (Spring/Summer 2011): 1–15.

33. Marie Cornwall, "The Institutional Role of Mormon Women," in *Contemporary Mormonism: Social Science Perspectives,* ed., Marie Cornwall, Tem B. Heaton, and Lawrence A. Young (Urbana: University of Illinois Press, 1994), 239–64; Claudia L. Bushman, *Contemporary Mormonism: Latter-Day Saints in Modern America* (West Port, CT: Praeger, 2006), 111–29.

34. See Linda P. Wilcox, "The Concept of a Mother in Heaven," in *Women and Authority: Re-emerging Mormon Feminism,* ed., Maxine Hanks (Salt Lake City: Signature Books, 1992), 3–22.

35. See Todd Compton, "The New Mormon Women's History," in *Excavating Mormon Pasts: The New Historiography of the Last Half Century,* ed. Newell G. Bringhurst and Lavina Fielding Anderson (Salt Lake City: Greg Kofford Books, 2004), 273–302; and

Newell G. Bringhurst, "Mormon Biography: Paradoxes, Progress, and Continuing Problems," Bringhurst and Anderson, *Excavating Mormon Pasts*, 323–25.

36. See Sara Hallier, "RLDS Periodicals—Past and Present," *Saints' Herald* 130, no. 1 (January 1, 1983): 20–22, for a survey of these publications.

37. Savage, "A Journey Toward the Ordination of Women in the Community of Christ," 111–38. See, for example, Lucy Mack Smith, *Biographical Sketches of Joseph Smith the Prophet and His Progenitors for Many Generations* (Lamoni, IA: The Reorganized Church of Jesus Christ of Latter Day Saints, 1912; Independence, MO: Herald Publishing House, 1969); Ruth C. Smith, *Concerning the Prophet Fredrick Madison Smith* (Kansas City, MO: Burton Publishing Company, 1924); Mary Audentia Smith Anderson, ed., *Joseph Smith 1832–1914: A Centennial Tribute* (Independence, MO: Herald Publishing House, 1932); Mary Audentia Smith Anderson, ed., *The Memoirs of President Joseph Smith III (1832–1914)* (Independence, MO: Herald Publishing, 1979), reprinted from the *Saints' Herald*, 1934–37; Mary Audentia Smith Anderson, *Ancestry and Posterity of Joseph Smith and Emma Hale* (Independence, MO: Herald Publishing House, 1929); Vida E. Smith, *The Young People's History of the Church* (Lamoni, IA: Herald Publishing House, 1918); Mabel Adelina Sanford, *Joseph's City Beautiful: A Story of "Old Nauvoo" on the Mississippi* (Independence, MO: Herald Publishing House, 1939); Frances Hartman Mulliken, *A Restoration Heritage* (Independence, MO: Herald Publishing House, 1979); Pearl Wilcox, *Latter Day Saints on the Missouri Frontier* (Independence, MO: privately printed, 1972); Pearl Wilcox, *Saints of the Reorganization in Missouri* (Independence, MO: privately printed, 1974); Pearl Wilcox, *Regathering of the Scattered Saints in Wisconsin and Illinois* (Independence, MO: privately printed, 1984), Pearl Wilcox, *Roots of the Reorganized Latter Day Saints in Southern Iowa* (Independence, MO: privately printed, 1989); Carol Braby, *Heritage and Hope* (Independence, MO: Herald Publishing House, 1984).

39. Inez Smith Davis, *The Story of the Church: A History of the Church of Jesus Christ of Latter Day Saints, and of Its Legal Successor, the Reorganized Church of Jesus Christ of Latter Day Saints* (Independence, MO: Herald Publishing House, 1938; Independence, MO: Price Publishing Company, 1996).

40. See, for instance, Paula Brown (pseudonym), *The Mormon Girl* (Lamoni, IA: Herald Publishing House, 1912); Jessie Ward, *The Call at Evening* (Lamoni, IA: Herald Publishing House, 1920); Gladys Mae Walter, *The Solid Rock* (Independence, MO: Herald Publishing House, 1941); Elva Teresa Oakman and Lillie Jennings, *It Can Be Fun! Religious Games for Young and Old* (Independence, MO: Herald Publishing House, 1948); Biloine Whiting and Josephine Skelton, *North of Heaven* (Independence, MO: Herald Publishing House, 1948); Madelyn Galbraith, *Feather in the Wind, A Novel* (Independence, MO: Herald Publishing House, 1952); Madelyn Galbraith, *Village in the Sun* (Independence, MO: Herald Publishing House, 1975); Margaret Wilson Gipson, *Emma Smith: The Elect Lady; A Novel Based on Her Life* (Independence, MO: Herald Publishing, 1954); Louise Scott Wrigley, *Play Poems; A Group of Thirty-four Short Poems Suited to Actions for the Nursery and Kindergarten Children* (Independence, MO: Herald Publishing House, 1955); Louise Scott Wrigley, *God is Love* (Independence, MO: Herald Publishing House, 1955); Louise Scott Wrigley, *Stand Tall* (Independence, MO: Herald Publishing House, 1961); Louise Scott Wrigley, *Your Right to Radiance* (Independence, MO: Herald Publishing House, 1961); Louise Scott Wrigley, *Look Up Heart* (Independence, MO: Herald Publishing House, 1962); Louise Scott Wrigley, *A Woman Searches* (Independence, MO: Herald Publishing House, 1966); Addie Spaulding Stowell, *The Walls of Zion* (Independence, MO: Herald Publishing House, 1953); Naomi Russell,

Once upon a Christmas Eve, and Four other Continuity Scripts that present the Christmas Story in Song (Independence, MO: Herald Publishing House, 1958); Naomi Russell, *Discovery: A Collection of Poetry* (Independence, MO: Herald Publishing House, 1976); Ruby Tinkham, *The Unwilling Saint* (Independence, MO: Herald Publishing House, 1959); Jo Montgomery [Josephine Skelton], *The Quiet Miracle* (Independence, MO: Herald Publishing House, 1962); Olive D. Church, *A Time of Rebellion: A Novel* (Herald Publishing House, 1968); Edith Brockway, *The Golden Land* (Independence, MO: Herald Publishing House, 1968); Mildred B. Grenier, *How Big is the Sky?* (Independence, MO: Herald Publishing House, 1968); Elsie Doig Townsend, *None To Give Away* (Independence, MO: Herald Publishing House, 1970); Elsie Doig Townsend, *Always the Frontier* (Independence, MO: Herald Publishing House, 1972); Elsie Doig Townsend, *If You Would Learn … Go Teach* (Independence, MO: Herald Publishing House, 1973); Lucille Oliver, *The Crystal Mountain* (Independence, MO: Herald Publishing House, 1974); Elaine Stienon, *Lightning in the Fog: A Novel* (Independence, MO: Herald Publishing House, 1977); Elaine Stienon, *Utah Spring* (Independence, MO: Herald Publishing House, 1979); Ruth Ann, *Miracle of the Tulips* (Independence, MO: Herald Publishing House, 1980); Colleen L. Reece, *The Ninety and Nine* (Independence, MO: Herald Publishing House, 1984); and Evelyn Maples, *Endnotes: Poems* (Independence, MO: Herald Publishing House, 1989).

41. David Howlett, "The Body of Zion: Community, Human Bodies, and Eschatological Futures among the Reorganized Latter Day Saints, 1908–1934," (master's thesis, University of Missouri–Kansas City, 2004); and David Howlett, "Zion as Fiction: Gender, Early RLDS Novels, and the Politics of Place," *John Whitmer Historical Association Journal* 25 (2005): 93–106.

42. See Danny L. Jorgensen, "Sisters' Lives, Sisters' Voices: Neglected RLDS Herstories," *John Whitmer Historical Association Journal*, 17 (1997): 25–42. Savage, "A Journey Toward the Ordination of Women in Community of Christ"; Lester, "Women in the Reorganized Church of Jesus Christ of Latter Day Saints," 728–32; and Jeanne Murphey, "From Emma to the First Presidency."

43. "Just Amy, Autobiography; My Experiences as a Negro in the Battle Creek Branch of the Reorganized Church of Jesus Christ of Latter Day Saints," P101, f88, (miscellaneous collection) and "Amy's Poems," all found in the Community of Christ Archives, Independence, Missouri. My copy of "My Experiences as a Negro in the Battle Creek Branch of the Reorganized Church of Jesus Christ of Latter Day Saints" was provided by Roger D. Launius after I was denied a copy of this document by the archives. Also see Roger D. Launius, "A Black Woman in A White Man's Church: Amy E. Robbins and the Reorganization," *Journal of Mormon History* 19, no. 2 (Fall 1993): 64–85.

44. My copy of the autobiography of Emma Anderson is from family sources since she is my great-grandmother's eldest sister, but, it is identical to the copy in the CofC archives. Louis Murdock, my aunt by way of her marriage to my mother's eldest brother, sent me her autobiography, and I encouraged her to share a copy with the archives.

45. See Savage, "A Journey Toward the Ordination of Women in the Community of Christ," 139–41.

46. RG24-3 f23–35, Community of Christ Archives. This set of materials includes typescripts and cassette tapes, as well as thirty-five folders in three gray document boxes. Some of my description below is based on reviewing these materials before they were processed and packaged, as noted above.

47. RG24-3 f1–22, Community of Christ Archives; also see Savage, "A Journey Toward the Ordination of Women in the Community of Christ," 139–40.

48. See Savage, "A Journey Toward the Ordination of Women in the Community of Christ," 140–41.

49. Also see Brunson, "Precedents Lost."

50. Edwards, *Our Legacy of Faith.*

51. Richard P. Howard, *The Church Through the Years: Volume 2, The Reorganization Comes of Age, 1860–1992* (Independence, MO: Herald Publishing House, 1993), and Richard P. Howard, *The Church Through the Years: Volume 1: RLDS Beginnings, to 1860* (Independence, MO: Herald Publishing House, 1992).

52. Roger Yarrington to Danny L. Jorgensen, 17 June 1993, copy in my possession.

53. These oral history interviews are used here with the permission of Gail Mengel, women's ministries commissioner for Community of Christ.

54. Jorgensen, "Sisters Lives, Sisters' Voices," 31–37.

55. See Danny L. Jorgensen, "Cutler's Camp at the Big Grove on Silver Creek: A Mormon Settlement in Iowa, 1847–1853," *Nauvoo Journal* 9, no. 2 (Fall 1997): 39–51; and Jorgensen, "Conflict in the Camps of Israel: The Emergence of the 1853 Cutlerite Schism," *Journal of Mormon History* 21, no. 1 (Spring 1995): 24–62.

56. See Danny L. Jorgensen, "The Scattered Saints of Southwestern Iowa: Cutlerite–Josephite Conflict and Rivalry, 1855–1865," *John Whitmer Historical Association Journal* 13 (1993): 80–97.

57. Emile Durkheim, *The Elementary Forms of the Religious Life*, trans. Joseph Ward Swain (New York: Free Press, 1915); Peter L. Berger, *The Sacred Canopy: Elements of a Sociological Theory of Religion* (New York: Doubleday, 1967), especially pp. 3–52; and Mary Douglas, *How Institutions Think* (New York: Syracuse University Press, 1986).

58. See Laurel Thatcher Ulrich, *Good Wives: Image and Reality in the Lives of Women in Northern New England, 1650–1750* (New York: Oxford University Press, 1982); Mary P. Ryan, *Womanhood in America from Colonial Times to the Present* (New York: Franklin Watts, 1983); Elizabeth Fox-Genovese, "Religion and Women in America," in *World Religions in America*, ed. Jacob Neusner (Louisville, KY: Westminster John Knox Press, 1994), 222–33.

59. Barbara Welter, "The Cult of True Womanhood, 1820–1860," *American Quarterly* 18 (Summer 1966): 151–74. Also see Danny L. Jorgensen, "The Mormon Gender–Inclusive Image of God," *Journal of Mormon History* 27, no. 1 (Spring 2001): 95–126, especially pp. 109–15.

60. Savage, "A Journey Toward the Ordination of Women in the Community of Christ," 190.

Emma Locine Whiting Anderson

BORN
March 8, 1853, Silver Creek, Iowa
DIED
June 10, 1922, Independence, Missouri

"We all are here of what we meet
To make the very best,
And run the race, with patience,
Till we enter into rest."

Bemidji, Minnesota
February 24, 1915

Dear Children,

I have had for years, a selfish desire to write my autobiography not with any thought of its ever being printed; it could never be interesting enough to any one for that. So the desire must be a purely selfish one because I could always find something else to do if I would. I began writing it in the rough (that is on wrapping paper or any old paper), about two years ago before my dear husband had left us a year, so I copy from that.

I was born at Silver Creek, Mills County, Iowa, March 8th, 1853. My father's name was Francis Lewis Whiting. He was born in Ohio, September 22, 1830. He died at Clitherall, Minnesota, September 11, 1909. His parents were Elisha Whiting and Sallie (Hewlett) Whiting. My father was the youngest of twelve children whose names were William, Edwin, Charles, Louisa, Harriet, Emeline, Chancey, Almon, Jane, and a babe not named, Frances, Sylvester, and Lewis.

My father was married to my mother on February 12, 1852 at Silver Creek, Iowa. Her maiden name was Ann Janette Burdick. She was born in the state of New York, February 19, 1831. Her parents were Gary Burdick, born September 1, 1794, died January 4, 1854, and Mary (Baker) Burdick, born February 16, 1801, died March 24, 1872 at Clitherall, Minnesota. Of her parents I know nothing, except that their names were Baker. Her only brother was called Henry Baker. He and his wife had a large family of children. One daughter Sylvia married a Mr. Dailey of New York. Two daughters were called Janette and Katy.

My mother was the third child of Gary and Mary (called Polly) Burdick. Their children were Oscar, Jackson, Ann Janette, and Jesse. My Uncle Oscar enlisted with the Wisconsin Volunteers in the Civil War and was killed in the first battle. Jackson Burdick died at Independence, Missouri, about the year 1890, leaving his wife and eight children. Uncle Jesse died at Cheney, Washington, in August 1913, leaving his wife and four children. My mother is still alive at eighty-four years of age.

My grandfather Elisha Whiting was one of the younger children of a large family. His father died, and Elisha was bound out to a man to be provided for and educated, and learn a trade. The education was very limited in those days. The trade was wagon and chair making. Grandfather and Grandmother Whiting were made acquainted with the Restoration of the Gospel in the early days of the church, 1830s or there about. My grandmother was the first to unite with the Church of Jesus Christ of Latter Day Saints. Grandfather had listened with interest and had not objected when his wife wished to be baptized. But not starting out in obedience to the gospel when first led to believe, he afterwards allowed the daily lives of some who were "called to be Saints" but had not yet overcome all evil, to hinder him.

I call to mind now, an expression of Brother J. J. Cornish lately in a sermon, concerning our being surrounded by so great a cloud of witnesses so let us go on unto perfection, for if we do not lay aside some of these things some of our neighbors might stand as witnesses against us here after. For if we do not lay aside every weight, and the sins that so easily beset us, and show forth the beauties of the Everlasting Gospel in our lives, our neighbors might testify against us and say we did not live right, so they had not reasons to suppose we had the truth.

So, my grandfather's family for some time had divisions in the family on the subject of religion and life was not pleasant for my grandmother, but her faith was steadfast and her prayers were heard. When after a time my grandfather became very ill, the doctors gave him up to die. He became speechless, could not swallow and what the doctors termed the death hiccoughs had set in. At this time, my grandmother bent over his pillow and asked him if she might send for the elders. He could not speak but managed to try to nod an assent, and she sent for them. They came, anointed his head, laid their hands upon his head and prayed God to heal him, if it could be his will, and ere their prayers were ended, the hiccoughs ceased. When they took their hands from his head, he asked for a drink of water, and was able to swallow the water they brought him.

From that moment, his recovery commenced, and in a very few days not being willing to wait longer, for what he felt he should have done long before, he was carried in his chair to the creek near their home and was baptized by immersion for the remission of his sins.

When the Saints moved to Missouri, my grandparents were among the number who settled at Far West. My father remembered the time told of in the "Lucy Smith History" [book] when the mob had surrounded Far West, and Joseph and Hyrum Smith and others were invited (commanded) to surrender themselves. I have seen my father cry when talking or reading of the time when the mob yelled and howled so when they had these men in their control.

When the Saints were driven from Missouri, my grandfather and family were with them. The mob burned their house and shop and they were not allowed to take their stock. Among what was left behind was some sheep, one of which had been a pet lamb whose mother died, and it was raised by hand and was given a name and would always come when called. Afterwards some of the older boys ventured back with a team to try to recover some of their own corn and property, and as they were nearing one man's place they began to say, "Those sheep look just like our sheep." So as they drove past, one of the boys began calling the name of this pet sheep and the pet heard them and came bounding over the fence and right up to them. But they were in the enemies' country and felt that they could do nothing after the exterminating order of Governor Boggs, concerning the Saints. So they went back without their property, except a load of corn from their own field.

Uncle Chancey Whiting married Editha Morley, a daughter of Isaac Morley, while in Illinois, and when their first child Isaac Morley Whiting was about a year old, a mob came to my uncle's home. He was gone, but they told my aunt they would give her an hour to get her things out of her house, when they should return and burn her home, as they were determined to drive the Mormons from the country. She knew that remonstrance was useless, but she had the courage to ask them if they would any of them be kind enough to help her carry her cook stove out of the house as she could not manage that alone. Some of them very kindly complied, and then they left.

She moved all the rest of their furniture and belongings out onto the little garden where there would not be so much danger of it burning, and when Uncle Chancey returned home at night, he found his house burned to the ground and his wife sitting in her little rocking chair in the garden holding their boy and guarding their possessions. I heard Uncle Chancey relate this story one of the last times I ever talked with him. He and his wife are over the river now and beyond the reach of mobs. But these are only some of the trials endured by some of the early Saints.

Uncle William Whiting and wife died leaving three small children: Edmund, Martha, and Mary.

Uncle Charles Whiting and wife died leaving three children: Elisha, Cordelia, and Martha Jane.

Uncle Edwin Whiting followed Brigham Young to Utah and followed him into that abomination, polygamy, also. For he died many years ago leaving several so-called wives, and numerous children and grandchildren.

Uncle Almon Whiting married Lucia Leavitt, a niece of Eliza R. Snow. She died a few years later. Afterwards he married Lydia Garfield. He is dead, but his widow and a family of children are still living.

Sylvester married Rebecca Redfield, they had seven children. She died a few years ago. He is nearly eighty-eight years old. He died June 19, 1915, the last one of that once large family. But I cannot write the history of all my uncles, aunts, and cousins. And there is nothing of my own life worth writing about. Still I shall write something anyway.

Of my aunts, Emeline married Walter Cox who went to Utah afterwards and into apostasy, having several wives at his death. By their works ye shall know them.

Aunt Louise married a Mr. Talcott. She was about the age of Queen Victoria. She got married about the same time as the Queen did, raised a large family of children, and died about the time that Queen Victoria did.

Aunt Jane married a Mr. Bruce but died a few years later. Aunt Harriet died young.

My parents embraced the gospel before the death of the martyrs, Joseph and Hyrum Smith. Mother was at their funeral, and I think all of their brothers and sisters were members.

When the Saints were driven away from Illinois, my grandparents settled at Silver Creek, Mills County, Iowa. That is what the settlement was called then. I am told no such place can be found on the maps now. That may be, but I presume the creek and the place still exists, at least they did forty-seven years ago when we visited there with my parents at Warren Follett's and Nathan West's. There my parents were married, and my sister, Lucia, was born March 21, 1855, and I was born there also. I was two years and two weeks older than her.

When I was over a year old, I took the whooping cough, and once, when choking and strangling and whooping, I went into convulsions and was given up for dead, but in answer to prayer, as I believe, I revived and was permitted to live for some reason—good or bad only time will tell.

Before this time, quite a number of the Saints had gathered at Silver Creek and organized a branch of the church. In 1849 or there abouts, Alpheus Cutler and family moved there and for a time he was chosen president of the branch. My father had become disgusted with the way many of the Saints who followed Brigham Young's false teaching were doing, and had almost lost hope and faith seeing so many go into polygamy after the death of Joseph Smith the Prophet.

But Alpheus Cutler began to call the people's attention to the three books, the Bible, Book of Mormon, and Book of Covenants, and to tell them that they did not need to go to Utah or submit to the rule or teaching of Brigham Young and his associates in order to be saved. This seemed right and sensible to my father, so he concluded to cast in his lot with Alpheus Cutler.

While there, Brigham Young heard a rumour at Winter Quarters, that Alpheus Cutler had gone to Silver Creek and was teaching against him and his colleagues, so he sent George A. Smith, and several others to investigate. Alpheus Cutler told them he was trying to teach the law laid down in the books to the people. They commended him in this, and in a public meeting bore testimony to the people of the calling and ordination of Alpheus Cutler, under the hands of Joseph Smith, to a mission among the Lamanites. I mention this here, merely to explain what was not explained to me for many years, for when I heard of this event, I supposed they meant that George A. Smith and others bore testimony that Alpheus Cutler was ordained to lead the church, or be presiding high priest over all the church, or president of the high priesthood as it is called in the Book of Covenants. And it was not till seventeen years ago that my father explained this to me. He said that George A. Smith and those with him at that time, never did believe it was Alpheus Cutler's right to lead the church, or be president of the high priesthood, but of this, more later, perhaps. At any rate, I am thankful that Father Cutler by his influence kept a good many from going to Utah, for they were as sheep without a shepherd and many knew not where to look. Persecuted by enemies, robbed of hard earned savings and possessions, driven from homes and harassed by poverty, it's a wonder they kept the faith to any degree.

Alpheus Cutler did not remain at Silver Creek many years for he with a chosen few, among whom were Hyrum Murdock, Nicholas Taylor, a Mr. Patten, and Lewis Denna, an Indian who had united with the church some time before this. This company ... moved to some place (in Kansas, Valley Falls I think) then called Grasshopper, to carry out this mission of Alpheus Cutler's among the Indians. But whether God recognized the work done or not, I know not. I heard Mrs. Denna say years afterward that she thought a few were baptized, but they were never connected with what was called the Cutlerite Faction. Mrs. Taylor told me before her death that the Indians did not appreciate the fact of the white missionaries coming into their country and settling on their lands, and trying to build a flour mill and etc., and there was trouble very soon at any rate.

By the summer of 1855, a branch of the Saints had located at Manti, Fremont County, Iowa, so I have been informed, and my parents moved there, this summer or fall. I do not know just when Alpheus Cutler and his family located here, but they were there as long ago as I can remember, and before that.

Alpheus Cutler was again chosen president of the branch and soon their little company concluded that Alpheus Cutler held the highest authority of any one after the death of the Martyr, so they proceeded to uphold him by vote, at each session of their semi-yearly conferences, although he was never at any time ordained to that office. So I was brought up to believe that Joseph Smith was a true prophet, but that Alpheus Cutler held the presiding authority over all the elect after the Martyr's death, and that all who refused to accept Alpheus Cutler as leader, or to be rebaptized by some of their officials, were really apostates, as all except Alpheus Cutler himself had been required to be rebaptized, he claiming that he would not break that link between him and Joseph. A query now ... in my mind would be, if it was anything that would break a link twixt him and the prophet, it would not be right for any of them.

Well, as a child I was of a sickly nature and nearly every fall, I would have a long siege of fever and ague, till when I was ten or eleven years of age people began to predict that I would die of consumption. Meanwhile, other children came to my parents' home. My sister, Ella Janette, was born December 6, 1857; my brother, Arthur

Wellington, came February 29, 1860; [and] my sister, Mary Bell, usually called May, born January 17, 1864 (she died near Bemidji, Minnesota, July 22, 1911).

My memory often turns back to my childhood home at old Manti, Iowa, near Shenandoah, although there was no Shenandoah then, just Prairie. I first commenced to attend school when only four years old. I believe my first teacher was Ambrosia Morse, who afterward married Johnathan Cox. I have a dim recollection of attending a school, taught by Charles Sperry, also of another taught by a Mr. Hyde, and one by Mr. Snow. I remember a school taught by Polly Gaylord, for I liked her so well.

But most of all do I remember my old teacher James R. Badham. And in the beginning of the Civil War in the United States, when the companies of soldiers would come marching through the town, he would always give us recess, as he knew we could never keep our minds or our eyes on our studies when a regiment of soldiers were tramping by, or a company of cavalry with their fifes and drums sounding so musically, and their pretty flags waving so beautifully through the air.

Those were scenes never to be forgotten. James Badham was the one who first advocated the idea of a Sunday school for the benefit of the children of Manti. Some or most of the older ones thought it a sectarian idea and not of much account, and all the grown up ones that I remember of seeing at our Sunday school, except our teacher, James Badham, was Aunt Rebecca (Redfield) Whiting.

Well, the Sunday school did not last long, and I have never known of the Cutlerites undertaking to start a Sunday School again, although in my heart I was always in favor of it.

The Reorganization of the scattered members of the original organization, who refused to follow Brigham Young, and his pernicious teachings, such as polygamy, blood atonement, Adam God the theory, and etc., began its work somewheres about the year 1852, but grew in favor slowly, as the years went by. It was a new country, the Saints were poor. After all their persecutions, facilities for traveling and sending news were few and far between, nevertheless letters were sent by members of the church to Alpheus Cutler, by those favoring a reorganization, of the broken fragments of branches, who desired to remain true to the books and the teachings of the true prophet, Joseph Smith, who had been assassinated June 27, 1844. These letters invited the Saints at Manti to cast in their allegiance on the side of the Reorganization.

But the little faction at Manti had already gone ahead and reorganized, according to their own ideas (I say reorganized because every faction had to reorganize, not one of them could leave the organization, as it originally was. They had to reorganize, each according to their own ideas). They had chosen Alpheus Cutler president of the high priesthood. He had chosen his eldest son, Thadeus, as his first councilor. Chancey Whiting as his second councilor, etc., so as this little faction had already set up an organization, they were not ready or willing to investigate the claims of anyone else.

So when Joseph Smith the son of the martyr came claiming that he had been called of God to the same position his father had held in the church, the majority of the little company at Manti were not ready or willing to accept his claims, and felt that it was really an insult and a persecution for them to continue to send their missionaries to their vicinity to preach and try to convert their members.

The Cutlerites had set up their "Secret Endowment Chamber" and all who were allowed to enter there (as it was supposed by them) were given the holy priesthood according to Melchesidek, or it was bestowed upon them. For they claim that those who enter there "attain to these two priesthoods," and thus become the kingdom and elect of God. They believed that regardless of what the books teach on this subject, of which I may write later, they really believed that they were the church and kingdom and the only ones recognized and accepted of God.

They had no use for the Reorganization, that is, the majority felt that way, nevertheless, quite a few of those who had been their members turned away and accepted the claims of the Reorganization.

Thadeus Cutler (son of Alpheus, and his first councilor) and wife and some of their children were converted to the new idea. Sallie (daughter of Alpheus Cutler) Anderson and her husband B. B. Anderson (who afterwards became my father and mother-in-law) joined the church of the Reorganization, so did their daughter and husband, Jerusha and Jackson Burdick; also Nicholas Taylor and wife; Wheeler

Baldwin and wife; William Topham and wife; William Redfield, wife and children (except my Aunt Rebecca); and some others. It was a source of grief and annoyance to those left who felt in some way that they had been wronged and that those who had left them were deceived and lost.

Well, I believe the Cutlerite fraternity meant to be honest, they believed in part, and were blessed in part; they believed in a restoration of the Gospel, they believed God had spoken from on high in these latter days, they believed God could hear and answer prayer and heal the sick.

I well remember when I was about six years old, that I had a terrible time with earache. I had moaned and cried nearly all night and a good portion of the day. When my mother came to my bedside and told me that my father and Uncle Chancey were coming to administer to me, and for me to try to pray in my heart at the same time, well I did not know how to pray, having never been taught a prayer only as I had often heard my father pray, but I did the best I could. When they anointed my head, and laid their hands on my head, and prayed God to heal me, I never knew when their prayer was ended, for the pain had ceased and I was asleep.

This circumstance gave me a belief and faith in God's power to heal the sick, which has never left me, but has grown stronger with the years, although it has not always been God's will to answer every prayer by healing the sick or removing all pain. I do not believe it was ever calculated, that mortals should have faith sufficient, to command every trial to flee away, or every pain to cease, or every difficulty to be removed, for in such a case how could the Lord have a tried people, and how could death claim us when our time had come. I think it would be a greater calamity than any other, if we could never die. Just think what a vast sanitarium this whole world would be. 'Twould take quite an institution just to hold David and Solomon and their wives and concubines.

Oh, I'm glad we can all die sometime. While we do believe it is good to have a faith and confidence in God and in His plans so that if it is His will, we may be healed, and if it is his will to take any of us from this earth, we may have strength and faith to say, Thy will be done. No doubt our faith is weak and we need to grow in grace and the knowledge of the truth and live more worthy of the blessings promised the believers, for I know God can and has healed the sick many times in this our day. All the honor and praise be to his holy name.

Whether we be old or young, bond or free, male or female, Cutlerite, Josephite, scientist or sectarian, Catholic, or Protestant, let us have faith in God. Search the scriptures, whether we be in the faith or not. Seek for his guiding spirit to lead us into all truth. It is a good thing to believe in God the Father and in Jesus Christ the Saviour and in God's power to heal the sick or to grant other gifts or blessings of the Holy Spirit, and any truth which any of us believe will never have to be given up, in order to receive more light. Yet I know that many of all these different faiths or beliefs take every blessing gained in answer to prayer, as a sure sign that the peculiar belief or faith or church they have united with, is the one and only true church or faith.

Would it not look more consistent to believe that these things are a sure sign of God's mercy and love to all people, and that these things are truths which all people ought to believe? God does not withhold his mercy and love from people even if they are deceived in some part of their belief, but is willing to bless them according to their faith, even if they do not know everything. Perhaps when we get over on the other side we will find none of us had come to perfection of understanding on all points. I know that among the little faction in which I was brought up, every blessing received was taken as a sure sign that their church was the only true church and they held all the authority and priesthood on earth that God recognized. From what I have heard, I think all the factions that arose after the death of the martyr made the same mistake.

I was recently talking with a fine old lady, Mrs. Shoven of Vanscoy, who knows but little of our faith, and she told me of her being healed in answer to prayer, and that was the reason she was a believer in Christian Science. I asked her if she believed it was God who healed her. "Why of course I do," she replied.

"Well," I said, "I believe that is a truth that all people should believe that God can heal the sick, and I have often had the same experience you tell of, though doing as we are commanded in James 5:14, 15: 'Is any sick among you, let him call for the Elders of the church and let them pray over him, anointing him with oil, in the name of the Lord, and the prayer of faith shall save the sick, and the Lord shall raise him up.' I have many times received blessings in that way."

"I call that having faith in God's power to heal the sick, and you call it Christian Science. It may be we are more nearly united in faith than we realize because of our different ways of expressing it."

She seemed puzzled for a while and finally asked, "But do you believe in present day revelation?"

"Yes, certainly," I replied. "The gift of healing is only one of the gifts promised the believer. The other promises are just as true. Paul says concerning spiritual gifts, 'brethren I would not have you ignorant,' and he mentions visions, dreams, tongues, interpretations, prophecies, and etc., so while we believe in God's power to heal, let us not disbelieve in God's power to reveal whatever he chooses in his own way. Let us all examine ourselves, whether we be in the faith or not by the sure word of God. 'To the law and to the testimony,' Isaiah 8:20."

As a child I do not think I was as good or as agreeable as the common run of children. The same can be said of me yet, so if my goodness was all there was to be written of, my autobiography would be short indeed.

Well, the war and the division in the church lines and the death of Alpheus Cutler which occurred June 10, 1864, all combined to cause a feeling of unrest, and the little community decided to move. So, in the fall of 1864, my parents, Sylvester Whiting, Marcus Shaw, and Jesse Burdick rigged up their covered wagons and with their families started out for some promised land, camping by the way. Along in November, I think, we reached Redwing, Minnesota, and were greeted with a snow storm, that night. So next morning the men decided we had gone far enough till spring, so after some trouble, they succeeded in renting rooms in the town for the winter, so we could be in shelter. I was now eleven years old. I had been baptized, when nine years old by my uncle Chancey Whiting and supposed that I was a member of the true church. The Reorganization had continued to send missionaries to Manti, and I had attended a few of their meetings, but I had no idea that my parents could be mistaken about anything, so shared their prejudices.

"One of the little foxes" that helped to spoil the vine, so to speak, was a belief, of which I am loath to speak, but in the interest of truth, I may as well make note of here. A suspicion that some of the neighbors (never themselves), were guilty of witchcraft, and thereby afflicting their neighbors, or who ever, they might feel a grudge against. I don't know when this evil began to get in its baneful work among those who should have been Saints, but my father who was not very ready to give credence to all these suspicions, said some fifteen years ago, that he believed it had been handed down in some families from generation to generation ever since the early settling of the colonies when they used to burn the witches at Salem, until someone had the wisdom or forethought or something to accuse the governor's wife of the crime of witchcraft. That set him to thinking and he began to put a stop to having everyone burned at the stake, whom someone else might accuse.

Well it seems the little community at Manti had hitherto been content with accusing some of their own members of this grave charge, but now there was a division and (of course as we don't know for a surety just who might be bad enough to work at witchcraft) to torment or to afflict their neighbors, why naturally there was a chance to think it might be some of those unfaithful ones, who had left us and joined the Reorganization, and thus in our eyes had stepped down a long ways from the way of truth and righteousness.

I well remember when a certain young lady of the Cutlerite faith was taken very ill until her life was despaired of, and all the faith and prayers and home doctoring had failed thus far to restore it. It was thought best to try some method or trick which it was believed would send the affliction back on to the one who was bewitching her. Whatever the plan was, it was tried and (so I suppose) the fever had probably come to the turning point that night. In the morning, we heard, she was much better, while the wife of an elder in the Reorganization was taken very sick. They had both, this elder and his wife, belonged to the Cutlerite faction, but shortly before this had joined the Reorganization. This occurrence was taken as proof (nearly) positive of who had been causing this trouble. Needless to say both parties recovered in due time.

They say old people live in the past. It may be, for I can remember many things of the past, while now I often forget where I put my specs. Well, during this winter at Redwing, my sister Lucia, and my cousin Almon (Uncle Sylvester's son), and myself, attended for a few weeks an Episcopalian Sunday school. It was at Redwing I saw the first Christmas tree. It was arranged for the whole Sunday school, in the courthouse, and our classes were arranged to march from the church to the courthouse, then up two flights of stairs, into the large room; and as we were going up and came into sight of the immense tree all lit up with candles and ornaments brightly, it seemed to me that we were marching right up into heaven. But we were not, though we had a fine time, and were treated to cake, candies, nuts, popcorn, and a little book for each one. We reached home, about nine o'clock, just as our fathers were starting out to find us, for they had expected us to be home at dark. We lived in a house back near the bluffs, and took several walks that winter along the top of Barns Bluff. I often wonder if Redwing looks now as it did then.

During this winter, Isaac Whiting, wife and sister, came from Iowa and rented near us, also Edmund Whiting and family, Calvin Fletcher and John Fletcher and families. We stayed there until April sixth, except my Uncle Sylvester and family who moved to Crow Wing before this, about February.

On April sixth, we again took up our pilgrimage toward the north, hoping to find a refuge from the troubles that assailed us in Iowa, and to be able to serve the Lord in peace, and to carry the Gospel to the Lamanites as that had been Alpheus Cutler's mission, and we who were left must needs carry out that work.

We waited to start early that morning of the sixth of April, but it takes so long to take down and pack up and load all your possessions into a covered wagon or two (if you don't believe it, just try it). You may think you haven't got anything, but just try to move and you'll find out. Well, we were very late in starting, and when we reached Brother Marcus Shaw's house, the elders entered the house and held a season of prayer. We all ate a lunch in our wagons and were on our way rejoicing. I believe we only got about nine miles that afternoon, when we camped, ate a hearty supper. There's always plenty to eat for the first few meals, cooked up ahead on such occasions. Us children romped and played till it began to rain, then we were hustled into the wagons and to bed.

Our wagon was fixed with boards projecting out from the top of the high box over the wheels to make the beds wide enough or long enough, so we could all sleep crossways of the wagon. There were seven of us all told, so the beds reached the whole length of the wagon. Slats were fixed across the wagon from one side to the other of the projections, upon which our beds were made, while underneath the beds were trunks, boxes, bundles and, oh yes, always a cook stove in the back end of the wagon bed. In the daytime, half the slats and the bedding had to be piled back on top of the other half to give space in front for a spring seat and to get at the dinner box.

Well, it turned cold in the night and when we woke in the morning it was blowing and snowing something fierce. My father told us to stay in bed for a while, and he dressed, climbed out into the storm, hitched the team onto the wagon, and the rest of the men did the same thing and drove to a more sheltered place in the timber and hills. It shook us up good and plenty, the road was so rough, but we only laughed.

Well, we stayed there two or three days till the storm abated, then on we went in the cold, trying to drive a few cows, and endure whatever we had to as well as we could.

There were seven families. Some of them set up their cook stoves in the wagons and had a fire burning as they drove along to keep themselves warm, but my mother's stove was too large for that so we had to tough it out the best we could.

When we reached Crow Wing, we camped there a few days, and our elders held a consultation with some of the Indians. But no converts were made. Then we started on. I forgot to say that when we camped near St. Cloud, we heard first of the assassination of Abraham Lincoln, and as all our men were strongly in favor of the course Abraham Lincoln had taken in the war, we were sorrowful to hear that he had been murdered.

Our road lay through a rough country, no good roads, but long stretches of old corduroy, that needed repairing badly, just the bare logs and poles with no dirt or hay covering. I shall never forget those awful corduroys, for I had caught cold and been sick, and was so sore all through my bowels that every jolt was agony. I would walk as long as it seemed I had strength to go, and my mother would beg me to ride; then I would climb in the wagon and lie on the bed, when jolt, bang, bump!! and it would seem like a knife piercing my body, and I would beg them to let me walk again, though every step hurt me. I was glad when that corduroy ended and we came to a bridge over a creek or river, just in time to put out a fire that had reached the bridge and just begun on the timbers. A few hours later there would have been no bridge to cross on.

All this was taken as the guiding hand of the Lord, and maybe it was. The Lord is not slack in his watch-care no difference how wayward his children are. But I am satisfied that greater blessings and fewer trials might have been ours but we "would not."

At last after a few days, we came to Ottertail Lake, which looked very large, being about fifteen miles long. We camped there a day or two, then on to West Battle Lake where we camped near the north shore perhaps three or four days. Then at last, on the sixth of May 1865, we reached dear old Clitherall Lake and there we made our homes. In a few days a log house was in process of erection, my father's house, the first in that place, and we were glad to feel a roof over our heads. How we children did like to play around the sandy shore of that wonderful lake. But I believe there was some lurking fear of Indians in those early days, by the women folks, for our nearest white neighbor was a Scotchman (I believe) who lived at Ottertail Lake, and had a native woman for a wife. Our next nearest white neighbor was a man at Chippewa, now called Brandon, about twenty-five miles south. There was a company of soldiers at Pommedeterre [Pomme de Terre], and another at Abercrombie thirty-five or forty miles away. Our nearest store and post office was at Alexandria, forty miles away.

The people had often to go clear to St. Cloud or Minneapolis over one hundred miles to get their wheat ground into flour or their wool carded into rolls or to buy flour, sugar, shoes, or clothing.

It was only two and a half-years or thereabouts since the terrible massacres in Minnesota, but we tried to be friendly with the Indians by whom we were surrounded, and we prayed the Lord to protect us so we never had any trouble with the Indians.

Along in July, the main body of the church came from Iowa, having been about three months on the road, driving sheep, cows, etc.,
along the way. I think there were fifteen or twenty families. There was
the widow of Alpheus Cutler, Lois by name, and familiarly called
Mother Cutler by all the neighborhood, and her granddaughter, Emily Pratt, whose mother was dead. There were Almon Sherman; Henry Way; Dewitt Sperry; Clark Stillman; Hyrum & Lyman Murdock;
Square [Squire]Eggleston; Uriah Eggleston; Erastus Cutler (he had
come with us, but his family came with the big crowd); Mr. Oaks;
William Mason; Edmund Fletcher; a Mr. Olmstead; James Badham;
and a Mr. Cameron; Lewis Denna; Chancey Whiting, etc., with their
families. Some, however, could not see the advantages of living in
Minnesota and returned that fall to Iowa, notably Square Eggleston;
Uriah Eggleston; Erastus Cutler; Mr. Olmstead; Edmund Whiting;
Mr. Oaks; James R. Badham, etc. Perhaps the camping out trips did
me good after all, as aside from a run of bilious fever at Redwing, and
my trouble over the corduroy roads, I began to have better health, as
we had got out of the fever and ague zone.

There was no school at this time, so I attempted to play at teaching school, this summer after I was twelve years old, out under the
shade trees. My own two sisters next to me, my cousin Ally, and Sarah
and Eddie Fletcher (children of Calvin and Mary [Miller] Fletcher)
were my scholars. I tried to follow my old school teacher, James Badham's, plan in teaching. The parents thought it a good plan, and tried
to get the children to be good and try to learn. I guess they tried to
mind for I don't remember any serious trouble.

We were favored with very good crops that first summer considering the small fields and cold backward spring. The men were able
to break up and get under cultivation, the limited supply of garden
seeds we had brought with us or been able to buy. But all of this little
colony were poor in this world's goods, and we had to practice economy and go without many needful things. I remember my mother
colored some unbleached muslin with oak bark to make me a much
needed dress and a piece of birch bark with some red calico for a band
was made into a sunshade (for a hat), and some buckskin moccasins,
bought off a squaw furnished me a Sunday outfit.

Those first few years were very busy ones with few amusements or recreations. Twice I remember a little riffle of excitement caused by the advent of a small company of soldiers into our neighborhood (which was named Clitherall). I don't know whether [they were] soldiers stationed at Abercrombie or Pommedeterre, but there were soldiers stationed at both of those places for a few years after the Indian troubles. Our little community would do their best to entertain the soldiers by several families making room for as many as possible in our houses.

We were surrounded by Indians who sometimes, especially in winter time, would visit us in companies of twenty or more, and go from house to house and have what was called a begging dance. They would file into the room and stand in a circle one behind another and dance in their quiet way with a sing-song music for a short time, and then on to the next place. We were all poor enough in this world's goods in those days, but we always found something to give them, a little bread, flour, potatoes, ruttabaggies [rutabagas], or something from our scanty stores we would divide with them. I don't think any of us went hungry on account of it, though flour was very high in price. At the close of the way, calico was sometimes fifty cents a yard, also common unbleached muslin. We managed to live though. I remember my Father and Uncle Sylvester bought a barrel of regular old brown hardtack of the soldiers and we children were glad to make a meal of hardtack and water with a little sugar. If the water was warm, and we would soak the crackers a while, we could eat them.

The next spring 1866, we thought it best to set out gooseberry bushes around our door yards so as to have fruit near home. So one bright day, us children gained the consent of our parents to go after gooseberry plants. Myself and Lu, Ellis and Arthur from our family; Loueza Keeler, a stepdaughter of William Mason, who was older than I; our cousins Ann, Alfred, and Lide. The last three brought their small wagon to haul the bushes home, and we went over near the outlet on West Battle Lake. I must have been of a piggish disposition and bent on doing wonders, for I chose the largest clump of gooseberries I could find. I worked and dug and chopped and rested and went at it again. The others were more sensible and chose small new shoats or not very large bushes and soon had a wagon load. We concluded to send the boys home with that load and sent word for mother to send us out a pail with hardtack, sugar cups and spoons and we would stay all day. We were tired and hungry and could hardly wait for the crackers to soak in the lake water, and sugar so we could eat them, but we pronounced them good.

After we had rested a while, I went at my large gooseberry bush again and finally succeeded in loosening all the roots, and we loaded my one large bunch and the others' small ones in the wagon and hauled it home. I worked labouriously to set it out in the corner of our garden fence by the Lake, where everyone who passed by could see it. It was a beauty when all leaved out and I imagined how nice it would look when covered with berries, but imagination was all I ever enjoyed about it, for in all the years I lived there I never saw any berries on that great big corner bush, though it grew larger for years.

Now, in 1916, I cannot find a vestige of my old gooseberry bush. The ones the other children set out were all right though and bore fruit, but the house is gone and the garden is part of a field, and all is changed but the land and the lake. The dear old trees are larger and I love them as a part of my dear old home, a home where love and prayer were our daily portion, where we all learned to work and economize and where reading was so scarce that I was just hungry for something to read. I had read the Book of Mormon before I was thirteen years of age, and found it an interesting history. I read the most of the Bible when fourteen, but as I could not understand the prophetic books in the Old Testament, I skipped over a lot of that. Our old Wilson school readers were treasured as jewels rare. That first winter a few spelling schools were held at Uncle Chancey Whiting's, with Charles Sperry as teacher. The next year Zeruah Sherman taught a three months term of school and Marcus Shaw taught writing and arithmetic evenings. The summer after I was fourteen, I was hired by the parents to teach the smaller children. There was no county organization, as yet, and the parents had to pay out of their own pockets and cash being scarce in the pockets I received eight dollars a month for my efforts at teaching in summer. In winter they would hire Miss Zeruah Sherman and the larger children would attend. She received twenty-five dollars a month.

That fall my father and family returned to Iowa, to get my grand-mother Burdick, as mother could not rest easy in mind till her moth-er was with her, so again a long trip was taken in a covered wagon. When we reached Sidney, Iowa, where Uncle Almon Whiting lived, my father rented rooms for us for the winter, and he worked in his brother's chair shop, at making chairs. My sister Lucia and I wished to go to school to our old teacher, James R. Badham, who was teach-ing at Manti, fifteen miles from Sidney, so I worked for board at James Badham's and Lucia stayed at the home of Amos Cox. The next July we were again on the road, in a covered wagon on our way back to Minnesota, but we were not alone. Uncle Almon Whiting and family, and our cousin Nelson Talcott, Uncle Jesse Burdick and family, and two young gentlemen, Edwin B. Anderson and Jacob L. Boyd, were with us, so there were four covered wagons jogging along the trail.

Our wagon was heavily loaded, as there were eight in our family now. Grandma's easy chair was fixed in back of the spring seat, and facing a side entrance, as mother had fixed a sort of door in the wagon cover between two bows, which could be unbuttoned and swung back, so one could look out at the side. Father had fixed a step between the wheels, and we could climb into the wagon at the side. But when the two young gentlemen of the party suggested that Lu and I ride with them in their wagon, our parents consented as we were so crowded in our wagon. Lu and I thought we could sit together on the back seat, and view the scenery from under the rolled up wagon cover, but we found that the young men had made a plan between themselves that one of them would sit in front and drive half the day, and then take the back seat and let the other be the driver, so we girls had to make a bargain with each other that one of us could sit by Edwin half the day and then that one must sit by Jacob the rest of the day, as we both liked Edwin better than Jacob, so that rule was strictly adhered to ex-cept for one afternoon when it was known that the young gentlemen had been drinking slightly.

We girls refused to sit by either one, but took the back seat and refused to speak to the young gents. They kept trying to say some-thing funny to make us laugh. Lu would giggle occasionally, but Em wouldn't smile. At last one of the young gentlemen said, "Em sits there as sober as if she didn't care a cuss," and I retorted quickly, "Why should I care for a cuss," and went on with viewing the surrounding scenery.

The next day Edwin told me that he should never drink intoxicating liquors again, and if he hadn't kept his word I should never have mentioned it here. They had only drunk enough then to make them a little more talkative than usual. I believe if every young girl would show their aversion to everything wrong in a sober serious manner, it would have a better effect on their young acquaintances than to laugh at such things.

It was very pleasant and healthful riding along through the country and a much better way to view the surrounding scenery than to ride on the train, but it is not pleasant in stormy weather. I recall one afternoon of a very hot day when, as we reached the top of a long hill, we saw a storm cloud moving fast in our direction, and the drivers hurried the teams down the slope to get to a more sheltered place ere the storm broke. As we reached lower ground, how the men did hurry to unhitch the teams from the wagon and drive them close up to the side just as the hail came pelting down at a lively rate. Of course the wagon covers were unrolled and fastened down snuggly, and Lu and I pulled a quilt over our heads as the hail knocked the rain right through the cover onto us. For a while it was all darkness and confusion, as the roaring of the storm almost prevented us from hearing the drivers "steady, steady," to keep them quiet during the storm.

The storm was soon over and we jogged along our way, thankful that the storm was no worse. At last, we could see dear old Clitherall Lake. I think we had been on the road five weeks, camping by the way, sleeping in the wagons, rather crowded in my father's wagon as there were eight of us.

This morning we knew we were nearing home, so Lu and I were very happy, and in honor of our nearing home, and friends, we donned our new print dresses, which we had recently made, every stitch with our own hands. Few people had sewing machines in 1868, and with our light sewing aprons and white collars, and a ribbon at the throat, we felt ready for the day. The young men made some remark like, "Well, if you girls didn't go and dress up," as we were climbing into their wagon. We were quite happy and excited when we could see the little village off across the lake, for we knew that all the young folks and half the old would be sure to call on us before night; so in my joy I unthinkingly swung the little popple twig in my hand carelessly up and down, still glancing off toward home, till to my surprise I see I was hitting Edwin's hand that held the lines. I glanced up at him rather embarrassed. He was smiling and he said rather mischievously, "I will dare you to do that again." Of course I quickly sung the twig on purpose that time, and as it touched his hand, I felt myself folded in his arms, as he stole a kiss. Well, that was the first time, but not the last. I freed myself from his arms and looked up in time to see Aunt May watching us from under their wagon cover, and laughing.

In a short time we reached home and were greeted heartily by all the friends and relatives. In fact they are all kind, sociable, friendly, old-fashioned people. They didn't care whether you ate with your knife, fork, or spoon, whether you wore hat, cap, or sun bonnet, or went bareheaded. The children went barefooted in summertime, to church even, and a neat calico dress for women and a checkered shirt without collar or tie for me was good enough for all occasions. There were no saloons or pool rooms, no gambling dens or worse dens. Enough of the restored gospel (which is the old Jerusalem gospel) had got into their systems to make them want to be decent. I thank the Lord for that. Doubtless we had enough failings, but no Sunday passed without church services, and no one thought of forgetting family prayer at night, or of asking the blessing at meal time.

Everyone was busy, the girls must all learn to cook, keep house, wash, iron, patch, sew, knit, and spin. We did not have any organized "woman's auxiliary," but it was all a part of woman's work to teach such things. I remember some hits on social purity given by good old grandmother Cutler, when some of us girls were visiting her granddaughter Emily Pratt, to the intent that love and marriage were a part of God's plan, and not to be looked upon in a light and frivolous way, nor entered into without due consideration and prayer. My own mother also taught the same truths, so that I was early led to believe such things—a subject for prayer for guidance of our Heavenly Father and not a subject for ridicule or nonsense.

This summer, I was again invited to teach the little ones, and was paid twelve dollars a month. The next winter I attended school taught by Brother William Corless. I remember him as a good kind man, respected by all who knew him.

The next summer of 1869, I again tried to teach a three-month-term. I don't think I ever knew enough to merit the term, teacher, really. I was now sixteen, and having become convinced that Edwin B. Anderson meant what he had said, and was strong enough to keep his word, I now promised to become his wife. Sometime after this, he was baptized by one of the Cutlerite elders and thus we were united in faith. The next winter, I attended school part of the time, and stayed home part, to help my mother, as a new baby sister had come to our home, on December 10th, 1869, and I loved little Sylvia Cordelia. I had been much pleased before her birth to be allowed to help make the little wardrobe, and never thought of feeling vexed over the expected event, as some daughters have seemed to feel in these latter days.

Time passed on, I was very busy with sewing and piecing quilts, as all my wedding outfit must be made by hand, and no girl was considered as having an outfit unless she had bedding for one bed. I did a very little crocheting, of edging, for lingerie and pillow cases, but otherwise there was plenty of necessary work to be done and little time for lace making. On the evening of the fifth of April 1870, a company of about forty-five relatives and friends gathered at the home of my parents to attend the wedding of their daughter Emma, to Edwin B. Anderson. Too young, you say. Of course, but we were not worrying about it then. In fact, as I look back now, in 1916, I am not worrying about it now. I only had a chance to live with my husband a little more than forty-two years, not near long enough, I felt, when he was laid to rest near Vanscoy, Saskatchewan, Canada.

Now perhaps it would be fitting to write somewhat of my husband's people. His father was Buckley B. Anderson, who was born in Huron County, Ohio, January 14, 1819, and died July 4, 1895, at Lebeck, Cedar County, Missouri. He was married to Sallie M. Cutler in 1837. My husband was their sixth child, born July 24, 1848, at Platt, Platt County, Missouri. Buckley B. Anderson was a son of John and Lydia (Hanks) Anderson. John was the son of Lemuel, and Lemuel was the son of George, which is as far back as I have any record. My husband's mother, Sallie (Cutler) Anderson, was a daughter of Al-

pheus and Lois (Lathrop) Cutler, which is as far in the line of genealogy as I have been informed, except that her mother's name was also
Lois. A dear old Bible name handed down for several generations.
The Lathrops were of English decent. From our earliest traditions,
the first Whiting brothers were of English and Welsh descent.

I again taught school or made the attempt, this summer of 1870,
while my young husband busied himself with farming, and building
our new home. It was not what would be called a first class house
with all modern conveniences, but a log house of one room. Our first
furniture was all home made. My father made the chairs. Of course
we bought a new cook stove, and a plain set of white dishes, while my
first tablecloths were made of unbleached muslin, and bleached by
continued washing. Too poor, you say. Well, I can't deny it, but people
can be happy with love in a cottage.

My husband owned a yoke of oxen and a cow. The farming furnished our breadstuff and vegetables, and my school wages were carefully expended for necessities, for the coming winter. Our two pigs,
that we were feeding to supply our winter's meat, came up missing
that fall, and we imagined they furnished meat for a camp of Indians,
who camped for a week or two a half mile from us. At least bones
of pigs about their size were found near the camp after the Indians
were gone, and as no one near had sold any sow meat to them we had
grounds for imagination.

In the spring of 1871, on May 29th, our first child came and we
named him Ernest Morell, and I thought it quite an item to learn
how to keep all my work done and care for a crying baby.

In 1872, the little church of which we were members undertook
to go into what they called "a oneness" or an organization of equality
where they were to be equal in temporal things, and considering it to
be our duty to comply with all church requirements we were of the
number. We always had dressed plainly, but now we were counseled
to lay aside all unnecessary adornment, so for several years no trim-
ming was allowed to adorn our apparel, neither collar nor jewels, nor
ribbon bows were worn. Sunbonnets for women and girls in summer,
and warm hoods for winter, were the only style—a very good style for
poor folks in a new country, but a little on the extreme.

On the fifteenth of November 1872, our second son, Lewis Ethan, was born. Then I had to learn how to care for two babies and do the necessary work. I also began to suffer about this time with toothache and neuralgia. And for about twenty-five or thirty years continued to suffer, at times terribly, with decayed teeth until I finally got rid of them all and obtained false teeth that could not ache.

On the fore part of January 1873, we were favored with that notable snowstorm that reached throughout all of Minnesota, North Dakota, Iowa, and I know not how many other states. It was an ideal morning. And the men thought it a fine day to finish up their threshing in the big field. They had put in all the fall threshing for neighbors who had settled near us but not of our faith, and so were very late in finishing our own threshing. My husband was in the field with the rest. I think they had nearly finished when all of a sudden they knew a storm was coming. I had company for dinner that day, Sister Joseph McEntyre, and we were visiting as contentedly when all at once her husband came in the house and said, "Do you know it is storming?"

We looked quickly out of the window and saw the fine snow gathering thick in the air. I knew he had come from the field, and asked where Edwin was. He replied that he had gone to the village only one and one half-miles from our home with a load of wheat. I urged Joseph and his wife to stay all night. But he said no, if they would hurry they could get home all right. They lived about a mile from our house, so they started. I wrapped up and carried in the night wood. It was only a few minutes till the snow was so thick in the air, I could see only a few feet from the house. It was a terrible blizzard and turned cold so fast, and dark so soon.

I prepared the supper, but felt terribly anxious for how could Edwin see his way home when I could only see a few feet from the window.

At last as I had risen for the second or third time from my knees, where I had been pleading with God to protect my husband and bring him safely home, he entered the kitchen. We now had more than one room. What a weight rolled off my mind, my husband was at home.

He told me he had let the horses guide themselves while on the lake, but they were a little off the track when they neared the shore,

Edwin and Emma Anderson family 1910. Used with permission of Perry Exley.

but Uncle Jesse Burdick had happened to come down to the lake shore with a lantern and seeing the glimmer of the light he knew they were off the track and swung them into it in the right place to come up the bank. It was then timber from there on home so he had no more difficulty. It was a fierce storm that lasted three days and nights. Many there were who did not reach home till the storm was over. My own father-in-law and others with him who had moved near Audabon [Audubon], Becker County, Minnesota, went four miles to town that day and did not go home till the storm was over. No one ventured away from home who was at home, and many lost their lives in the storm that passed over so large a tract of country. Farmers were fortunate who had plenty of fuel and could feed their stock. On the prairies some burned their furniture for fuel. This is but an incident as we journeyed through life.

1873 and 1874 passed by uneventfully except that in the fall, September 1874, my parents received an addition to their family, and my little new brother was named Francis Lester. He was dear to me then, and he is dear to me now, though he is forty-one years old, and now in March 1916, I am sixty-three years of age.

On January 19, 1875, my first little daughter was born and we named her Celia Annette. She was a dear little babe destined to remain with us but a short time. A short time before her death, which occurred September 12, 1875, I dreamed of seeing my husband standing by a mound of fresh earth with such a look of sadness upon his face. I saw that fulfilled in a few weeks. We had the measles in the family. I myself took them and the babe took the disease from me. I did not know she was dangerously ill but thought when she broke out she would be all right. I gave her some sage tea to try to drive the disease out, but she would throw it up. She seemed quieter one day, slept most of the time, but did not pay much attention to anything. I was young and did not know much about the disease. There were no doctors in the country. Next morning we found her dead in our bed when we woke. It seemed to me that my hair began to turn gray from that time. It seemed so terrible to me that we should have been asleep, and our baby dying. But in the years that have gone by since then, I have heard of many like cases of a nursing babe dying suddenly if the measles do not break out on them soon.

Life is full of sorrows and disappointments, yet there is some joy and gladness and love in a home, and prayer in the heart helps us tide over the deepest sorrows. Perhaps our sorrows help to lead us to prayer. Some might ask, "And were you always loving and prayerful?" and I must say, "Oh, no, far from it."

I had naturally a very hasty temper and with many trials to contend with, I must say I all too often allowed my temper to overcome me, and many times in our lives, I have asked my husband to forgive me for some unkind speech, while a few times he asked me to forgive him, but if people love each other they can forgive, and overlook a great deal. I don't see how people ever could get along without love. Their trials would surely overcome them.

This summer of 1875, before the death of our babe, the Reorganized Church of Jesus Christ of Latter Day Saints had sent a missionary, T. W. Smith and wife to Minnesota. They went first to Audabon, where my husband's father and mother lived, and also near where Almon Sherman, Henry Wat, Dewitt Sperry and family, and Mother Cutler lived. They had disagreed with the remainder of the Cutlerites, and moved there before my father-in-law came from Iowa.

Emma and her sisters. Used with permission of Perry Exley.

T. W. Smith preached there and baptized them all, except Father and Mother Anderson. Then my husband's parents had joined the church in Iowa.

T. W. Smith and wife, Mother Cutler, Father Anderson, and Mother came down to our neighborhood about sixty miles and took up their missionary work among us and our neighbors. My husband was nearly convinced that they had the truth then, but when the old rancid question of bewitching people, and afflicting them, came up, it was more than he could swallow, and I took it as sure proof that there was no truth to be found outside of the little Cutlerite Faction. That was worth noticing. I never stopped to think that those who believed this thing had been Cutlerites and had believed such things then, and if it was an error they had carried it with them into the new church they had now joined. They really believed that some of our little church members were afflicting some of their church members. I believe that was a mistake, but I do not know anything about it. I do not know what people might do if they were mean enough to want the devil to afflict someone. Having been very fallible myself and very easy to fly mad and say something I was sorry for, yet never having even wished bad luck or affliction to come upon anyone. I judge others by myself and think that everyone will have all the trials they can stand and more, too, and yet no one be to blame for it among their neighbors. So I now set that belief down as a traditional error once had by a few of the Cutlerites and a few of them united with the Reorganization. The Lord knows all about it but I find nothing in the word of God to uphold such an idea.

We read in the Bible of the Witch of Endor and she pretended to call up the spirits of the dead and that art, whatever it was, was highly condemned by the word of the Lord.

Nowadays, there are some who believe in trying to call up the spirits of the dead but they have a new name for it now. They call it witchcraft. No one would have anything to do with it, if they called it by the Bible name. The Book of Mormon says when Jesus comes he will cut off witchcraft out of the land. I believe this is what is meant by the books. But enough on this question.

I could not think my parents mistaken, so would not try to investigate the position of the Reorganization at this time. Some of our good brothers and sisters did investigate and join them, which was a grief to us.

July 1876 came and the grasshoppers came to our region of country and nearly all vegetation was destroyed. We saw hard times, the next two years. On July 16, 1876, our son Victor Royelle was born. We shortly moved into Old Town as it is now called to be near my mother's while my husband went away to work. Becker County had not suffered from the grasshopper raid, as Ottertail County had, so my husband went to his father's region of the country and went to helping thresh, thus earning enough to tide us over the winter. My father-in-law also sent us several sacks of potatoes. I remembered the prophecy of T. W. Smith that if the little community at Clitherall rejected the gospel he had brought to us, we would go down, both spiritually and temporally.

In the summer of 1877, the grasshopper eggs began to hatch out and again the hoppers took our crops. Edwin and I rigged up our covered wagon and moved up to his father's place for the summer and fall. My sister Lucia and her husband, Alva Murdock, and their sweet little Bessie, soon followed us. We moved into Father Anderson's shop and my sister and I lived together while Edwin and Alva worked for the farmers and threshers, at whatever they could find to do, and thus were we provided for. "But the short and simple annals of the poor" are not always very interesting. It tells of hard work and trials while the love and happiness in the home can hardly be portrayed with a pen.

In the fall, my sister and husband moved back to Clitherall. The ensuing winter, my husband and his brother Richard took a job of tie making and wood chopping in the timber near Detroit, Minnesota. We moved to the shanty in the woods the day before Christmas, and as my husband had told our three little boys that they could have a Christmas tree, if we got to our woods camp in time, they were planning on it, and so was I, though my means were very limited.

I had knit them some mittens out of red yarn, and hid them away for weeks. I only had three cents of my own, but when we neared the little town of Audabon, on our way to the camp, I asked my husband for some change.

"Why! What for?" he asked.

"Why," I replied, "you have told the children several times that they could have a Christmas tree and they believe it, and are planning on it, so much. I do not want them to be disappointed."

"Oh," he says, "that don't make any difference and we are liable to need every cent I've got for necessary things."

"Well," I said, "I do not believe in telling the children something that I never intend to carry out, so if you have any change let me have some. It won't take long to buy a little something," for man-like, he didn't want to stop in town as we had a long drive before us, but he gave me a quarter, and I went in the store and bought ten cents worth of pretty red apples, five cents worth of striped stick candy, and a nickel a piece for a tiny red and blue tin pail. Then I got a little red tin cup for three cents for the youngest, and felt very well satisfied.

It was after dark when we reached our camp, and Richard was there to help set up the cook stove and bedstead. We hastily prepared supper and ate it, and the children were soon in the trundle bed asleep. Then I insisted on my husband cutting an evergreen bush, which he nailed up on the wall and I fixed twine around the red apples and hung them on the tree, also the striped sticks of candy, the red mittens, and some small cakes with raisins. In the morning, our three children were pleased over their Christmas tree and never found the least fault with it. So little does it take to please the humble poor.

Well, in a short time we had a dozen men to board. At first I would have the breakfast on the table at six a.m., but Richard thought we better have it earlier, so we tried having breakfast at half past five, but the boarders didn't like to get up so early so we settled on breakfast at six. I managed to do the cooking for all hands alone for a while, but found it too much, so my husband's sister helped me a few weeks. Then my sister May came up from Clitherall, and helped me the rest of the winter.

The snow went off early that spring and we moved back to Clitherall. My husband then concluded to take a homestead near East Battle Lake, on the north side and go in for himself, so he settled up with the Bishop Warren Whiting and turned in his buildings to the society of equality, so as not to be in debt to them. We had been holding the land we were on as a preemption for the church, but let them have it back to hold it for themselves if they wished. We did not leave the church, though, at this time.

We built a home on our homestead and managed to raise a very good garden the first year, built a pasture fence and a good sized log house; most all the houses in the country were of logs at this time. This winter my husband was away most of the time, at work in the woods, and he hired Emer Murdock to stay with us and do the chores, haul and chop wood, etc. Early in the spring, he was home working to open up a farm on our brush land. On Aug. 6, 1879, our daughter Alice Eugenie was born. Those were very busy years.

A school district was soon organized so our boys could attend school. After this, a railroad was built through our region of country, which made work and wages more plentiful for all the settlers. This fall my sister May married Freeman Anderson and Arthur W. married Lois Murdock. On October 30, 1881, our son Edwin Bryon came to live with us. And I now began to find it a little difficult to keep all my sewing and patching done up along with all the rest of my work with seven in a family. I had no sewing machine and I still continued to knit all the winter socks and stockings for the family. I sometimes took some sewing to my mother's or some of the neighbors who now had machines and so I learned to sew on a machine. We now began to be visited with sewing machine agents who wished to sell us a sewing machine. My husband would have risked running in debt for one for me, for he knew I needed one badly, but I would not allow it. I saw how hard it was for him to pay for machinery for the farm work, and I decided that I would never have a machine until we could pay for it.

Thus the years went by. The little church we were still members of had gone down spiritually, till they ceased to hold meetings entirely for some time, an unheard of thing among them before. I sometimes thought of the prophecy by T. W. Smith, to the effect that if we rejected the claims of the Reorganized church, that we would go down both spiritually and temporally. The grasshoppers had come in a year from then, and now in a few short years, they had given up holding services. I compared this prophecy, with the only prophecy I ever heard Uncle Chancey Whiting utter, and that was when we had first entered into the order of oneness, or equality. He had been chosen and ordained, as president of the high priesthood, before this, and according to the Book of Covenants, it should be his gift to be a prophet, seer, and revelator. I had always been looking since his ordination for him to give some evidence of having the gift of prophecy, so when he said in a public meeting, "I tell you when this order of oneness that we have entered into becomes fully understood there will be thousands come in under this order." Well that was about forty-three years ago (as I am writing in 1916), and nothing of the kind has been fulfilled yet.

Well, the winter of 1884 arrived and the Reorganization again sent a missionary to our country. Elder Thomas Nutt came and commenced holding services in our Girard township. At first in the homes of the neighborhood, we consented for him to preach in our homes. After awhile I began to consider the matter thus. If there is anything to our Latter Day Saint belief, we must believe the books. The Bible surely points out an apostasy after Christ's day, it as surely foretells a Restoration of the Gospel, by an angel and plainly shows the coming forth of a Book which is truly fulfilled in the Book of Mormon, and the Restoration of the Gospel to Joseph Smith. I believe that Joseph

Smith was a true prophet, and we are admonished to take the books for our guide.

Now according to the Book of Covenants, "Every president of the High Priesthood shall be ordained by direction of a High Council or General Conference." Alpheus Cutler was never ordained to that office at any time, or in any way, as I have been told by the widow of Alpheus Cutler and by both of his daughters, Lois Sherman and Sallie Anderson. Also my parents have admitted the same, so why should I believe he ever held this authority?

Joseph Smith, son of the martyr has been ordained, according to the law laid down in the Book of Covenants. I have heard the followers of Alpheus Cutler tell that he said of himself, "I am neither a prophet or son of a prophet." And yet held the office to which that gift belonged by right, or pretended to hold it. Other things as absurd came to my mind, when I allowed doubts to enter; there were plenty of doubtful things to come up. So when on the fifth of March 1884, we heard that there were to be some baptisms at the Lake, I had the desire to be baptized, but I had hardly the courage to say so until Brother Jedd Anderson came and told us that Ernest and Lewis wished to be baptized and asked if we were willing they should be. I replied it would look sort of strange for us to consent for our children to be baptized if we did not have faith enough to go forward ourselves. "Well," he says, "Come on yourself if you believe."

He went away and I told my husband. I didn't believe I should ever have any faith in the authority of the Cutlerite faction again and that if he was willing to be baptized now I was. He said, "well, if you are ready, I am."

So we hastily made ready and were baptized in the ice cold waters of East Battle Lake that afternoon. A hole had been cut in the ice, and I think eleven of us were immersed according to the Bible mode of baptism. A step which we have never regretted.

I had been a member of the Cutlerite faction for many years and yet had not believed everything that some of them did, so now I found that I could belong to the true church and still not believe some things that a few did believe. Some questions that troubled me, mentioned heretofore in the autobiography, never troubled me again. I think it takes a long time for people to overcome all of their mistakes or traditions and perhaps none will come to perfection of understanding in this life. Still, I believe we should study the word of God and try to understand and obey that, and have charity and sympathy for others not of our faith. Suffice it to say God has confirmed his word by signs following the believers since we united with the Reorganization to my complete satisfaction, though I still pray for my Cutlerite friends and relatives whom I believe to be honestly deceived.

On July 20, 1885, our daughter Bertha Francis was born and we all loved our lively little girl who could jump so sprightly when a year old in her little jumper. In 1886, we sold our homestead and then I told my husband, "Now you may get me a sewing machine." And he bought me a fine new Home, which has been a blessing to me for twenty-eight years or more. In the fall of 1887, we moved to Missouri and located at Independence. We remained there one year and a half.

On March 10, 1888, a dear little babe came to us which we named Raymond Arthur. He was not very well and for several months before his death was a great sufferer. He died October 18, 1888, and was laid to rest in the Independence cemetery. Before his death (as before the death of our first little daughter), I was warned of the trial coming to us, but was shown if I would be faithful I should have my children again in the resurrection. May God help me to be faithful.

In the spring of 1889, we moved to Cedar County, Missouri. On December 23, 1889, our daughter Grace was given us. Emma Grace was her name. We rented a farm the first year and then moved onto a piece of land which my husband had bought. We were not very prosperous and though we worked hard and lived economically, we kept getting poorer. The boys grew up, and had to go away to find work. Our stock died, for no reason as we could see.

On July 13, 1892, our twins were born, which we named Robert Earl and Ruby Pearl. When they were three months old, our last cow, which was a good one and well as far as we knew, came up by our gate and laid down and died, so we had to go to buying milk for the twins to have enough to eat.

On March 19, 1893, our house caught fire and burned to the ground. The most of our clothing and bedding and other things were burned. We moved next day into a little house a mile away. A week

later, Victor took very sick with [some] sort of pneumonia and pleurisy combined. After being sick about a week and growing worse all
the time, he was healed instantly through the administration of Elders G. Beebe and Jedd Anderson. To our Heavenly Father be all the
praise.

After that we had much sickness in the family, and though we
received blessings often in answer to prayer yet sickness would come
again. We almost despaired of ever raising Ruby. She had so much
sickness. A short time before the twins were a year old, we were
thrown out of a rig when riding, and into a rocky ditch, or gulley, and
I suffered a compound dislocation of my right elbow. Doctor Marquis
of Cedar Springs was summoned, and he and my husband's brother
Jedd managed after the fifth trial, which caused me great pain, to set
the elbow back into proper place. It was a week before I could move a
finger of the hand, three weeks before I could commence to squeeze
a dishcloth in my hand so as to help wash dishes, six weeks before I
could help wash clothes, but in all these six weeks Victor, who was
about seventeen, and Alice, fourteen, would each take a tub and board
and work hard all one day in every week to get our week's washing
done.

Lewis was at this time in Minnesota to find work. Ernest went
into Indian Territory, or Oklahoma, to work. This fall of 1893, my
husband was sick a while, both twins were sick, Victor was sick again,
and again was healed through the administration of the Elders. At
this time one of our neighbors, a Mrs. Dunham, came over to call on
us. She did not believe as we did, and she asked, "how is Victor?"

I said, "He seems better for a short time now."

She said, "I see you had the Elders here again."

I said, "Yes."

"So I suppose you think Victor will get well, do you not?"

I replied, "Yes, if it is God's will."

"Well, don't you think if it is God's will he would get well anyway?" she asked.

"Well," I replied, "He might, but don't you think that if we do as
God has commanded we will be full as apt to be blessed of the Lord.
In James, you know, we are commanded to send for the elders if we
are sick and you know some people do not deny God's power to heal

the sick. We Latter Day Saints are among the number. The Bible says some will have a form of Godliness but deny God's power, 'from such turn ye away.' We do not deny God's power to grant any of the blessings promised the believers."

She looked as if I had hit her hard. She was a Campbellite in belief.

This fall or early part of winter, Lewis came home on a visit and he took a sick spell. When he got better, he advised us to go back to Minnesota. My husband found a chance to sell the forty acres he had bought and took the most of it in horses and colts, so he rigged up two covered wagons and on the seventh of May 1894, we started on a pilgrimage to Minnesota again.

Ernest was still in Oklahoma, Lewis had returned to Minnesota, so there were nine of us in the family. When we were two weeks on the road, we found our five youngest children had been exposed to the whooping cough for they began to whoop, and we had whooping times from then on. I believe we were about six weeks on the road. I was very glad to meet my parents, brothers, and sisters, and other relatives again.

We moved into a house which was vacant, and stayed that summer and winter, my husband and sons working at whatever their hands found to do. On February 22, 1895, we celebrated Washington's birthday by another burn out, and lost lots of our bedding and clothing in this fire. I must not forget to say that after both these fires, our kind friends and neighbors came to our relief with many needful things, which we greatly appreciated. May God bless them all for their kindness to us in our times of need. I wonder if we will understand better hereafter why all these trials are permitted to come upon us.

This summer of 1895, we rented a farm of Orris Albertson and raised a fine crop. The children and I tried to help all we could. I crawled over the onion field time after time with the children helping me to pull weeds. In the fall we had to put forty bushels of onions in an outdoor cellar because there was no sale for them. The next spring my husband had to take them all out and dump them on the ground because there was no sale. Our potatoes which the children and I worked so faithfully to help dig and cellar, were partly fed to cows and a few sold for ten cents a bushel. In the spring our wheat brought about forty cents a bushel. Still we had a plenty to eat and lived some way. The next year we rented the St. Pierre farm north of Battle Lake. Crops were poor this year too. The next year we rented a small farm of Alva Murdock. In 1898 and 1899, we rented the Ricker farm in Girard. While here, Lewis enlisted in the Cuban Spanish War, with the United States.

The fall of 1899 we moved to Bemidji, Minnesota, over one hundred miles north. Our daughter Alice had taught a term of school near Deer Creek and this summer had taught near Buena Vista in Beltrami County. Our sons, Ernest and Victor, and my husband's brothers, Freeman and Myron, had taken homesteads near Bemidji, so we moved up there and lived on Victor's homestead.

I know I'm missing many interesting events, among which that I counted as our blessings were the chance to attend several reunions and district conferences when a part of our family would go with tent and covered wagon and stay over two Sundays. We were in Fergus Falls at a reunion two years, at Wadena one year, and at Detroit one year. I mean we attended reunions over two Sundays at those places, not that we stayed one year or two years at those places.

In May 1900, we were pleased to have my parents, my sister Lucia who was now a widow, and my youngest sister Corda, and her husband and family make us a visit. My husband's parents had both died before this. While on this visit, Corda's husband was baptized by Elder I. N. Roberts, which was a cause for joy to us, but of sorrow to my poor old parents who still held their prejudice against the Reorganization. Shortly after their return home, my sister Corda united with the church. My sister May who was the wife of Freeman E. Anderson, and sister Ella, wife of Winfield W. Gould, had united with the church shortly before I did.

We worked hard while at Bemidji but began to have more for our comfort. Lewis came from the Philippines for which we were glad. The men worked at wood chopping and hauling in wintertime and trying to get farms open in the Jackpine regions in summer. Our home was always open to missionaries, and we were pleased to have them with us. Here Edwin was ordained a Priest. I remember Brothers Nutt, Holt, Foss and wife, T. W. Smith and wife, who were welcomed at our home either before or after we had joined the church, also Alexander Smith who gave my husband, myself, and Alice, our patriarchal blessings. After we moved to Bemidji, T. C. Kelley, I. N. Robert, Bro. McCoy, E. A. Stedman, F. A. Smith and others visited us, and all sought to strengthen us in the Gospel.

On June 10, 1900, our oldest son Ernest was married to Miss Lilly Hand, and our oldest daughter Alice was united in marriage with Leon A. Gould at our home, ceremonies by I. N. Roberts. Leon and Alice soon left us for Lamoni, Iowa, where Leon took up the work of stenographer for the patriarch, and Alice wrote us faithfully of how kind Aunt Lizzie Smith was to her when she went as a bride and stranger to a strange land.

Ernest and bride soon went to housekeeping on his own homestead, and our family began to dwindle. We tried to start Sunday schools and prayer meetings, shortly after reaching Bemidji for we believed in taking our religion along with us wherever we went, for it is the religion of Jesus Christ.

In 1901, Freeman Anderson and family, and my husband, myself, and our daughters Bertha, Grace, and Ruby, and our son Robert went with teams and covered wagons to Clitherall to the reunion. While there we were pleased to witness the baptism of my sister Lucia Murdock and her two children Ralph and Mae into the family and fold of Christ. This summer Ernest and Lilly's son Lester Lawrence died.

When we returned home from the Reunion we found Alice and Leon there but Leon left us in a few days to start on a long mission to Australia leaving his wife with us. That fall, Leon's only brother Winfield (always called Winnie) died with typhoid fever at his parent's home in Ottertail Co., which was a grief to us all, as he was such a dear good boy beloved by all who knew him.

Alice wrote to Leon every week and received letters from him often, but he could not get her letters as he was going from one island to another and his mail could never catch up with him, till he reached Australia. While on one of the islands, the missionaries were warned through the gifts, of sorrow awaiting some of their number, and of course Leon would wonder if it could be Alice. Their little daughter, Alice Leona, was born November 28, 1901, at our home, but it was way into January 1902 before Leon got the letters telling him about his little new daughter, or before he heard of his brother's death. He read that first in the Ensign. In March, Alice and baby left us to visit our relations at Clitherall. While there, the baby was healed of a terrible affliction of eczema, or something like it, through administration of the elders. When Leon came home they went to Lamoni to live. Bertha and Lewis went there soon to work for Alice at the Saint's home for the aged.

Time passed on. Our son Victor, our nephew Ross Anderson, and John Hedeen a neighbor, went to Canada and took homesteads about twenty miles southwest of Saskatoon, Saskatchewan. In the winter of 1904, Victor returned on a visit and married Miss Anna Hedeen; they went immediately to their Canadian home, but she only lived a few months, when she died of a Blind Tumous [tumor?], or the effects of the operation by doctors to remove it. Thus trouble comes so unexpected. In the early winter of 1905, Victor returned to Minnesota and worked near home all winter. I was shown in a dream that we would go to Canada soon.

A new railroad was built near our house. We boarded a dozen or more hands for nearly three months, then Victor chartered a car to take our stock and household effects to Canada. Ernest and wife and little Thelma (they had lost their first baby, a boy named Lester Lawrence) started for Portland, Oregon, where Lilly's mother resided—the same day that we started for Canada. Perhaps it was the twelfth of April we started, I am not sure now. Anyway we boarded the train about three a.m., on Wednesday morning. At eleven p.m., Thursday evening we were at Brother Richard Anderson's. We got to Saskatoon about six p.m. and hired a rig to take us out twenty miles, so we were good and tired when we got there, at eleven o'clock at night. Next day we drove over to Victor's home and so were at home in a strange land.

The next Monday, Victor reached Saskatoon with the car, and our boys Byron and Victor, Uncle Rich and John Hedeen, all went with teams to help haul the effects and drive the cows to our place. My husband filed on a homestead joining Victor's, and from the first day I got there I loved our Canada home. About the third Sunday after reaching there we started Sunday school. The next winter a branch was organized. My husband was elected president. He had been ordained a priest while at Bemidji and later an elder at a Clitherall reunion.

We tried to make all the missionaries at home at our house—as far as possible who came there. They were always welcome. I recall Elders Kimsley, J. L. Mortimor, H. J. Davison, Samuel Tomlinson, Elder Beckley Beckman, E. E. Long, Elsworth Moorman—I think his name was. U. W. Green, F. A. Smith, and Bro. Hilliard, and Bro. Charles Derry.

Well, we did the best we could with our limited means. We worked and prayed and trusted. Our children left home for homes of their own. Ernest's dear wife died at Dayton, Washington, December 13, 1906, and the next March, Ernest and little three and a half-year old Thelma came to live with us in Canada. Our daughter Grace married Omar L. Nunn, September 4, 1907. Ross Anderson married our daughter Bertha April 12, 1909. Victor married Miss Jennie Leach May 30, 1909. Our son Byron married Miss Nora Hourie, May 8th, 1911. Ruby was united in marriage to Mr. Algot Ward August 16, 1911. Lewis married Miss Addie Caress November 29, 1911, so that our number was decreasing in our own home, but increasing in our children's homes.

And now I think I will tell you of my husband's and my own visit to our daughter Alice's and other relatives, as to go off on a trip on the train to visit anyone was a new and unexpected event to us old worn and weary pilgrims.

In the spring of 1909, Leon and Alice and their four children and Lewis had left Lamoni, Iowa, and went to or near Bemidji, Minnesota to live. I had relatives near there and also at Clitherall. It had been nearly five years since I had seen any of them.

Abraham Lincoln believed in God and in his personal supervision of the affairs of men and nations. He believed himself to be under the control and guidance of a Supreme Being. I wonder how far us Latter Day Saints believe this. I remember how badly I wished to make a visit to Minnesota in the early winter or late fall of 1909. I knew Alice needed my help for a while, and it seemed as if I could hardly give up the idea that I ought to go that winter. Bertha had come to Canada the year 1907 and would be there part of the time, and Ruby could do the home work. Well, I thought, we are not able to furnish the means for such a trip. I wanted pa to go with me, but he thought that would be impossible.

Along the last of November we very unexpectedly received fifty dollars that a brother owed us. We had not thought he could pay it that fall. About the same time a young man whose homestead joined ours and who had stayed with us a good deal till he seemed one of the family, heard that his mother was sick who lived near Bemidji, too, so he was to start for Minnesota the last of the week. My husband said I could go, but he did not think he had better try to go that year. The children all were in favor of my going. John Hedeen was willing I should go when he did, as I was timid about traveling alone.

The night before we were to start, I was suffering with an affliction which had troubled me for years and could not sleep well and my thoughts ran this way. I am not very well and we need this money for so many things especially to pay as tithing, as we never can make out to pay the tenth of all we own, so will I not be robbing God, as well as the family if I take this trip? So I about decided to give it up, though I felt very sorry to not go. When in the morning I made my decision known, the children all objected and Edwin said, "I think you merit a vacation and you better not give it up," but I was afraid it would be wrong and so hastened to do some sewing for Alice thinking if I could only get them made, I could send them with John Hedeen.

Ross and Bertha came with the little gifts they wished me to take to Alice and seemed much disappointed to think I would think of giving it up. John Hedeen came to see if I was ready and said, "Well I am sure you are better able to go now than ever before."

Robert kept saying, "Oh! Ma will take Christmas dinner with Alice." Till finally I said as we were eating dinner, "Well, if you will empty that trunk I will be ready in time." The boys dumped things out of the trunk in a hurry and in half an hour I was ready. My trunk was packed and we climbed into the rig and started.

We had to ride sixteen miles to Sister Van Eaton's place that afternoon, and on the way there I suffered so acutely that I told my husband that night, that it was a foolish thing for anyone so afflicted as I was to ever try to go any place and that like as not when we got to Saskatoon, I would decide to go home with him instead of going to Minnesota. Well, I tried to pray over the matter, asking the Lord if it was right for me to go on this trip for Him to bless me so I might not be tortured so in my body, but go rejoicing in him.

Well towards morning, I got easy and fell asleep, and was blessed with a dream to the effect that it was God's will that I should go and that I should be blessed in my body, that I should not try to plan too much for myself, but if I would trust him, I should find he was directing all things for my best good. When I awoke and thought of my dream I said, "Could it be possible that I could be relieved of this affliction so that I could make this journey in comfort? I believe I will try it and perhaps hereafter I can see why the Lord is directing me to go now."

I was free from pain all the morning, rode seven miles to reach Saskatoon, walked around town a good deal to make some necessary purchases, went to the depot about noon. My husband bought a return ticket for me for about thirty-one dollars. He thought I could stay about three months and Lewis would be ready to come home with me, as he intended to go to Canada in the spring. About one o'clock, we entered the train. I thought to myself, I don't know when I have felt so well as this whole afternoon, surely the Lord has blessed me. I believe my husband had prayed for me, too, though he did not tell me so. At home when the girls were putting up my lunch, I had told them I didn't feel as if I would need anything to eat all the way down. But ere the train had left Saskatoon, I was hungry, and enjoyed every meal. This was on Saturday. I was well all the way. We reached [Bemidji] Monday forenoon and took dinner at a restaurant. John Hedeen hired a rig to take us and our trunks out into the country. We reached his mother's first and found her better, then on to Leon's and Alice's.

They did not know I was coming, so I took them by surprise. I found Alice sitting up for the first time in six days as little Arlo Bryan was then six days old. Leon's sister Ethel had seen the rig drive up and said, "Alice, there's someone come, and she looks like your mother."

I went right into the house, for little Winfield opened the door for me and I said, "Don't be scared, Alice, it is only someone from Canada."

How she laughed as she said, "Why, Ma Anderson, is it possible?"

We were all glad to see each other. I had never seen any of her five children except Leona, and she was only six months old when they had gone to Lamoni. Well, when I told Lewis my plans he said he could not get ready to go to Canada by the first of March. I wrote home and asked my husband to try and make it possible for him to come down and make a visit this winter, for I thought it would be terrible to have to go so far alone. When he wrote to me he said he would think of it, but feared he could not make it.

It was the sixth of December that I reached Alice's. I stayed at Alice's all through December, except nearly every Sunday when Lewis and I would go over to Freeman Anderson's and visit my sister May and go to church, which was held at the school house or in private dwellings.

New Year's Day passed and 1910 was ushered in. How I looked all day for my husband, for I thought, if he does come at all he will come before the new year because the excursion rates run out by that time. But the day passed and he did not come. On Sunday Lewis and I again went to Freeman's neighborhood. Sunday school and church were held in the school house that day. Freeman's folks had not gone yet and said for us to put our team in the barn and ride over with them. When I entered the house, I thought they all looked pleased about something. Pretty soon Maurice Anderson, our nephew from Canada, came into the room.

I said, "Why, Maurice, when did you come?"

He said, "Oh, I got here the day before New Year's Day."

"Did anyone come with you?" I asked.

"Yes, Guy Anderson (another nephew) came."

"Well, why didn't you bring my old man with you?" I asked.

"Oh," Maurice replied, "He did talk a little about it, but he was so changeable minded I guess he thought it wouldn't be wise for him to come now or something or another."

"Well," I said, "I don't know as it would be wise, but I wish he could have come."

Maud and Blynn were laughing, so I wondered why, and Maud said, "why, Aunt Em, would you care at all to see him?"

"Would I?" I replied, "I was telling Alice and Leon this morning that though I had not seen my mother or sisters or brothers for so long, yet I would give more to see Edwin today than anyone else on earth."

"That seems strange," said May, "For such old folks."

"Strange or not," said I, "It is true."

Then as we were riding along to the school house, May said, "Well, Em, maybe you won't have to go home alone anyway now that Maurice and Guy are here."

"Oh," I said, "I don't suppose they would care to have an old woman along with them." How disappointed I did feel to think Edwin wasn't here to go with me down to Clitherall and to visit all around and go home with me.

Well, when we reached the school house, May made me go in first, and when I got into the inner door I stopped speechless, for there sat a man whose back looked just like my Edwin. I couldn't believe my eyes till he turned his head and I knew it was him. Then I rushed over to him and shook his hand and said right out loud in Sunday School, "Oh, they didn't let me know you had come." How everyone laughed at me then, all knowing how surprised and pleased I was. That was one of my happiest days. It seemed that the children back home had all combined to encourage him to come. Some of them had given him some money to be sure he had enough and had packed his suitcase and lunch box before he had said he would go, when they knew Guy and Maurice were coming. He wanted to come but feared it would not be wise.

Well, Alice and Leon were as surprised to see Pa that night as they had been to see me. We visited around Bemidji a while then went to Clitherall and visited there, but not long enough for Pa. We hurried back to Bemidji to go home with the young folks, for Guy married Miss Jennie Smith, and Maurice married Amy, and Frank and his young wife made up their minds to try Canada, so there were six young folks going with us when I had feared I would have to go alone. But my husband looked solemn when we were leaving dear old Clitherall and kept looking out the car window at Orson's field as long as we could see any of it. Till I said, "Edwin, I am going to try to feel as sister Lu told us to, as if I am not leaving for good, but am coming back."

"Well," he said, "that's a good way to feel if you can think so."

And I thought to myself, Edwin doesn't feel as if he is ever coming back in this life. Then when we bid our daughter Alice goodbye, Oh! what a look of sadness came over his face, and I noted it, and thought, "Pa doesn't think he will ever see her again." I could have cried with fear of it, then, but must needs control myself. How glad I am that we made that short visit then. I wish we had stayed longer. "But of all the memories coming now and then, the oldest are, it might have been."

We had a fine trip home. We went through part of the great Eaton Store, at Winnipeg, but though I wished to see more of it, Edwin cared nothing for any of it, only sat and waited till I was ready to go. We reached home safely. In the summer of 1911, I came down to Bemidji again with our sister-in-law Eliza Anderson to see my sister May, Freeman's wife who was very sick. We stayed about a month. May died a couple of weeks after we had left her; the first one of my mother's children to end her life work. Our dear old father had passed over the river in the fall of 1909. Well, such is life and death in the midst of life. We mourned the loss of our dear ones but not without hope of an eternal resurrection.

Maurice Anderson, son of M. M. Anderson died with appendicitis while Eliza and I were still at Bemidji, leaving his young wife Amy and babe, dear little Dorris, so there was mourning both at Bemidji and Vanscoy.

All this year I had known that my husband's health was not so good. In the winter of 1911, he had been sick a few weeks with what he called rheumatism, as his feet and limbs would swell. He never seemed to recover from this so as to feel as well. After I had returned from Bemidji, he took a short vacation and went with Lewis to Sedley to a conference, and was gone nearly a week. After this he seemed anxious to get all his business affairs settled up, as far as possible, made final proof on his preemption, etc., so that when all the payments were made there would be no trouble about the proofs.

About New Year's time 1912, he was again taken sick, the same as the year before. He got a little better, so he could chore around a little, but was very weak. He still thought it rheumatism. At last we prevailed on him to see a doctor, who pronounced it leakage of the hart [sic]. One Sunday when we were alone, he told me he did not know as he was ever to get well.

I said, "If you think so, Ed, don't go till you bless me, for I do not feel as if I could bear it." (I had received evidence ere this that he would die.) So we knelt in prayer and he then anointed my head with oil and prayed God to bless me. I received a spirit of peace and reconciliation to God's will, and he died the twenty-third of May 1912.

Well, I thought there would never be anything more worth writing after my husband's death. But I have found that life goes on. The Lord still has blessings for us and we still have our trials to endure.

Now as I write this page October 10th, 1920, the hand of affliction is upon me and I am so lame I am now going on crutches since I wrote the former page. I have lived for a time in Canada, Montana, Minnesota, and Missouri. At present I am in Missouri at the home of my sister Cordelia Perry's and I am thinking of sending this book to my son Robert, and his wife Martha.

With love and all good wishes. Hoping that all my children will learn to trust in our Heavenly Father and carry all their troubles to him in prayer.

——Emma L. Anderson

Elsie Florence Andes Doig Townsend

BORN
October 15, 1908, Far West, Missouri
DIED
April 16, 1994, Missoula, Montana

Interviewed by Donna L. Ellison on February 24, 1986, in Manhattan, Montana.

Where were you born? And where did you grow up? Tell me about some of these things.

Well, I was born in Far West, Missouri, right across from the temple lot. My parents and their family of five children went to a homestead in northeastern Montana in 1910. I was not quite two years old, so I don't remember Missouri. My father put up a one-room [sod] house.... All seven of us lived that year in that one-room sod house. I grew up in Montana. We lived there from 1910 to 1930. My father, Sam Andes, was a priesthood member.

Were you reared in the church, Elsie?

Yes, we always went to church. Our first meetings in Montana were held in our house. In summers, we even met in my father's blacksmith shop. At the age of eight, I was baptized by my father in the little [illegible word]. My first reunion was in North Dakota. I was just seven years old. We drove there, but on the way we had an accident. The car landed upside down, and my leg got hurt, but we went on to the reunion. At the last prayer service, I stood and bore my testimony. I loved God, and he loved me, and then I sat down so embarrassed, because I was not old enough to be a member. I had no right to take part in their prayer and testimony service, but I am glad I did.

What about your mother, was she active in the church?

My mother, Florence Wildermuth Andes, was born in Lamoni, Iowa, the first white child born there. Her father, Eli Wildermuth, was a missionary all his adult life for the RLDS church. It was in her grandfather's home in Wisconsin that the early meetings of the Reorganization were held. You will find them, in fact, in volume 2 of the *Church History*. When living in Montana, Mother was happy to have more church members come in and take up homesteads nearby. Working together, they built a church just across the road from our house in 1914. The lot they built on was given to the church by Joe Higgins, mother's brother-in-law. The church was heated by a little coal-burning stove, lighted by a kerosene lamp. A shed in the backyard had stalls for horses that pulled the wagons and buggies to bring the members to church. Father was president for years. Often at prayer meetings, father held his youngest child in his arms, presided over the service, and led the singing. Always we went to church. When I was just eleven, my father had me play a little pipe organ for Sunday school.

Did other missionaries stay in your home? Did your parents have contacts with them?

[The] missionaries who came to Andes, Montana, always stayed in our home. We were so near the church, of course. Also, my brothers gave up their bedroom and slept in the hayloft of the barn. My mother's brother, Joe Wildermuth, who was a missionary to North

*Elsie Florence Andes married James Stuart Doig on August 19, 1934. Used with permission of
Mary Charlotte Gamel.*

Dakota and Montana for years, usually brought one of his children
with him, and, always, they stayed with us. Years later, her brother,
Lester Wildermuth, came as a missionary to western Montana and
came to my husband's and my ranch home, at least one week a year
to "rest," he always said.

But he put up that chart of the church doctrine on the wall, and
he converted my husband [James Stuart Doig]. The next summer at
reunion, the people were going down into the water to be baptized

and he was standing there. [Lester] put his hand on my husband's shoulder and said, "Don't you think you are ready to be baptized?" And Jim said, "Okay," and they went down into the water and he baptized him.

What other missionaries stayed in your home? I know you had several people in your home.

Well, when I lived in Bozeman, many appointees came to visit us. There was apostle George Mesley, apostle Percy Farrow, Wayne Smith, and many others. Any missionary who was in Bozeman stopped at our house. After that, when I lived in Independence, Missouri, we often had missionaries come to stay with us. Harry Black, then an appointee to Montana, came and was there for several days. He had led the Zion's League down to Independence for the week. In fact, the day he left, he stood to offer a prayer for us, and he thanked the Lord for people like Wendell, my [second] husband, who was so kind to Elsie, his wife. Ken Robinson and his wife and family lived in our home for three weeks after he came from Australia, after he had accepted his appointment and was going to school over in Kansas City. Later, they bought a house in Independence. Gordon Mesley and his wife came to conference. They came from Washington, DC, and they lived with us for that week.

When you were a youngster were there any difficulties in getting to church services?

Well, father often carried the gospel into the homes of the people around us. Mother lived it. She had time for all of the sick. She delivered ninety-eight babies ... in the area around about, during the years she lived in Montana. One winter when I was about twelve years old, father was asked to give a talk in a home twelve miles west of us where the neighbors would be gathered and waiting for him. He asked me to go with him to sing a duet with him there for the service. We rode horseback through the deep snow. Coming home it was dark. Father and the horses knew the way to our barn.

As a teacher in rural school for years, often for church I read the scriptures on Sunday and worshiped by myself, because I couldn't get to church. Later, teaching in towns where there was no RLDS

church, I played the piano for the congregation. In Ennis, it was a
Methodist church—I took my little children with me, and worshiped
with the congregation. In Ennis, at their United church, I taught the
high school class, played the piano for all the services for two years.
My five little children and I walked a mile to church, and I put them
on the front row and told them to be good. Then I had to sit up on the
platform all the time. One day I asked the pastor, "Would you think
it would be better if I didn't bring those children to church? People
have to look at them, and they do make some wiggly sounds." And
the preacher said, "Mrs. Doig, if other people brought their children
to church, they wouldn't be looking at yours." So.

When I taught in Ennis one weekend in February, I decided to go
to the valley below for the weekend. I could buy some shoes for my
little ones [because] the twins two years old couldn't wear the shoes
[handed-down from] the twins four years old. There were no shoe
stores in Ennis. We could go to our own church in Bozeman, also,
when we were there on Sunday to worship with our members.

Early Saturday morning, I took a big can of hot coals from the
basement furnace, and carried them out to the car and set them down
under the engine. The weather then was 30 to 40 below zero most
nights. I hadn't run the car since Christmas, and, of course, I had
no garage. Back in the house, I fed the children, helped them put
on their coats and overshoes. Taking two big pans of hot water out
to the car, I filled the empty radiator, got in the car, stepped on the
starter—the motor began to run. I left it running, went back into the
house, and carried my two sets of twins out to the car. I didn't want
a lot of snow on the seats, because they would be sitting on the seats
with their feet up there.

Our drive to Bozeman was good. The highway had been plowed.
We stayed all night at the home of my sister-in-law. On Sunday, how
we enjoyed worshiping with the Saints in Bozeman. At noon, however, it began to snow, and by 2 p.m. the wind was wild and the snow
was gusting hard. Loading my five children into the car, I began to
drive the sixty miles over deeply covered roads toward Ennis. Cau-
tiously, I made the sharp turns in the road. There were no other cars
on the road [since] it was Sunday. Also, never would there be a snow-
plow on the road that day. Nearing the pass, I carefully kept the car

in the middle of the road, afraid of slipping over the edge and falling into the canyon below. One by one, I made the sharp turns in the road—five of them. The last one was the most difficult, I knew, and the climbing was steep.

Almost to the curve, the car stopped—stuck in the deep snow. I stepped out, went to the trunk of the car, got out the shovel, began to get the snow off my trail, also from under the tires and under the car. Getting into the vehicle, I started the motor, tried to move the car forward. The motor roared and roared, but only slipped backward a little bit. I tried more shoveling and again tried to get the car to go forward, no luck. I stood gasping. I looked around. Ranches on both sides of the road, of course, but no houses nearer than three miles, I knew—no cattle up here this time of year, being fed at the barn way down below. I couldn't walk all the way to a house and carry those kids—it was bitter cold—strong wind and snow. We couldn't stay all night in the car, I knew. I just had a student in the high school who had frozen to death in his car, because he had tried to stay there all night. So, of course, I was praying.

Suddenly I looked up—a man was coming through the pasture fence nearby, a snow shovel over his shoulder. He called at me, "Need any help?"

"Oh, you know I do," I said.

He came to the car. "Pretty well shoveled out," he said. "I'll put my shoulder against the back fender and push hard. It is a steep incline in the road. You try to move the car slowly."

Before I got into the car, I said to him. "I can't stop to say thank you after I get moving, so I will thank you very much right now." With the force of him pushing, I got the car moving forward, climbed up over the pass.

"Mother," Stephanie said from the back seat, "Who helped you?"

I don't know, but the Lord knew that I needed help and gave it to me. Many times when I have told RLDS people of this experience, they said, "That was one of the three Nephites."

Elsie, you have had such marvelous experiences and you are so committed. What are some of your memories of reunions? I know that you have gone to so many of those in your lifetime.

Reunions have always been a learning experience for me, as well as a worship and fellowship. When I was in my teens, we began to have district reunions at our church at Andes. The leaders always slept in our house, of course. The summer of '28, G [Jeremiah Alden] Gunsolley came to our reunion. At that time, he was also acting as president of Graceland College just for that one year. All week I acted as secretary for him, because the year before when he had been there, he had given me my patriarchal blessing. But his wife was with him, and she acted as his secretary and took, in shorthand, all of his blessings. When he came this year, he said, "My wife couldn't come. She is sick. But isn't there someone here who could write in shorthand?" Nobody put up a hand. Then he said, "Is there someone who could write these blessings for me? Somebody stuck up a hand and said, "Well, if Elsie can write as fast as she talks, she can do it."

And so I tried. All week, I took down the blessings, and I learned so much during that week. He began to persuade me about going to Graceland College. Now, no one had gone from Montana to Graceland College, that I knew of, and I was too poor, and I knew I couldn't go. But that year during my school teaching, he wrote me several times about that. The next fall I went to Graceland—studied there for two years—met so many who later became officials in the church. I got acquainted with church members from other countries of the world—for instance, Arthur Oakman from England, Ed Larson from Denmark, and many others. I sent each one of my children to Graceland to learn to live.

How have prayer services influenced your life? You have told us something about prayer.

Prayer services often give me experiences of real communication with God. I know I tell about them so often. One outstanding prayer service that I attended at a reunion is Missouri. The leader stood and spoke in tongues, something I had never heard before in my life and never heard since. When he interpreted the words, the message to us was an inspirational understanding of the purpose of Sunday as a day of worship—not just an hour of preaching. I will never forget it—how it enlarged our knowledge of God's commandments—His purpose for us.

What is your interest in the words of the scriptures? You are always quoting scriptures. I enjoy hearing them.

Well, I have taught classes in church school often and to make these of any value to the students and to myself, I have had to study the scriptures again and again, also read church history and practically all the church books. Certain quotations are my special interest, such as, "Study it out in your mind," "Seek ye out of the best books words of wisdom," also "Seek learning even by study and also by faith," "Study and learn and become acquainted with all good books and with languages, tongues, and people." I believe if we knew more about other cultures, people of other lands, it would make it possible for us to relate to our members in other countries. If our missionaries study and learn about the people to whom they are going to tell the gospel, they will be able to understand better.

For instance, Chuck Neff once said in a sermon something about it being difficult for us to preach God the Father to people in Japan because of Shintoism, Buddhism. I wanted to know more about this. I read and read, and when I was in Japan a few years ago, I read the book on the table beside my bed in the hotel room—Buddhism, Shintoism. Meeting many Japanese people—friends of my sister— I could communicate with them so much better and answer their questions more understandably. I liked that [quotation], "Become acquainted with all good books and languages, tongues, and people." I took courses in Greek drama, Plato, Olympus, and Sinai because I enjoyed teaching Greek mythology at the college.

Then one day, the head of the English department of the University of Kansas City called me to say, "We are organizing a group to take a tour of Greece. The English teacher is going and about twenty-five students—come go with us." Of course, I went. What a wonderful tour. Seeing all those faces I had taught so many years was a great experience. Also, it improved my teaching. Being a world church, we know that members who live in other countries need to know more about us here in the United States, too, so they can relate to us, and we to them. At world conference several years ago, I was a delegate in the Santa Fe Stake group. One morning, a black woman came and stood by us and said, "Is there an Elsie Townsend here?" She spoke very good English.

"Yes, I am Elsie Townsend," I said, and quickly she moved close to me. I took hold of her hand—and I don't know her name—but she said, "I'm from Africa. My friends and I have read your book and they asked me to meet the author—to talk to you. We understand you and your way of life now." We talked together that day until the conference meeting began. What joy she gave to me.

Of course, the basic reason for reading the scriptures is to improve our lives, to help us communicate better with the Lord, to prepare for his coming.

You like music, too. I know you sing hymns and play them for church, and I know that every morning you play the organ in your own home. Tell me some of the ideas you have of singing.

Well, when I went to Graceland, I took music as my major and every subject in music that was available—I had to take it. I took my first degree with a major in music. But I found that singing had been vital in my life. Singing in the "Messiah" at the Auditorium with my son and several of my daughters gave me great joy for several years. In fact, one year we were over in Kansas City and it was put on television.

Now, in our home when I was growing up, Father always liked for us to sing hymns with him. He had a very old fold-up pump organ, which he had brought to Montana in 1910, and he could play some on it. His voice was tenor, and my brother sang bass. I sang soprano, and my mother and my sister sang alto. Every evening, we had family worship. Mother and Father would read from the scriptures, and one would offer a closing prayer.

Later, serving in youth camp many times, I found out how uniting singing around the campfire could be. But, I was older before I realized the value of singing as not only a worship experience, not only a fellowshipping experience, but also a worship experience.

Living in Independence then, my husband and I joined the People to People [Student Ambassador Program] and each year had men, women, or youth in our home for a week—people from many places in the world. Ed Larson, our leader of People to People there in Independence, finally suggested that we take a trip to Europe as a group and visit in the homes of the people who had come to the United States and been in our home. Over twenty-five of us from Independence joined Ed. He had meetings to prepare us, to teach us more about the countries in which we would be traveling. Before we left, Ed had corresponded with the pastor of our RLDS group in Norway, who had promised us that his congregation would meet us, and we would be with them.

Arriving in Norway, we went to a building where the Saints were waiting to see us—the second night it was. They were sitting in a group on [the] side of the room. On the other side we sat in our group. Standing before us [was] the pastor, now he is the father-in-law of Cliff Carlson, who had met the daughter at Graceland, and they had married, and they lived in Independence. He spoke good English. Now, the leader told us that the members of his congregation were going to bear testimonies, and he would translate them to us. One by one, we were given their messages. Then, he said, "I like [illegible word] better because that means 'until we meet again.' [illegible word] just means 'goodbye.'" He turned to go. Quickly, one of our group called out, "Oh please, let us tell you about our projects— our problems in Independence." He turned back, nodded his head, explained to the natives in their language. Several of our group gave testimonies, which he translated.

Then ... I raised my hand—I always open my mouth and stick my foot in it—and spoke, "Please let us sing together."

He shook his head. "No songbooks here," he said.

"But there is a piano," I said. "I'll play the familiar hymns by memory."

I walked to the back of the room and began to play "There's an Old, Old Path." Eagerly, our group sang in English and their people sang with fervor in their language. We sang the first verse of that hymn, and then I played "Redeemer of Israel," and many of the old well-known songs. On and on with feelings we sang, looking into each other's eyes, sharing each other's emotions—not only fellowshipping, but now we were really worshiping together as a unit. How happy we were, as we shook hands, and said, "goodbye, and thank you."

That was a marvelous time, I imagine. Do you remember a time when you struggled with the results of a faith experience?

I was always taught that if we would pray, the Lord would answer our prayers—would bless us. I thought he would give us what we asked for. But I find we don't always get what we ask for. One experience that shook me up—and I learned from it: I was in the grove near Palmyra praying, kneeling beside my twins, Jim and Joan. My Jim, a spastic, was recovering from a second emotional collapse. I prayed earnestly for him and the Lord answered me: "You must learn to accept and try to understand." That wasn't the answer I wanted. I felt hurt, but the message has taught me over the years at least to begin to accept.

Later, another experience aided my understanding. In reunion in New Mexico, all week long I had prayed silently for my daughter, Marilyn, who having been a Fulbright student (and should have been in Germany), returned home with a terrible headache that continued on and on never ceasing. She was with me at the reunion, and so was Beverly, my other daughter. So I didn't pray aloud.

Finally, that last morning, I was praying, "Lord, don't speak to me through these leaders. Don't speak to me because you will tell me bad things that I have done that have kept me from having my prayers answered. It must be that I am not good enough to be able to have my prayers answered."

At the end of the reunion at the prayer meeting, apostle Arthur Oakman stood and said, "Sister Elsie, the Spirit tells me that I should say something to you. All week I have been held back for some reason, and now, before we end this reunion, I must say to you, your prayers are heard by God. But they will not be answered as you ask. You must learn to pray, 'Thy will be done,' and the Lord will do what is best for you and for the person for whom you are praying. You should continue to pray to God to communicate with him."

After the service, he walked into the back of the room. We came out, and he put his hand on Marilyn's shoulder and said, "Marilyn, how long has it been since you have been administered to?"

She said, "Quite awhile."

He said, "Come on, go over here to where I am staying and let me administer to you." He did, and she did.

Studying this for years, I have learned many things. Also, many mornings I play on my organ and sing, "Have thine own way Lord, have thine own way." And I receive a blessing of peace.

Was there a particular special time when you took part in enriching the people of the congregation? You have worked in several congregations.

Coming to live in Bozeman in 1947, I found that the little branch had no priesthood. In the store (before Sunday), a few days after we had arrived, Sister—I can't think of her name—asked me to be church school director.

"We have a feud in our congregation," she said, "and we are divided into two groups. We don't even speak to each other, hardly, and we need somebody to be our leader now."

I was so scared. I had never been an administrator and I am not a good supervisor at all. But that first Sunday I had to do it. I had those five children, seven years old, nine, and eleven, and I wanted them to know the joy of worship. I didn't want them to think that Sunday school and church were unhappy experiences. Earnestly, I prayed and then went and taught the adult class. I didn't know whether anything happened at all that was good, but at least I was going to try.

Then, just a few weeks later, Cliff Carlson began to attend. He was a junior in our college, Montana State University, but he had been two years at Graceland. In a few weeks, the district president came to ordain Cliff as a priest. We were glad to have a priesthood member, but he hadn't attended church much in his life. He had lived in Montana, and his father had not been a member, and he hadn't been to church much.

Now, long after that, he said to me, "Elsie, if you will offer the opening and closing prayer, and bring the bread and wine, and set up the table, I will serve communion next Sunday." I read the Doctrine and Covenants—I could find no quote that was negative about a woman doing that, so I did. After the service of the bread and the grape juice, Cliff had us offer prayers and bear testimonies. We were woven together. The spirit touched our hearts. The feud just slipped away, and we were so closely united.

**I know when our family moved here in 1955, everybody had such
a love and caring attitude toward each other. You must have been
instrumental in that, Elsie. Did World War I or II have any effect
upon your personal life?**

Well, when World War I occurred, I lived in Andes, Montana.
Mother and Daddy leased our home to a couple that had bought our
store. We moved into our barn, all nine of us. We kids [slept] in the
hayloft—the boys in one end and the girls in the other end. My parents slept in the granary room. Our cook stove stood outside—right
out in the open air whether it was raining or not, and we ate at a table
that was set up in a cow stall. No piano or organ to play now. But we
still had our worship service every night.

Now, the piano my mother had [brought]—my father had taken
it to the church and also the old organ. Finally in the cold fall, we
moved into my uncle's empty house nearby, but when father got the
letter of his brother's death in the navy—he read it aloud to us. His
voice broke with every sentence, and together we shared his sorrow. It
wasn't a happy experience. But it made us a close family.

During World War II, my youngest brother was drafted into the
Air Force. In the last session of his training here in the United States,
he was in Boise, Idaho, training to be a navigator on a bomber. He
wrote to me, "Elsie, can't you come to see me here before I am sent
overseas?"

I puzzled about that. I was teaching in a high school in Montana.
My housekeeper was with us only on school days. But this was nearly
Easter time, I would have the three days of no school—Friday, Saturday, and Sunday. I gave her extra pay to stay with our children, so I
could go see my little brother. Thursday evening, I climbed on a bus,
rode all night, arrived in Boise, and gazed out of the window—there
was my brother in his uniform looking up at me.

He took me to a hotel room, then said, "Elsie, I want us to go
shopping. There is a store downtown where I saw a book with clas-
sical music compositions in it. Just like the one you gave me several
years ago. Remember you are the one that started me out on learning
to play the piano. Every summer you gave me lessons, and I started
to take lessons from regular teachers. My degree from the college is
in music and literature. Say, do you remember the time you had me

play for Aunt Anne's wedding?" It was in my home and I had asked him to play.

So, he bought me the book and autographed it and I used it ever since. What a good weekend we had together. Sunday afternoon, I went back home. Just six weeks after this, he was wounded on a B-29 bomber over Austria. When he parachuted to the ground, the Germans shot and killed him. They said, "We don't want to take care of any sick people."

My mother had a severe heart attack. As soon as school was out, I moved to Warrensburg—me and my five kids, five rooms of furniture—and moved near where she lived. I found this house, and when school began in the fall, I begin to teach at Knob Noster about twelve miles away. My youngest twins, who were five years old, could go to kindergarten. Now they could walk all the way from the school to my mother's house at noon, as soon as school was out, and she would take care of them until I returned home from school. Yes, I hated war. Most of us do, but it made a reason for me to move near my mother, and my children had another parent—a grandparent.

I know because of your belief that you have had many experiences. Is there any other experience you want to relate? About these wars?

Another experience I had of World War II—that [concerned] my next-to-the-youngest brother, who was drafted early in the war time. He was in Washington and wrote to me. "Elsie, do you know of any chance for Alma (that was his wife) to teach a school near you?"

I checked. Yes, there was a vacancy in the Dry Creek Rural School. I talked to the trustees. They hired her. Every Friday, I went out to get her after school (of course, I was teaching, also) to come to stay at our house during the weekend and then to go to church on Sunday. Just before Christmastime, a trustee said to me, "We're going to have to let her go. [She] doesn't fit in with our school. She is so lonely." What could I tell Alma?

Nothing of this I ever did tell, neither did I tell her husband this—[and] don't you tell them—but I wrote to my brother to ask him to come to get her to take her to Washington to get an apartment near the army camp to be with him awhile before he would be sent overseas to fight in the war. He wrote to tell her he was coming.

He came next week, repaired his old car, which was setting out here at my place in the country, and in the morning they left to drive to Washington. The weather was 20 degrees below when they got in the car. Their car had no heater in it, so I had filled a big jug with boiling water, heated two rocks down in the furnace, and I put these things in front down near Alma's feet to give her a little bit of comfort. In March, my brother went with the 163th Infantry. Alma came to live with us. She said, "Elsie, I am glad I was with him these three months. I am pregnant now, and I will have something wonderful to look forward to all of this time." I enjoyed her happiness too.

In the context of the gospel, what are the beliefs that have really spoken to you? You have told us some of them, but I would like to hear some more.

Well, always I have believed in God. I didn't have to see him to worship him. An experience I had a few years ago supported this belief in God and enlightened my heart. My sister asked me to go to Japan with her. Her husband had died. The dignitaries there wanted to [use] part of his ashes on which to perform a Buddhist ceremony. He had been seven years in charge of all the scientific research in Japan—all of the universities after the war. When he [first] came there, he found that six men had been sentenced to execution by General MacArthur.... He didn't believe they should be executed, so he said, "Let's let them live and let's use their minds for something good." And he persuaded the president to tell General MacArthur to take away this execution sentence.

Of course, I hopped on a plane and met my sister in New York and flew to Tokyo. We took part in the Buddhist memorial over my brother-in-law's ashes, and we visited in the homes of her family. When we arrived in Japan, she said to me, "Now, Elsie, no talking of religion. You know I gave up my church years ago because of my husband's command."

The last night in Japan in our hotel room, as we were preparing to go to bed, she said to me suddenly, "Elsie, you still go to church, why?"

For a second I paused to ask the Lord how to answer. "I go to church because I love God. I want to understand more about Him.

And I want to live my life as Jesus taught. I need to learn more," I said to her.

She said to me, "But you can't show anyone your God. Here in Japan they show you their Buddhist [statues]. You and I even climbed up inside that one near that largest one they have. In fact, we climbed clear up to the forehead and peeked out, didn't we?"

Puzzled as to how to answer, I sought the Lord earnestly and he helped me. My answer was, "God loves me. I love him. I want to live my love for him to demonstrate by loving others."

When I arose from my knees after praying, I glanced over toward my sister and there she was on her knees saying a prayer—the first time in forty years. Ever since then, this thought [that] was given to me has been a blessing. I do want to learn to live the gospel.

What else can you tell us, Elsie?

Well, I shall like to tell of another experience that has been an inspiration to me to help me understand God and his caring. Teaching and taking care of five small children was a very difficult thing to do. When my husband [James Stuart Doig] died on the ranch, I chose to go back to schoolteaching because I reasoned that in a few years my children would be old enough to be in school, and they would be there in the same house that I was, and then we would have the summer together. Well, in Ennis, I was teaching music and English in high school. Two weeks before Christmas, my housekeeper said, "I have just received a letter offering me a permanent job in the post office in Manhattan. I will be leaving you this Friday."

What could I do? I called my sister-in-law down in the valley asking her to come to help me for two weeks. Then I would go to Bozeman at Christmastime to find a housekeeper, I hoped. Anna came, stayed for two weeks, left on Friday, and that night as I went with my kids to the bedroom to have our little worship, Beverly was taking off her clothes and rubbing her body. "Mother," she said, "Look what I have got. See these big pimples all over me. I itch and burn."

Quickly I went to her. "Oh, chicken pox! There are many who have that in this town right now. And Aunt Anna said she never had the chicken pox. So we can't go down into the valley at Christmas, and, besides, we will be under quarantine." We all of us had our little

Bible worship. I read them a story. I hid my distress, because I had always said I didn't want my children to grow up watching me cry. We said our prayers. Telling them good night, I went to the living room, dropped onto my knees before the little Christmas tree decorated with strings of popcorn and cranberries, and one little set of bulbs. The only light in the room was the tiny little bulb at the top of the tree. The tears flowed down my cheeks. I said softly, "Oh, Lord I can't do it by myself. I need someone to help me." And then once I stopped to listen, the Lord took my heart and gave me this message very clearly—"You are never alone. I am always with you." I was filled with the peace that surpasses understanding. The Lord does continue to speak to us—to give us wisdom and knowledge. Our church teaches us, and I am glad I do believe it.

An illustration of this gave me understanding I did not have before. In Bozeman, completing my master's degree at the university one summer, I was told that I would have to take an oral exam one time before the heads of all of the departments in which I had taken majors and minors. There were six, and they were going to sit around the table and ask me questions. The day before my test, I met a friend, and she came out of the exam room. She was crying. She had failed her test and was not going to be given her master's degree that summer.

Scared and upset, that night I prayed and prayed, "Please Lord help me to know all the answers tomorrow." It was a typical gimme, gimme, prayer. I stopped for a few moments and listened. The Lord said to me that I should not pray that way, but pray that I might be able to answer the questions in such a way that I would prove that my religion had made me a better teacher. Saying, "Thank you, Lord," I got into bed and thought of this most of the night.

Next day, I walked into the testing room. There were these six people sitting around the table. I was still shaking with fear. Then suddenly I was filled with peace. The words that came to me and warmed my heart were, "Know the truth and the truth shall make you free." I was blessed with the freedom to speak. The oral test was a beautiful experience. On and on it went for two hours. They kept saying, "Let's don't quit yet. We have more questions we want to ask her." They asked me to tell them all kinds of things about my teaching.

Next day in the class, a friend said to me, "You know, Elsie, doctor (What is his name? I have forgotten), you know he talked to us in our eight o'clock class this morning a long time about the oral test in which you were the one interviewed. He didn't say your name, but I recognized you as the person, and he said, 'That's the kind of person we need in our classroom.'"

I had learned more about praying than I ever had before. I hope I can pray with more intelligence and more understanding.

Another concept of the gospel that I understood better, was an experience at a reunion in Missouri. Marjorie and Marilyn, my eight-year-old twins, were ready for baptism. I made arrangements for this at the summer reunion, so then, we walked down by the edge of the lake. Apostle George Mesley came to us, lowered himself to his knees, put one hand on the shoulder of each twin, and said gently, "Marjorie and Marilyn, those are your names. Your mother gave them to you, because she loves you. Now you are to take on the name of Jesus Christ, because you love him and he loves you. Let your life show this love." Never have I forgotten that message—how much it has meant to me and to my twins.

Because of the death of your husband, the father of your five children, what learning experiences have you had, Elsie?

Well, when my husband died, my friends and relatives all said, "You can't possibly take care of five little children by yourself. A little girl three years old, twins just two, and twins just three months old—and you would have to earn a living for them also. You must give some of them away."

One brother, a doctor, happily married for ten years but had no children, wrote to me, "Give me one or two—our home would be a good one." Others offered to adopt them. I had a brother, who was on the faculty of the University of Kansas, and he said, "I would like to have a child. We have got one, but my wife has a bad heart and can't have another one. Can I have one?" Another one had his doctor's degree in chemistry, and he had a very good salary—wages—and he said, "My wife can't have any children. We want to adopt a child. Send us one of them."

Finally, I wrote to my oldest brother, "I will let you have Joan, the tiny baby. You know she just weighed four and one-half pounds when she was born, but she is a darling. Well, I will have to give her away, I guess. When will you come and get her?" He telephoned me, "I can't leave my class right now. But I will be there soon."

Just two weeks later, all my kids got the flu. Their temperatures were between 102 and 105. Joan developed pneumonia. She cried and choked, and I had to take the phlegm from her mouth with my little finger, or she would have choked to death. Besides caring for the children, I was working at a little service station that was connected with the house—making almost enough money to pay for the groceries. I had plenty of things to do. Joan became so hoarse—I couldn't get her to cough, so I had to take her to the hospital. I got a neighbor to come and take my place for the time I was gone.

The next day I called the hospital. Their answer was routine—"about the same." The second day, the doctor called me. "Your little daughter is dying," he said. "She won't take any milk. She cries all the time. Will you come? She needs your love."

This time, I got my sister-in-law to come to take care of the sick children and the service station. I hurried to town to the hospital, and down the hall to the ward. I could hear Joan cry, and I recognized her cry. In the room, I instantly picked up my baby and begin to sing to her. She quieted down after a few moments, but when I quit singing, she began to cry again. So, I talked and petted her, singing to her, and she became quiet. To a nurse I said, "Hey, bring me a bottle of milk, please."

I tried to put the nipple in her mouth. She refused it. Again I petted her and begin to sing, and with no difficulty, I was able to get Joan to take a full bottle of milk. Quietly, she went to sleep. I laid her in her little bed, but, instantly, she began to cry again. Taking her into my arms, I talked to her. The nurse brought a rocking chair, and I relaxed in that chair and rocked my baby. The nurse brought another bottle of milk, and, after a little while, she drank that.

All day long I held that baby. Finally, about midnight, I was able to get her to lie down and sleep in the bed for two whole hours. Yes, I slept in the front entry on a davenport. They woke me in two hours, and said "Your baby is crying again." I had to repeat my care of her.

By noon next day she became quiet—so quiet that I could feel no breathing, could hear no heartbeat. The nurse took her temperature. "Very low," she said and shook her head. I called the doctor on the telephone and asked him if he could come.

As I waited for him, I stood at the doorway leaning against the door casing and said silently, "Please, dear Lord, if you will help her to get well, I promise I will not let her go. I will keep her and love her."

The doctor came and explained her condition. He said he was sure she would revive. By evening, the doctor let me take her home. He said, "We are not doing anything for her here that you can't do at home."

And I did! I wrote to my brother, "Keep your cotton-picking hands off my kids, all of you! I am going to keep them." I learned that the Lord hears our prayers and answers them in a way that is best for us.

Your children have grown to do so many things in the church. I know them all, and I would like for you to tell about your children—your wonderful children.

Well, first, I want to tell you something that I have found in the record that you wanted to know. Yes, I have the old diaries that my grandfather wrote during his missionary work of the church. I would be glad to send it to your office if you would be interested. Also, I have the record of the church reorganization group meeting in his father's house in Wisconsin. I have a small trunk filled with letters—many of them written by my little brother when he was a navigator before he was killed in the war. In fact I have written these in a manuscript we have entitled "Unfilled," but I haven't had it published at all. I would be glad to give it to anyone that would like to read it.

Well, about my children. They were such darling little babies. I loved them so. I was away from them so much, I know, but they grew up to be five children that I love. And I am so glad that I didn't give them away. This was the name of the book I wrote about them: *None to Give Away*. The Herald House published it for me. Thank goodness. It is a story of the things that we had to go through in those six years, and then, finally, I married again.

Well, if I could tell you something about my children—I love to brag. My oldest daughter, Beverly, is an international consultant for the Burroughs Computing Company—all over the world. Two years in Australia, two years in Munich, Germany, two years in Sweden, two years in England, and so forth. Of course, when Christmastime came, Beverly would get on the telephone and say, "Mother, I know it is a long way to Australia, but it is lonely here."

My [second] husband, [Oliver Wendell Townsend], and I would hop on a plane and go over to be with her. One time when I was there, she made arrangements for me to meet the people at the church reunion and to give a speech to about two hundred of them. Oh, that was a wonderful experience! But anyway, I met the church people in many countries of the world because of Beverly. She took her master's degree at the University of Wisconsin. Her work was first with the navigation, and then with the planes, and United States work. She has had good work, but she didn't get married.

Now, my older twins, Marjorie and Marilyn, I sent them to Graceland.... [Marjorie] went to the Sanitarium and took her nurse's training. One thing I can tell you, if I have time—one thing that happened that I thought was so wonderful. Trying to make five children learn to like a stepfather wasn't easy. When I married again, they were six and eight and nine, and they didn't want me to bring in a man in the house. They had never had a man in the house. You know, it is not easy to take a stepfather and make him loved by children who had never known a man. If he tried to touch them, they would jerk back quickly away. And if he tried to talk to them, it wasn't easy....

A few mornings after we were married, at breakfast, Beverly said, "Pass the salt, Wendell."

He said, "Beverly, why don't you call me Daddy?"

"I can't call you Daddy. You are not my Daddy."

"Yes, but I want to be your daddy. Can't you call me Daddy?"

"No, our daddy is up in heaven. I am not going to call you that."

He said, "Beverly"—and then he said something that I think was really clever. He said, "Beverly, when you go to school and you say 'Mother and Daddy' that is okay. But, if you say 'Mother and Wendell,' you have to explain it."

He tried to make himself into a daddy, and he did a good job. I have written a whole book on this. The Christian Publishing Company in New York wanted me to write the sequel to *None to Give Away*, and I did. It was about making a daddy out of a stepfather. But my children wouldn't let me publish it. They said, "No Mother, let's not." My book, *None to Give Away*, has made me very happy—for so many, many people say it was good to help them try to attack the impossible. Or do things that you can't do.

Well, Marilyn, the other twin (they were identical twins. No longer do they look like identical twins, but they were identical twins)— Marilyn took her first degree (went to Graceland, of course) … at Colorado State University, and then she went to University of Michigan and took a master's. She also was a Fulbright student in Germany. She took a lot of work there, and now she has her own business in computers in Michigan.

Joan and Jim are only 45—which is plenty old enough, isn't it? Joan is a very beautiful girl. She took her work at the University of Michigan and now has just finished completing her master's in Colorado. She married a young man—that was such a happy experience.

As I said, making a daddy out of a stepfather isn't easy. Let me give you an example—when Marjorie was going to be married. She had finished her training at the Sanitarium, and she was twenty-two years old. She said, "Mother, I am going to be married to Don. He loves me and we are going to be married. Mother, will Daddy give me away at church?"

I said, "I don't know. Daddy hasn't been as interested in religion as I have always been, but you go ask him."

So, she went over and put her hand on his shoulder—the first time in her life—[and] she said, "Daddy, will you walk down the aisle and give me away at church?"

He said "OOH! That is a big church (it was at South Crysler). Oooh, that is a big church…. Well, if you want me to, I will." And he did. That next day when they were married, I put three handkerchiefs in my purse, so I would have plenty to cry on—cause I knew you cried at weddings—the mother always cries. I never used one of them. When they walked down the aisle, [Wendell] looked so happy. He looked like a cat that just swallowed a canary, and the canary feathers were still on his mouth. He looked so happy when he said, "Her mother and I do." We knew that he had become a daddy to her.

The next year when Joanie came home from college (she was a junior at the University of Michigan)—she was there, oh just a few days—and the telephone rang. Again, Beverly said, "Mother, it is lonely down here. You said you couldn't come to see me and I can't come to see you. Will you send Joanie down for a couple of weeks?"

I always do the things they ask me to do. I have never learned to shake my head. So, I put her on the train and she went down there— came back in two weeks. When I went and got her, she looked so mixed up. She came home and was walking around through the house and she said, "Mother, I am just a crazy mixed-up kid. Mother, help me out."

I said, "What are you talking about?"

"Well, mother, you know down there in the Army is Al Green. I knew him at Graceland, and we dated some, but I didn't know him for a long time. Mother, Beverly had him over to the house, and we went to church with him, and he came to our house and everything."

She said, "Mother, now Al says he loves me, and Al says I love him, and I don't know. Mother, tell me about love and marriage."

I said, "I don't know anything about it at all."

"Oh mother!"

"Now, you go ask Daddy."

She went over and took his hand. The first time in her life, she took his hand, and she said, "Daddy, come and talk to me about love and marriage, will you?" And they went out on the patio. (I always talk so much, he had to get away from my talking to be able to talk to her.) They went out on the patio, and, for two hours, he talked to her about love and marriage.

He explained to her that marriage isn't just something like you see on television where they lay and kiss each other, and make up, and they get married, and that is all there is to it—that marriage is something you work at ... you have to understand each other. He told her all kinds of things about love. Love isn't just a simple little thing like in a love book.

She came back in, and she said, "Mother, I know that Al loves me. I know I love him. Mother, may I use the telephone and call him?"

She did. She said, "Al, it won't be until next year. I have to finish a year of college. But, Al, I want to marry you." They did, and for twenty-two years they have had the happiest marriage. I am so glad.

Then, my other child is a son. My son is a spastic. I don't know what could have done the damage in the motor area of his brain when he was born. When he couldn't walk at two years old, I was so worried about it. I talked to Anna, my sister-in-law. She said, "Elsie, you have got to give him away. You can't keep him. You can't take care of him. Put him in an institution."

After she left that night, when I was giving him a bath—he couldn't walk yet, he couldn't do things for himself—I said to the Lord, "Please, dear Lord, shall I put him in an institution? What shall I do?"

I had begun to realize that I would rather have him in my home and love him, than let him go. I kept him, and I am glad that those words, "none to give away," still were with me. Over the years, it was so difficult to try to do the things for him. I took a master's degree in education, but I also took it in counseling to see if I could help my son. My college students said, "Well, if you didn't help your son, you have helped a lot of us—so don't worry about it." But, I was still discouraged.

At the age of fourteen, I started helping him to have voice lessons because the teachers in school wouldn't let him sing when the teachers came in to teach the class to sing. They said he didn't say their words at the right time. They wouldn't let him sing with them even. So I thought, if I could have him take voice lessons, maybe at least he would learn to articulate.

Right next door to us, there in Independence, lived Paul Craig. Now, Paul Craig was the one who started the Graceland College music department, and then, after he retired, he was there in Independence giving voice lessons. He was also the head of all the music of the church for years in Independence. Well, he was older, but I liked him, and we were good friends. I explained to him about Jim. He said "Yes, I know about Jim. Send him over and I will give him voice lessons."

Well, every morning I would practice with Jim before going to school and practice with what he was supposed to be learning, and then, in the evening after school, I would practice with him again. He began to sing, and he began to speak much more clearly. Do you know just before Paul Craig died—he was in the hospital at the San[itarium]—and I went up there to see him. I was talking to him and saying good bye, and he said, "Elsie, your son was like my son. Did you know that?" I didn't know that.

Well, Jim didn't improve much, but he did some, anyway. Over the years, I have had to learn that I must accept what the Lord told me in the grove in Palmyra, "You must learn to accept and try to understand." When we were leaving Independence—South Crysler congregation—and coming to Montana, the pastor came to me and said, "Elsie, don't worry so much about your son. You know he hasn't done the things you wanted him to. He hasn't become a doctor or a famous lawyer, but listen, Elsie—when he comes to the church and sings a solo, I love to have him, because every word he sings touches our hearts. He sings them so we can hear them, and understand them, and he touches our hearts. Then, when he comes on Wednesday night to the prayer service, if he offers a prayer or gives a testimony, his words are the ones that bless us and give us real ministry. So, don't worry about him anymore."

So, I came to Montana these last three years ago—I came to Montana to live. I left him there in Independence.

I have heard Jim sing, too, and he does have a beautiful voice. How many years were you in Independence, Elsie?

I was twenty-seven years in Independence. Of course, being in there that long you get involved in so many things. I loved to work in Sunday school at South Crysler, and we had pastors that were so good. Of course, I wanted to teach classes. They started me out with the second grade class. I had been teaching in high school and college, and I knew I couldn't manage, but I decided I would do it if I could. Finally, not too long ago, they asked me if I would be church school director. I said, "I can't be. I am no good at that."

They said, "Well, do it anyway." So I took it. One young man there, [Don Coffman], was teaching in the schools in Independence. I asked him to teach the senior high class—the Zion's League-age class.

He said, "Elsie, I can't teach in Sunday school."

I said, "You are a good teacher in school and I know you can."

And what he did that year just made us all so happy. He started out—he said, "What text shall I use?"

I said, "It doesn't matter. Pick up the one you like or make up one yourself." He began to use his own ideas, and what he did for those Zion's League people you can't imagine! For instance, he would go and talk to the priest in the Catholic church and get permission to bring his class at Sunday school time to the Catholic church to worship with them, and then bring his class back to our church after an hour. Then, the next Sunday, he would have someone come in and explain to his class some of the things in our church that were not quite the same but why we had them.

The next time it was the Mormon church. He made arrangements with the leader of the Mormon church for a class to go over there. They went over, and they came back, and the next Sunday I couldn't miss attending that class because—I have forgotten his name, but he was somebody that did so much missionary work for the RLDS church in Utah—he came to talk to the class, and it was a really good class. I enjoyed it. He did this with all of the churches around and about....

One night at prayer meeting, the pastor got up and said, "I have a call for Don Coffman to be ordained an elder. Is there anyone that has a confirmation of this call?"

No one said a word. I sat there and I had a strong confirmation, but I had just been in the hospital with a heart attack and I thought, "I can't stand up and talk, I will fall down." Then I thought, "No, but I owe this." I stood and gave a confirmation, and told something of what this young man had done. He was ordained, and do you know what he is now? He is the pastor of the South Crysler church. They say he is doing a wonderful job for them.

Independence work—working near the headquarters—was a wonderful experience for me. In the first place, the RLDS Professional Teachers Association was organized a long time ago, you know. When I came there, they had just started the organization, and I couldn't miss going to that. They asked me if I would work on a newsletter that they put out, and I worked with Cleta Finley.... We worked on the newsletter and we had very good meetings.

Then I got interested in helping with the Neighborhood Council organization to improve Independence. Now, these weren't just RLDS people—but there were a lot of us who were RLDS. We did some things for Independence that resulted in Independence being given a special honor in New York as one of the best cities in the United States.

Then I started doing things in the stake. In fact, for three years, I was in charge of all higher education for the stake. Let's see—I think we had twelve congregations first. I would go to the different congregations, and I would talk to the Zion's League-age classes, and sometimes they would have me talk to the adult classes, and we had very good experiences.

Then, for three years, I was in charge of all the communications in Santa Fe Stake. This was interesting. I decided to see if I could get all the congregations to put out a newsletter to see if we could improve the attendance, and also to get different attitudes and understanding of people who didn't go to church, but could read a newsletter. I got nine congregations to put out newsletters. We had some classes and did things for them. Then, I thought, "Well, I am going to do one for South Crysler." So I did.

Then, another thing that I thought was a very good experience—just two years before we left, they asked me if—let's see, it was Pershing Tousley, a bishop of our church. He had been asked to come and take over this work in the church, and he had been teaching at Graceland for years. He ... called me, and he said, "Elsie, will you come and work for me. Just free."

I said, "Sure. I am doing nothing. I am retired."

He said, "Will you come and do some research?"

I said, "What?"

And he said, "About the Aaronic priesthood."

I said, "I can't research the Aaronic priesthood. I am a woman."

He said, "Haven't you taught thousands of students how to do research in high school and college? Can't you do research for me?"

I couldn't say no, of course. I went up there, and he said, "Now, I want everything read that has been written about the Aaronic priesthood, the Bible, the Book of Mormon, and the Doctrine and Covenants. But, [first], I want you to go up to the library in the Auditorium up on the sixth floor and read everything there is in the way of booklets or articles or class work, or anything on the Aaronic priesthood.

Well, I started to read, and I was just so thrilled at some of the things I found out about the Aaronic priesthood. I didn't know they had the ministry of angels. I was interested in one thing, because at least once a week, when I would go up there [to the sixth floor], I would look over the desk and there would be [apostle] Arthur Oakman, and we would have a good conversation before we went to work. Well, then, I went and took notes every week I met with this man and took my notes in [to Pershing Tousley].

Finally ... after several weeks, [Pershing] said, "Now, Elsie, will you read the Book of Mormon, the Bible and the Doctrine and Covenants?"

I said, "Oh really?" and he said "Yeah." So, I started to read and try to find out about the Aaronic priesthood and the Book of Mormon, the Bible, and the Doctrine and Covenants. There are so many things that are in the Book of Mormon that I didn't know were there. And that was a wonderful experience! For three months, I worked every week and I got a good light.

The next [month?]—right after Christmas—apostle Gene Austin called me and said, "Elsie, will you come and do research for me?"

I said, "On what?"

"Well," he said, "Come, let's meet together and we will talk it all over." So, we did. We met (let's see—we were meeting in the Auditorium weren't we?) in his office I believe—in an office in the Auditorium. He said to me, "Listen, I want some research on Peace groups all over the world—not only in the United States, but all over the world."

Then, he said, "I, also, want anything you can find about women in any of the books, because the president of the church wants notes on his desk for the next conference." I was really concerned about that one.

Well, the first one about peace organizations—I went to libraries and looked up everything I could find. Then, I thought, you know, I helped a student—I helped pay his way in the University of Hawaii to get his degree on the Chinese people and their culture. He wanted to study over there in Honolulu, and I had had him in high school years before, and so I had helped. When he got through with college, you know what he has been doing ever since? He has been in the state department in Washington, DC helping with any correspondence or any leading with the people from the Orient, the Chinese particularly. He has been over there many times. I know that for several years he was an aid to our ambassador to the United Nations. He was there when he wrote to me. I thought, I can find out from him about peace organizations and places that I can't find in the library. I wrote to him. So, these experiences were so good, and now I am in Montana. I haven't done much ever since.

You certainly have helped our branch here. You were also a guide at the Auditorium. Do you have anything to tell about that?

Yes. Guide service [at the Auditorium] and, of course, I had to do it on Sunday afternoons, [since] I was teaching at the college full time. We didn't get paid either, but it was a really interesting experience to do guide service. We would meet the people and then take them around through the whole place. We were not to preach, but whenever we stopped at the museum room where we had the things like that, the people often asked questions—or if we were very long in a room where the Quorum of Twelve and others met, they would ask questions. And that was a very interesting experience. One time, one group said to me, "Mrs. Townsend, is this where the Lord is going to return? Right up on the top of this Auditorium?"

I said, "When Jesus comes again, I think he is going to come to all of us, no matter where we are."

And they were so kind to me. We talked quite awhile. One of them was a teacher … in Kansas City. It wasn't too long after that (I wasn't teaching then), and she called me and said, "Mrs. Townsend, will you do a guide service for all of my students here … I have had them read in the encyclopedia about your church, but I find that there isn't too much to tell us about it. Would you do a guide service for them?"

By this time I had quit being a guide, we were so old after all, and they had so many young, very young guys. I went to the Auditorium and said, "May I do a guide service for them?" They said, well, they would see that it was done [since] they came to study about our church. There was a whole bus load of [students] that came. I found that guide service was a learning way. I learned more than the people did.

Also, another thing that was very interesting—for several years, we had a bus on Saturdays before conference ... [to] take [people] up to the historical places of the church. Before we went, we had to learn more. As a group, several of us (two of them were editors in the Herald House, and they were people who had a lot of background) and we went up there. I didn't know as much about Haun's Mill as I learned as a guide. I didn't know as much about Richmond as I learned as a guide. Thank you for listening.

You have talked about a book you have written about—*None to Give Away*. What are some of the other things you have written? [Are there] any journals or other [books] that your family may have that these people might be interested in?

I have been writing articles for the *Herald* since 1949. At the beginning, I also wrote for *Stepping Stones*.... Later I [wrote] for *Daily Bread*, and *Restoration Witnesses*, and I was thankful when they printed my book. They are still trying to publish my articles. I have a small trunk filled with letters—many of them written by my little brother when he was a navigator before he was killed in the war. In fact, I have written these up into a manuscript which I have entitled *Unfilled*, because he wanted to take his degrees in literature and music—and here he was a navigator on a B-29. But, I haven't had them printed. I have also written other manuscripts that are filling the drawers of my desk, but I don't know how to sell books.

You wrote a book about your early family life when you were in Montana, didn't you? And one about your teaching?

My second book was *Always the Frontier*. That is the story of the family coming to Montana and settling there, and all the experiences that happened there. The third one is *If You Would Learn, Go Teach*.

That was where I tried to tell my students' problems and how they were solved. I really thought, all my life, I wanted to be a teacher who could show each student that he was of some worth. I didn't believe in going to hugging and kissing them, but I believed in showing them that I loved them because of the way we had our class. I so wanted to write that one [book], *If You Would Learn, Go Teach*, because I learned so much more from my students those days than they did [from me]. But, I am thankful I started teaching fifty-eight years ago.

You have been an inspiration to us, Elsie, and I certainly enjoyed listening to you and [I'm sure] there are many more experiences that you could tell. So, at a later time we will continue.

It sounds like bragging, but may I tell you this—I am written up in *Contemporary Authors of America* in Washington, DC in the Library of Congress. They asked to put me there, because they said the first book was a piece of literature. I am very fortunate that this has sold so well. I am also written up in *Women Writers of the World* in London, England. I am written up in *International Biographies* in Oxford. I think this is something that an English teacher would be happy about.

Beatrice Noel Deaver Darling

BORN
July 23, 1910, Webb City, Missouri
DIED
November 25, 1991, Independence, Missouri

Originally interviewed by Ruby Morgan on May 14, 1987, in Independence, Missouri. On February 18, 1988, Beatrice revised her history in a letter written to Miss Carol Anway, and addressed to the Auditorium in Independence, Missouri.

You will recall that last year I asked permission to edit the "Story of My Life," which Ruby Morgan had recorded for me. I had no idea that it would take me so long, but I am kept very busy here at Resthaven [Nursing Home], playing the piano and organ, directing the music for devotions, etc., so I am just now getting it finished.

The lady who interviewed me caught me unexpectedly, so I wasn't anticipating the sequence of events as I wished to tell, and omitted many events which I should have included. I am sure you will notice the difference by the returns.

Do you ever make a copy of these articles? If so I would love to have a copy.

I hope the enclosed meets with your approval. Thank you kindly.
Very sincerely,
Beatrice Darling

Preface

I have had a feeling for many years that I should write an article enumerating some of the outstanding events and experiences which have happened in our family.

My husband served as an appointee in the church for thirty-one years, and every summer was spent in reunions and youth camps. For many years, I also accompanied him, sometimes taking care of the music, and other times teaching the women's classes, and so often, when I related experiences to the women, different ones would comment that I should write up the stories so others could enjoy them.

Needless to say that it was no surprise when a representative from the women's department sought me last spring, asking for an interview concerning the events of my life. Time had caught up with me, so the following is the result.

The Life of Beatrice Deaver–Darling

My father, Albert Nathaniel Deaver, was one of several children born to Angeline and John H. Deaver who lived on a large farm just a few miles out of Mansfield, Missouri. Albert always ranked well scholastically, and when he graduated from High School he was awarded a scholarship in mathematics at the University of Missouri.

The following summer was a busy one, filled with anticipation and plans for the following year, besides the regular summer activities. The community always held an annual Fourth of July celebration in Mansfield, and people from the surrounding towns always came to share in the gaiety of the day.

It so happened that Albert and one of his friends noticed a group of young ladies having a good time, and they followed them at a distance, for a while, before approaching and meeting them. The remainder of the day was delightful, and later in the evening Albert took his friend aside and said, "Notice the little blue-eyed Princess. I

Beatrice Noel Deaver Darling. Used with permission of the John R. Darling Jr. family.

am going to marry her." She, in turn, had noticed his attentions, but was not too impressed, for she had a steady boyfriend back in her hometown of Ava, Missouri. Her name was Sarah Jane (Janie) West.

The next two months were exciting ones, occasional dates with Janie and making preparations for school. Then came the time for him to leave, but his family was quite disappointed when he stayed only a few weeks and then came home. He would never admit whether it was because he was not satisfied with his instructors, the boys with whom he was associated, his classes, or if he was concerned that he would be so far from the home front that Janie's affections might turn favorably to his competitor. Anyway, he found himself hunting for a job, and next we find him located in Webb City.

During the early 1900s, transportation was a problem. There were very few automobiles, and horse and buggy method was very slow, so that left only the train for traveling, but that did not keep Albert from his regular visits to Ava. It so happened that Albert and his family all belonged to the RLDS church, while Janie had been raised in the Baptist church, but she found the history of his church very fascinating, and during her off-hours from work, she busied herself reading stories and studying about the church.

The next year found her preparing her trousseau for her coming marriage to Albert. I can remember yet the beautiful blue taffeta, floor-length gown which we saw hanging in the guest closet, for we thought it was the most beautiful gown we had ever seen. And there was a gorgeous hat to match.

The first two years of their married life were spent with Janie studying in preparation for joining the [RLDS] church. Then a little boy, Neal, came into the family. During the next two years, Janie read the story of Beatrice Witherspoon–Burton, and decided that if she ever had a little girl that she was to be named Beatrice, while Albert was fond of the name Noel. So, when the little girl appeared on the scene the following year, her name turned out to be Beatrice Noel Deaver.

In the meantime, the young couple had bought a little home, built upon a terraced lawn with about a three-foot drop. The grass was pretty and a delightful place to play; and the only thing I remember of that whole period is what a tease Neal was, because he could run up and down along that terrace, then turn and laugh, because I was afraid to run. But I could sit down and scoot very fast. I did not like for him to laugh at me.

Sometime during the next year, while I was still two years of age, the folks decided to move closer into town, since the former place was out on the shore of Center Creek, [and] that always necessitated catching an interurban car in order to come into town. They had a family friend by the name of Ed Behr, who spent a lot of time with them, and he helped them move. I remember so well how he carried me into the new home and stood me up on the kitchen table, admiring me and telling me how happy he was that we now had a new home, and it was nearer, so he could see us more often.

We were a very happy family. Mother was baptized, Dad was called to the office of teacher, our activities moved smoothly from year to year, and during the next several years, four additional children joined the family: Don, Wayne, Paul, and El Doralynn. We lived about a mile from the church, but there were sidewalks all the way. Very few families had a horse and buggy, so we were in style to walk as the other families did.

When I was seven years of age, Neal and I began taking piano lessons. Dad had bought us a new piano just a short time before, and we were in the height of our glory when we could "fool" away time playing it. Mother also took a few lessons, so she could help us, and we progressed very fast. At school, it was the practice to have a pianist play a march as the pupils went in and out of the building, so I worked hard to attain the proficiency which would allow me to meet the occasion, and have the honor of playing for the marching. It was really a thrill, and I found myself playing from the sixth grade through junior high school, accompanying the junior high chorus and playing for assembly programs.

In the meantime, back at the church everything was changing. Mother had a very nice voice and had been elected as music director, so for the first time this little church, which had an attendance of one hundred to one hundred twenty-five members, she organized a choir. It so happened, that Neal had been playing in the school orchestra, so both he and I had been exposed to timing and the directing of music. In fact, we had been practicing in front of our mirrors and really having a "ball." So, we schooled Mother along these lines, and after much practice, we all became braver and ventured into a new field. With all three of us working together, it was really a stimulating experience. Neal and I were alternating at the piano, and helping in the choir as we could.

The activities of our church had quite a program for young folks. For the girls, there were the Blue Birds (ages seven to ten), the Orioles (ages eleven to fifteen), and Temple Builders (ages sixteen to adult). For the boys, there were the Scouts. I have always been very interested in these activities, and worked very diligently for the efficiency awards, progressing from one class to another, and when I was a junior in high school, I was asked to take a class of small girls in the Sunday school, their ages seven to eleven. I found them a real challenge. We worked out our lessons for the Sunday morning classes, and during the week, we went hiking, on excursions, had parties and bunk parties, and enjoyed a fine fellowship until I went away to college. I loved those little girls, and was sorry when I learned the group was broken up afterwards by divorce between the parents.

But let us go back to my junior year in high school, for it was then that I really became involved with the music department, playing for soloists, different programs, and playing for operettas. I loved it, but was kept so busy. I always had some chores when I got home from school in the evening, then, after dinner and the dinner dishes were done, I always had to practice my music until time for the family to retire. Then I got out my study books and did my homework.

These were the hours I spent with my dad, for I found mathematics was difficult, and Dad was a "whiz" at anything along that line. On Saturdays, during these years, I also began teaching piano to a few young students, including my younger brother, Paul. He was very musical. (He is now a concert pianist in New York.) I started him at two and a half-years, for we could not keep him away from the piano, so we decided he should be learning proper positions and techniques as a basis.

I taught him until he was a junior in high school for then I went to Graceland to teach, and the following year he went to Cincinnati, Ohio, and took second in the National Piano Contest. As one enters such a contest as that, they always ask the information of background, etc., and the judges wrote quite an article to our hometown paper, commending the older sister who could give the boy such an outstanding background.

Our little church in Webb City did not have a font, so as candidates became ready for baptism, we all went out to a private beach on Center Creek. We had some wonderful experiences. The confirmations were always held back at the church. As the members of our family reached the age of eight, special emphases were made in preparation for the occasion, making it very special—a spiritual celebration for the entire family.

Another occasion which the family enjoyed together was the attending of reunions each summer. At that time, we were in Spring River District, and our reunions were held in Joplin, [Missouri]. We began attending reunions when we were quite young, and there was a large number of young folks in our age bracket who counted it our vacation for the year. We anticipated getting together for reunions and conferences, growing in fellowship and spiritual stature. It was a wonderful time for all of us.

I recall so well the summers when Gus Koehler, Evan Fry, and Mabel Carlyle directed our music. Each was very fine and worked with us in our directing classes. I was usually at the piano, and even though my hours were quite monopolized with music, I felt so rewarded for my efforts. Soon after I graduated from high school our reunions moved to Columbus, Kansas, then later to Racine, Missouri.

Our folks were always anxious for us to become acquainted with the missionaries and men of the church, and invited different ones to our home for meals. Some of those who came were: Apostle Curtis; Apostle Hansen; Brother Lee Quick, who was district missionary; and Brother Amos Higdon, our district president. Patriarch F. A. Smith also came and gave me my patriarchal blessing.

I enrolled at the State Teachers College in Pittsburg, Kansas, soon after graduating from high school. It is now Pittsburg State University. Being well acquainted with the folks there, since we were all in the same district, I became very active in the church groups. During my junior year, I was pleasantly surprised upon receiving a letter from President George Briggs of Graceland College saying that I had been recommended for the position of typewriting–shorthand instructor at Graceland, and he wanted to come and interview me. We had a very interesting day, and I found myself with a job for the coming year. Only one drawback—my boyfriend would be back in Pittsburg.

It so happened that my brother Neal was head bookkeeper at Graceland, so he was delighted to know that I was also going to be there. It was a great year. I was studying music along with my teaching, but soon after Christmas the head of the business school back at Pittsburg College wrote to me and invited me to come back to Pittsburg as faculty stenographer. Oh, what a temptation. Yet, I loved my work at Graceland, so I wrote and declined the offer, fully intending to return to Graceland.

As I was en route home for the summer, I stopped in Pittsburg. It was enrollment day at the college and I got to see many of my friends. Then, the dean of the business school spotted me, and came directly over to me, and said, "Miss Deaver, please come with me." As I went with him, he explained how the position of faculty stenographer was still open, and they still wanted me. We went to the president's office (I was acquainted with him from former years), and I told Dr. Lyerla that I was planning to return to my teaching at Graceland. But he said [we would go visit the president] just in case I would change my mind.

So into the president's office we went, and after greeting him, [the president] said that he would like to give me three short letters. I took them in shorthand, then sat down to a typewriter and wrote them off for him. As he signed them, he said, "You're hired. We will see you in your office the middle of August."

I was floored. There I was with two jobs for the coming year, when I had ever so many friends who would "give their eye teeth" for either of them. That put a terrific responsibility on me, for now I had to decide which job to keep, then, write a letter giving up the other.

I loved both jobs and grieved deeply trying to decide which to decline. In July, Neal came home for his vacation and reminded me that time was running short for my decision. Then he came to my rescue. He said, "Sis, I am going to write two letters to President Briggs at Graceland. One will be your resignation there, and the second one will be that you are anxiously anticipating your return to Graceland. Then I will hold both of them at my back, and you will choose. That will be your final answer." I drew the resignation [letter], quickly signed it, and placed it in the mail. That was the end of a beautiful experience at Graceland.

In August, I returned to Pittsburg, Kansas, happy to be back and anxious to learn about my new job. Our office handled the placement bureau, kept the alumni files up-to-date and published the alumni directory every fall, and I was secretary to the chairman of each department. It was a lot of work, but I loved every minute of it. Everything went very smoothly, then, there was a big shift at the end of two years. The professor who had supervised the placement bureau decided to take his sabbatical leave and attend the University of Kansas for his master's degree, so the placement bureau was moved to the education department.

The alumni directory had become such a huge job that it was decided that the files should be kept without publishing the directory, which shortened my job in some ways and enlarged it in other ways. This all happened during one of the years when the economy was so low, many students were graduating and could not find jobs. It was a very trying time. My boyfriend was caught in this predicament, so he returned to his folks' farm, working there and listening for signs of a job anywhere.

It so happened that a young man, [John Darling], who had a scholarship in education and was teaching two classes in the department, also had a desk in the education office. One day, as my friend walked to the office with me, John noticed him and said, "Hmmmm, and who is that?" I remarked that he was my boyfriend, and John remarked, "Nice fellow."

My friend left and returned to his home that day. John had been helping me with some of the typewriting when my desk was crowded, but that day I noticed that he took a few of his books and left. For the next ten days or two weeks, we did not see much of John. He came into the office just long enough to get his books, then, he was gone.

Then one day, there was an activity for the entire student body. I was not going, for I was feeling a little "low." Things were not going too well between my boyfriend and me, because so many misunderstandings occur in letters. Then John bounced into the office and, noticing that I was not going, he said, "My car is right there in the parking lot. Let's jump in and join in the festivities." We went, and we had a delightful time. That evening when we got home, I wondered when I had laughed so much and had such a good time.

From then on, the atmosphere in the office changed. John was at my elbow, helping with the many problems which arose. Our boss was bedfast with arthritis most of the year, which required our running between his house and the office with correspondence, answering letters, and helping the head of the education department as best we could. I saw my boyfriend less and less, and I saw John more and more.

That year John gave me a diamond for Christmas. Then I began facing other problems. John was a member of the Presbyterian church. Where to from here? John's father had died when he was a boy of ten years, and his mother had returned to college for her teacher's certificate and was still teaching. We attended my church when we were in Pittsburg, but we attended the Presbyterian church with her when we spent the weekend in Cherryvale [Kansas]. We invariably had serious discussions after these sermons for it seemed that the Presbyterian preachers left so many questions unanswered, while the RLDS preachers helped us into a greater understanding of the scriptures.

For the last two years, I had been director of music for the Pittsburg, Kansas, Branch and was usually involved accompanying for the soloists and special music. When I wanted to visit back in Webb City, I had to plan ahead for someone to take my place. Of course, I wanted the folks back home to become acquainted with John, so we made plans and went over for the weekend. Some of the elders were not too considerate and tactful in dealing with people of other churches, and I was a little apprehensive as to what he might hear. I asked Mother who was preaching that morning, and when she told me that dear old Brother Williams was scheduled, I prayed a very quick prayer for help. The Williams family were fine folks, and we loved them, but the poor English that Brother Williams used was another story—and here John was an English major. Of course, we could always drive over to Joplin for church, but then it seemed that just maybe we had a job to do in this—a good job of praying.

Mother and I both prayed earnestly that night that the sermon would be one which would be of influence to John. The next morning we both felt good, and were both inclined to believe that everything would turn out all right. WHAT A WONDERFUL EXPERIENCE. Brother Williams was blessed with a fluency of speech we had never heard him use before. He had a freedom of thought and presented his topic in a beautiful way. Then, after the meeting was over, he and John spent a good half an hour discussing some of the points. WHAT A BLESSING THAT ENTIRE MORNING WAS.

From this point, John and I received many blessings in many different ways, and we realized that we were directed in many of the decisions which we made. He was to graduate that July, and was planning to teach through that time at the college. I decided to resign my job about the same time, then, we would be married the first part of August. The remainder of that year went fast. He was hired as principal and to teach fifth and sixth grades in Holton, Kansas, rather early in the spring, so we were able to finalize our plans and set the date for our wedding. Our district president, Brother Amos Higdon, was to marry us.

On the Saturday a week before the wedding, all the bridal party met for the rehearsal, and just before we began, Brother Higdon took me aside and said, "Bea, I never hated to marry anyone in my life like I hate to marry you to this non-member." And my answer was, "Brother Higdon, John is an RLDS to the very tip of his toes. He just does not know it yet." Then Brother Higdon answered, "I hope so."

After the rehearsal, Brother Higdon and Brother Charlie Wilson (who had brought Brother Higdon from the reunion grounds in Columbus) returned to Columbus, for the reunion opened the following day.

The following Saturday, August 4, 1934, was the hottest day in history. The grass had turned brown, and there was not a flower anywhere to be found. They all had to be ordered from St. Louis, but that failed to dampen our spirits. John and his mother arrived from Cherryvale (a two-hour trip) at seven-thirty that morning, not wanting to miss out on anything, and the entire household was buzzing in preparation for decorating the church. Mother had planted flowers and fire bushes, tending them with her tender, loving care through the summer in preparation for this occasion. It was such an exciting time, and everyone was so happy. The church looked so lovely, but they would not let me see it until time for the wedding at four o'clock. The flowers for the wedding came from St. Louis, packed in ice, and did well to last during the ceremony, but everything was lovely and turned out beautifully. What a wonderful day.

After all the years of schooling, teaching, and working, it was exciting to think that after one week of honeymooning in the Ozarks, we would have just one week to pack and start life anew—only now, I was the wife of a schoolteacher.

We loved Holton, and quickly found our places in the community. Soon I was invited to join the music club, and John settled into his position like an old pro. The second year, he was promoted into the high school to teach English and speech, and in time became head of the English department. In the spring of 1937, little John Junior became a member of our family, and it seemed that our happiness was complete.

During the summer of 1939, John learned that some special courses were being offered at Northwestern University, at Evanston,

Illinois, which would help him in his work. We talked it over with Mother Darling, for she was still teaching, and we felt that she would like to go along with us. After all, it would be nice to have a summer of work credited on her transcript from Northwestern University, and she was delighted to go along. My folks had no idea that we had any intention of attending school that summer, so our next step was to drive over and inform them of our plans.

They were very surprised, and began telling us that an apartment was no place to expect a child to be happy for a whole summer, and that Johnny would be so much better off staying with them on the ranch. He was two-and-a-half and Mother began urging us to leave him—that she and Dad would really have a ball with him, and she would promise to write to me every day. I knew he would be better off, and after all their talking, there seemed to be nothing for us to do but give in. John made a quick trip back over to Cherryvale for Johnny's clothes for the summer, then, the next day we left.

Only mothers who have left their little ones can know how terribly I was already missing him. We had also left his dog, Toto with him. He was an excellent watch dog. He would let Johnny go just to the edge of the lawn, then would cross his pathway and stay right there until the child turned around. Even Johnny's hitting him on the back and saying, "Move, Toto, move," did not faze him one bit. Yes, we knew he was well cared for, and in good hands. We returned to Cherryvale, quickly packed our bags, and found ourselves on our way to Evanston for the summer session of school.

Our summer was a great one. On the weekends, we usually toured parts of Chicago and enjoyed various programs out at Riverside Park. One highlight was a piano concert by Joseph Hoffman which was truly wonderful. One weekend, the university sponsored a trip across Lake Michigan to the House of David. We all wanted to go very much, but I had a terrible fear of something happening that would hinder our return to Johnny, so I refused to do anything or go anywhere that posed a risk. There were always other things to enjoy.

Then one day, John was recommended for a position as a critic teacher in the state university at LaCrosse, Wisconsin. His heart leaped with joy. He was quite young, and already THIS. The following weekend found us driving across Wisconsin and enjoying that beautiful country. Everything was so lovely and everyone so gracious. We fell in love with it, and John found himself signing a contract to begin teaching there the following fall.

That summer had been hard on us financially, for we had been paying rent in three places: Holton, Evanston, and while we were in LaCrosse, we had to take time to rent an apartment where we could send our furniture and live during the coming year. Since we would not be there when our furniture arrived, we left particulars with the moving company so they could place our furniture as they moved it in, thus making it more livable when we arrived.

We were glad when the summer school was over in Evanston, for so many things were crowding in on us. We had the trip back to Kansas, activities and business to close up in Holton, then the packing and moving to Wisconsin. But, first, and most important, was our trip after Johnny back in Webb City. HOW I HAD MISSED HIM. The summer had been so long. And now we were going after him. It seemed that the car just wouldn't go fast enough. I was so anxious. I firmly resolved that I would never, never do that stunt of leaving him again.

We saw him playing in the yard as we drove up, and he had grown so much in those seven weeks, we could hardly believe it was he. That was one happy reunion. The next day we drove to Cherryvale to take Mother Darling home, then journeyed on to Holton to get things in readiness for our move to LaCrosse, Wisconsin.

We left with one big regret—we were going into an apartment and there was no way we could take Toto with us. We had raised him from a tiny roly-poly little ball of fuzz, and now he was a beautiful collie. He and Johnny had created quite a picture when they were both small, and rolled and played on the floor together, but now he needed to be out where he had room to romp and play. With the promise that we would buy him another pal after we were moved and [got] oriented in our new living quarters, Johnny was a good sport and trusted the rest to us. It so happened that my dad had a friend who was needing just such a dog, so we knew that Toto was getting a good home.

We experienced quite a period of farewells in Holton, then receptions ... in LaCrosse before we were able to settle down into the business of living again. Everyone seemed eager to help us, and anxious for us to meet their friends. It was a very friendly place to live.

We soon learned that there was no RLDS church so, again, we began attending the Presbyterian church. The minister seemed to take a special liking to us and became a weekly caller. We soon learned that sometime between the dinner meal and ten o'clock Saturday evening we could expect him to make his call. He was a fine fellow, and we really enjoyed Dr. Niebruegge.

When we took Johnny to his Sunday school class, I made a habit of staying in class with him, trying to erase in his little mind the fact that Mommy had left him once, but that was not going to happen again. He made friends quickly, and I was soon able to leave him on his own. Then one day, as he was playing around in the apartment, I noticed he was coughing quite frequently. I listened closely, and surely enough, I heard a whoop. I almost fainted. I told myself, "Surely not that again."

It so happened that the first summer that we took Johnny to Cherryvale, he was only three months old, and several of John's old classmates came by to see "the little Darling." One girl had two small boys who had just recovered from the whooping cough, but she assured me that the doctor had given them a clean bill of health just the preceding week. However, while the little boys stood beside Johnny's bed, one of them had a coughing spell. I felt sick, and I said, "Helen Louise, are you sure those boys are over the whooping cough?" She repeated that the doctor had examined them just a few days before and told them that they were out of quarantine and free to come and go.

What could one do, but hope and pray? But that was all in vain, for in just a few weeks, Johnny had a full-fledged case of the whooping cough, and him so small and helpless.

John had a job for the summer, helping audit the books for a milling company there in town, and I found myself with a full-time job of nursing the whooping cough. I felt so sorry for the little fellow, for he could not keep any food down during the day. But he could keep food down during the night, so I fed him every three hours all during the night. I was really concerned about him, for at that age, he should have been gaining weight, so I fed him regularly during the hours he could keep his food down. It was a battle I was determined to win.

We found a very good pediatrician down in Coffeyville, Kansas, who introduced us to a foreign medicine especially for the whooping cough, which helped us through the summer. We had to change bedding often through the day, but were so thankful for the nights when the digestion was normal, for even if he was not gaining weight, he still was not losing ground. It was a very hard summer, but we were so thankful that we were able to weather it through.

Now, after that experience, one can understand why I was so shocked to think Johnny might have to repeat that experience. However, when we took him to the doctor, we were shocked anew to learn that nursing babies can have the whooping cough again. So we resigned ourselves to another quarantine, had our doctor order the same medicine which we used in Kansas, and accepted our fate as a time to do things together. Johnny was old enough to be a big help during this spell. We taught him to run for the bathroom when he felt the coughing spells coming on, for that floor was easier to clean than if there was an accident on the rug, and that saved a lot of work.

Life went on, but was quite uneventful during those months. Dr. Niebruegge continued his calls each Saturday evening, and proved himself a real friend, slowly working his way into our hearts. We had also found a lovely young girl who turned out to be a valuable baby-sitter, and this allowed us freedom to attend activities now and then. The next year we leased the home of an Army colonel while his family joined him in his assignment in Virginia. It was a lovely home, and only about three blocks from the university, which allowed John to walk to and from work.

We were still having to guard Johnny's health, for a bad cough continued to haunt him. The doctor told us of different cases which had developed into rheumatic fever, and to us, that was a naughty word; we did not want that to happen. Week after week, we tried keeping him in bed for three days after the fever went down, only to have him turn almost crimson with a high fever each time he was up.

Finally, the doctor said if we could carry him to the office and get him under the ultraviolet ray machine before his temperature went up, it would possibly break the pattern. At this juncture, we were willing to try anything, so we followed instructions and were so happy when it worked. It was the next spring before we ventured out again, and how wonderful it was for him to be over his coughing.

As Johnny began feeling better, he reminded us of our promise to get him a dog, and it so happened that we had friends whose cocker spaniel was expecting a litter quite soon. We put our name in for one, and as soon as it was weaned, we proudly took a little black cuddly "Bow" home with us. He was so precious, and was a real playmate for Johnny. We spent a lot of time with Bow, for we all loved him, and by spring, when it was warm enough for Johnny to go outside, Bow was already wearing a collar and seemed to enjoy the attention which wearing a leash and following gave him.

We had been inside so closely all year, it was really great to be outside. We had a nice lawn, and we almost lived outdoors that summer, getting acquainted with new surroundings and new neighbors. By the end of the summer, we faced another problem—Bow had an inborn tendency to chase cars, and we did everything to keep him from it. He just had to chase cars, and we knew that sometime he would get hit. We even rolled newspapers and scolded him, but nothing fazed him, and sure enough, he got hit. Even though it was inevitable, we all grieved, for he was such a smart dog, except for that one fault.

Since we were in the habit of having Bow around, we knew of other friends whose cocker spaniel was also expecting a litter, so we soon had another little cocker to take Bow's place. While we were waiting for the new pup to be weaned, John built a nice little dog house, and Johnny had fun helping his dad paint it and get it all ready. They painted it white with a brown trim at the top to match our own house. We were all so proud of it. When "Woofer" finally came, he was used to being with his brother and sister pups, and he was so lonesome, so we kept him in the kitchen until he could orient himself to his new surroundings. Then, after a few weeks, we could tie him out in the yard during the day.

We bought Woofer with the understanding that his care was Johnny's responsibility. We all loved the dear little fellow, and he was so responsive for all the attention we gave him, but he was still Johnny's pet. On the other hand, Johnny was new in the neighborhood, and he was enjoying meeting his new friends and neighbors.

During these two years, I had been meeting and working with the Presbyterian women, and when their devotional chairman was absent, the leader was always asking for someone to volunteer voicing the prayer for the meeting. They always had their prayers written out and would read them. One day, the leader asked for a volunteer and I said I would be glad to voice their prayer. Imagine their surprise when I extemporaneously voiced a prayer for their meeting without any notes, any helps, or crutches of any kind.

From that time on, I was called on to help quite often. This got back to the minister, and one evening, when he was visiting us, he said that there was something he wanted to ask me. He said, "Mrs. Darling, I would like to know how you can voice such beautiful prayers and still not be a member of our church."

I looked at him very straight and answered, "Dr. Niebruegge, there is only one answer. Praying in your church just qualifies me to do a better job when I get back to my own church." And he replied, "I really believe you mean that." I believe he respected me for my answer.

Everything was going well for us in the Presbyterian church. During the year John was voted in as an elder in the church, and we both were becoming quite active. One day, a "little birdie" told us that Mrs. Ristow (the lady who owned our house) was thinking of selling it. We had been talking about how we loved the place, and thinking we would like to buy it, for it was so convenient and livable. So we decided that John would call her and talk to her about it. We were almost sure that she would be asking more than we could pay for it, but at least he could call and talk to her about it.

So, he called Mrs. Ristow and told her that we had grown to like the place, that we were thinking of buying a place of our own, and wondered how much she would be asking for it. When he quoted a price to her, she said that, of course, she could not sell it for that, but she needed time to think about it, and for him to call her back in two or three weeks.

We had taken good care of the house and made replacements as things needed it, but we had never said anything to her about small things. All we could do now was WAIT. We did a lot of praying about the matter, for we liked the place and knew it would be a nice home for us. John had a special, private nook in the basement where he talked to the Lord about certain matters. I never knew about this until sometime later. But he made this a special topic of prayer, for we wanted it so very much if it was the wise choice for us to make.

The morning that John was to call Mrs. Ristow, he petitioned the Lord, asking that if it was the right thing to do, we would be able to come to an agreement with her. It was with a degree of fear and trembling that he called her that morning, but she was so sweet and gracious, saying that we had been such good renters and had always kept the place looking so nice. Then, she added, "I'm an old woman, and I don't need the money. I have just decided to let you have the property at your price." WHEE-E. We were so happy. We knew the good Lord had certainly had a hand in that decision.

My mother had been sending us the *Saints' Herald* for some time, and often I would find articles which I wanted John to read. So, I would read all but the last few paragraphs (so I could truthfully say I had not finished it), then leave it open on the coffee table. Often, he would pick it up and read it, then remark that it was an interesting article. If he accused me of leaving it open purposely for him to read, I could always say that I had not completed reading it. I was anxious for him to know that we really had educational leaders in our church.

The next summer, Mother visited us, and we had a delightful time. It was her first trip to Wisconsin, and she was thrilled with its beauty. We were very surprised when she informed us that she had learned there was a small group of RLDS people holding meetings over in North LaCrosse, which was four or five miles from where we lived. We tried to call the home where the meetings were being held, but the folks were out of town at that time. They returned the week after Mother left.

One day, I called and invited her over for I was anxious to meet that Mrs. Batchellor who seemed to be leader of the group. We had a nice visit, but she was very aggressive in the doctrine of the church, which caused me to be rather apprehensive with fear that she might just "turn John off," and at that stage, I did not want that. She could not understand why, after John had been introduced to the church, he did not fall for it "hook, line, and sinker." But, he had never lived where there was a church and had an opportunity to study about it. When we attended his church, we often discussed the sermon afterwards, and it seemed that we were both concerned, for his preacher never quite satisfied our yearning to understand more about the gospel. It was at those times, I always added the thought that OUR ministers seemed to give us a more complete understanding in their sermons and scriptures.

When Mother went home, she left us a copy of *The Call at Evening*. I had read it when I was young, but I was anxious to read it again, and then I noticed John was also reading it. He took the book upstairs to his study where he had his Bible and pencils, and looked up every reference that was given. He had been an English major in school, and usually read a book in a few hours, but with this book he was different. When he came home at noon, he would come in the front door, kiss me "hello," then would hit the stairway up to his study and read until lunch was ready. In the evening, it was the same way. That continued for several days, and I became worried. How was I going to answer some of the questions he might ask me? I took my problem to God and prayed that I would be helped to know the right answers. When John had finished the book, he came to me with just one statement, "Honey, let's raise Johnny in your church."

Just a short time later, Mrs. Batchellor (the lady where the church meetings were held) called me to say that Apostle E. J. Gleazer and Bishop Clarence Skinner were going to hold a week of meetings in Sparta (a town about twenty-five miles northeast of LaCrosse), and she wondered if I might enjoy going with them some evening.

My heart leaped with joy. I told her that I would speak to John about it, which I did, and he said that he thought I would enjoy it. The meetings were planned for two weeks later, and after about three days, he asked me again when the meetings were to be held. I told him again, and he seemed satisfied. The next week, he asked me the same question, and when I told him, he said, "I wonder if they would mind if I went along to the meeting with them." The men [Apostle Gleazer and Bishop Skinner] were staying at the Batchellor home, so that gave us an opportunity to visit as we drove to and from Sparta. John seemed very interested and began borrowing books from different church members, and studying to learn more about the church.

The next year was a busy one. John continued his study very religiously. I was starting Johnny on his piano lessons, and he was quite excited about entering preschool and meeting new friends. We began visiting the RLDS group as it met in North LaCrosse, but it was so limited in every way. They were studying the books of the church, and that was what we needed, so we tried hard to orient ourselves into their program.

The following spring we faced another problem. The university had a policy that when the instructors proved themselves over a three-year period, they were automatically placed on permanent tenure. And there John was, approaching the end of his second year. There were several Presbyterian members on the school faculty, and accepting a permanent position before changing churches might have been viewed as a delaying tactic after going on tenure. So, John knew that he had to go to the minister and lay the matter before him. Of course, the minister was shocked and saddened that we would be changing churches.

As John walked home that evening, he was feeling so low, as though he had lost his best friends in the Niebruegges. He gazed at the beautiful autumn sky, and was watching the moon as it arose over the majestic Wisconsin bluffs, when he heard a most comforting voice saying, "Fear thou not, for I am with thee; be not dismayed, for I am thy God; I will strengthen thee; yea, I will help thee; yea, I will uphold thee with the right hand of my righteousness." What a wonderful feeling came over John, and he knew that, even if he lost his teaching position, at least he had been honest. But, he was not released from his position. He continued teaching until he resigned three years later to accept a church appointment. Dr. Niebruegge remained a true friend throughout the years.

John was baptized the next summer at Chetek Reunion by Seventy E. Y. Hunker, and when he told his mother about it, she remarked, "My religion was not good enough for you, was it, Son?" The following year, our son, Johnny, was baptized. Then the following year, Mother Darling was also baptized, both [were baptized] by Brother Hunker at Chetek Reunions.

The fall after John was baptized, we attended a district conference where President F. H. Edwards was guest minister. John participated in the prayer meeting that morning, and afterwards, Brother Edwards came to me and said that he felt a call for John to the office of elder, and he wanted to know how I felt about it. He explained that several of the appointees, who had worked in our area, had returned to Independence and spoken of the young educator at LaCrosse, and that morning he, himself, had witnessed John in action, and he was very impressed with him. I told Brother Edwards that John was an easy person to talk with, and was very approachable, and that I was anxious for him to talk to John himself, and become acquainted with him.

At noon, while we were enjoying a basket dinner, we saw the two of them going for a walk. Of course, I knew what it was all about, but there was no opportunity for learning about it until we were driving home that evening when John told me the essence of their conversation. He was quite moved, but he told Brother Edwards that he would have to wait for an answer, until he had a confirmation of the call in his own heart. Brother Edwards appreciated his answer and said that he would be keeping in touch with John, and wanted him to be sure to write to him when he was ready to accept his call.

During this last year, another occurrence had crossed our pathway. For several years, we had wanted a second child. Johnny had begged for a brother or sister, but we had given up hope. Then, one day, we began "riding the clouds." Yes, I was pregnant and we were so happy. After a few months, we shared our secret with Johnny, for everything was going well, and I was feeling so fine. Not for a moment had any thought of disappointment crossed our minds. We were all so thrilled, when all at once the ambulance swished me to the hospital, and all of our fondest dreams vanished. Only couples who have had similar experiences can know the disappointment and heartache we suffered. But, we had to accept it as a part of God's plan for our lives and look for the silver lining. Two additional operations followed before the cycle was broken.

Shortly after I went back to the hospital, Johnny came home with the mumps, and ... John had never had them. So, about the time Johnny was over them, John discovered that he [had the mumps]. WOW. What a family. We were so thankful to have Mother Darling helping to keep the home fires burning, with the aid of one of the college girls who had roomed with us during her years at the college. This happened to be Charlotte's third year with us, and she had

become a part of the family, always willing to babysit with Johnny
or help wherever needed. On days when she did not have morning
classes, she would walk over to the hospital (about two miles) [where
I was] and bring me up to date on the family news. We will never be
able to repay her for her many kindnesses. She was a DEAR. And we
all rejoiced when we recovered and could be as a family again.

Months passed, filled with study and prayer. Then, one Sunday
after we had been to church, John said, "I must tell you that I have
to write to Brother Edwards and accept my call." What a thrill that
was. In the meantime, several general church men had stayed in our
home, some for a week at a time, and others for just a few days, as
they worked in and around that area. Among those was Dr. Floyd
McDowell, and he was talking to John about the possibility of going
into the department of religious education as his assistant. He did say,
however, that the church could not let us have a home like the one we
had in LaCrosse. However, John hastened to answer that that would
not make any difference, if he were ready to accept the offer.

And so, after quite some time, John accepted the job as associate
director of religious education, helping Dr. McDowell. The following
summer, we sold our home and moved to Independence. That was the
summer of 1945, and Johnny was in the third grade. John's mother had
retired from her teaching, and had been living with us for two years.

After we arrived in Independence, for several days, Brother Elbert Smith and his wife, Clara, came by each evening just to check on
us, and be sure we were getting along okay. Johnny soon found friends
in the neighborhood. Then, one day, John thought that I should go
to the office and meet the office force. Who should be at the office
looking for a music person, but Blanche Green, director of the vacation church school activities. After she stated her mission, John said,
"You know, I think my wife could handle that for you." So, just like
that, I inherited a job which I continued until John's assignment was
changed. I was also spending one afternoon a week helping the Blue
Birds and Orioles with their music, and I loved every minute of it. It
is strange how quickly one can become involved.

Johnny was continuing his piano even through the weeks of
change, and had progressed very nicely. As some of his friends heard
him play, their mothers commented that they wished their youngsters

could study along with him, so I soon found myself with a nice class of youngsters.

Johnny was meeting new friends and making a nice adjustment to his new life in Independence. We were attending the Stone Church on Sundays, and after church school we all met and sat together for the eleven o'clock service. One morning Johnny came and told us that he had met a very nice elderly man who wanted him to sit with him during the service. The two of them sat in the balcony, and after the service, Johnny brought his friend, Mr. Andy Goode, around to meet us. It was a lovely friendship which they enjoyed, and oftentimes, Mr. Goode would invite Johnny to go home with him for dinner. Then, we would drive out after him in the afternoon.

Mr. Goode had a beautiful farm out east of town where his daughter and her husband lived with him. One Sunday, Mr. Goode gave Johnny a set of bantam chickens, a little hen and a cocky little rooster. We had a lot of fun with them, until one morning they were gone. Johnny searched everywhere for them, and late in the evening, he was still searching, when he heard a noise from the rooster. Looking up, he saw them sitting high in one of our tallest trees. The little hen came down to eat the next day, but the rooster stayed up there for two days, until we became worried about him. So John turned the water hose on him, which brought him down in a hurry.

One evening, Johnny was late in coming home from school. He explained it by telling us about a litter of kittens at one of the homes the children had to pass on their way to and from school. He ended the discussion by asking if he could bring one of the kittens home after it was weaned. We thought we had talked him out of that, when one evening, he came home carrying a sweet little yellow cat in his arms. He said it had followed him so far he was afraid it would get lost if he sent it back home, so he just brought it home for overnight.

That was the beginning of the cat story. He loved that cat. In fact, we all did, and because she had such pretty white feet, we called her "Mittens." Late the next spring, we realized she was going to have kittens. The first one was stillborn, but the second one was the perfect image of her. We watched them closely for a few days, then, we decided to call the new arrival "Sniffer."

Just a short time later, we were notified that the folks who owned our house wanted to sell it, and since we did not like the location, we began house hunting. There were only two houses available in Independence. This was during World War II when everything was tight, and there was no building going on at all. One of the houses was a small five-room brick home, which was too small, so we had to take the only other one, even though it needed a lot of repair.

The move took us into another area, and we were sorry, for Johnny had made good in his Scouting, and there was no Scout program available in our new location. However, he had made some new friends in the West College Church, so we allowed him to attend there, because of their fine Scouting program which they supervised. Among his new friends, was one named Charles Athey, and the two of them proved to be real buddies all through high school and college, and until their professions took them to different areas. They enjoyed such good times together. During these years, Johnny progressed in Scouting, even to earning his "God and Country Award." Then, he spent much time in helping other Scout members to attain their respective awards.

The dog which we had at that time was a beautiful collie. We had bought him when he was a tiny pup, and he had grown into a lovely dog, but when we moved into our present neighborhood, he quickly learned the habits of those dogs. We lived in the middle of a two-block long area, and when the postman came walking along with the mail each day, the dogs at the top of the block began barking. This seemed a sign to the other dogs that the postman was on his way. He did not like dogs, and carried a long strap to strike at them, which made them all the more vicious.

So, of course, Laddie joined them in their daily practice. We tried to see that Laddie was closed on the porch about that time each day, but everyone always knew when the postman was coming. One day, I had ordered some groceries to be delivered, and as the delivery man came around the house, Laddie proceeded to bark and follow him, and the man said that he even nipped at his trousers. Of course, that was a little too much. John was out of town at the time, but when he came home that weekend, we held a family huddle, for we knew we could not keep Laddie with his growing practice. The following week we were having the trees trimmed, and the man was in search of a dog such as Laddie. He fell in love with the dog during the days he was there, and gave him a lot of attention, and it was Johnny's decision that this man would be a good master for Laddie.

It was sad for all of us as Johnny and his dad gathered Laddie's belongings and drove them over to where the man lived in Kansas City. But when they arrived there, the man was sitting alongside of a few belongings which had been salvaged from his home, which had just burned. The man was so happy to have the dog's help in protecting his things. This story was written and published as a devotional by Aleta Runkle, and appeared in "Bread and Butter" under the title "So Great a Love," because Johnny loved his dad enough to sacrifice his dog, so his dad would not worry about what the dog might do while John was out in the mission field. All that Johnny said, as tears ran down his face, was, "the dog will do him more good than it did us."

When Johnny was fifteen years of age, he began working at the J. C. Penney store where Howard Anderson was the manager. He could only work during daylight hours and on Saturdays until he was sixteen; then, he became a regular salesman. He proved himself a worthy worker and continued working for the Penney company in each area he lived through his college years. The company kept track of him and employed him full-time after he graduated, during which time he became manager of the women's department, and did the ordering for the area stores.

John's work in the department of religious education had taken on a variety of activities. It was the year before Carl Meale came into the department to handle the Boy Scout work, and John was working with the boys who were particularly interested in attaining their God and Country award. Members in the office were also working on the Zion's League guidelines handbook, which included a program of study, worship, service, and recreation for a cycle of four years. John and Dr. McDowell were also conducting institutes across the country, and helping with reunions during the summer months. Johnny and I enjoyed attending reunions with John until Johnny reached the age to attend Boy Scout camp; then, my attending was scheduled around his Scouting and work periods. However, when Johnny went to Graceland, he found it was a great homecoming experience, with all the young folks he had met in the many areas where we had been with John.

During the nine years John worked in the department of religious education, he had many wonderful experiences. I would like to list a few. One weekend, he was scheduled to conduct an institute up in Illinois, near Chicago. When we came under appointment, we were driving a Dodge car, so John drove the car that weekend so he could take some necessary visual aids and equipment. The weather turned cold and icy, and the further north he drove, the worse the weather became. Then, he came to a big hill and the car began sliding on the ice. It continued skidding until it slipped into a ditch. John tried to get out, but there was no traction, so the car continued to stay there. He looked around and saw a farmhouse some distance away. So, getting out of the car and choosing his footing carefully, he made his way to the farmhouse only to find no one at home. He carefully retraced his steps to the car and knelt on the running board to pray for help. When he arose to his feet he saw a Jeep coming up beside him. It was a four-wheel drive, just the kind of car he needed to help him. The driver was very jovial, and they fastened chains to the Dodge, and pulled it back into the road, and up the next hill. John was very appreciative, and wanted to pay the man for his kindness, but the man refused any money, saying that he was glad to be of service. John knew it was an answer to his prayer, and has always enjoyed telling the story as an example of witnessing.

On one of his institute trips, John was going to be gone for two or three weeks up in Michigan, only he was going by train. It so happened that the weather was bad and stormy, and the train was late getting out of Kansas City. John was concerned, because he had to change trains in Chicago, and the stations were some distance apart. The snow was swirling very badly when he got off the train, and all the taxis were going in the wrong direction. He was laden down with bags in each hand, yet he waited and waited on the corner in vain. Suddenly, a big strong policeman appeared in front of him and asked if he needed help. When John told him that he had just a short time to make the train, and that all taxis were going in the wrong direction, the policeman stepped into the middle of the street, and gave one loud blast on his whistle, and the next taxi swirled about face, picked up John and his luggage, and made it to the station on time.

Another weekend, he was scheduled to conduct an institute in Iowa. The kick-off for the weekend was to be a banquet on Friday evening. It was during a rainy season, but that held no qualms for him. He left home rather early, barring any unexpected hazards. His road had been mapped out for him, so he was travelling along very casually. He had made one turn. Then, he began asking himself if he had made the wrong turn, for the pavement had run into a dirt road, and what was that at the bottom of the hill? But surely he could get through there, so he chanced it. The hole was deeper than he had thought, and the car began slipping more and more. Then, he was stuck.

There he was, umpteen miles from nowhere. Well, he would try it again, but the wheels just went deeper. But, if he got out in that mud and rain, how would he look to go into a banquet? Then, he thought, "God has helped me many times when I was in difficulty. Why have I waited so long before calling on him for help now?" So, he got on his knees and poured out his heart to God, and pleaded for help. Then, he moved back under the steering wheel, turned on the engine, and the car was lifted right out of the mud, and he traveled on up the hill on high. But you see, he evidently was on the wrong road, so he had to turn around and retrace his path through the mud and back up the other hill. But all was well, for his prayer had been answered.

Another time, John was traveling by train to an institute, only he was going through St. Louis, and was laden down with a bag in each hand. As he walked along a sidewalk, which had a high brick wall on the inside, he suddenly looked up to see two large, strong, rough-looking men coming toward him. He feared they had ulterior motives. All at once, he was aware of two personages walking beside him, one on each side. As the men came nearer, he lost his fear, and they passed him by. After some distance, the two personages also disappeared into the night.

The next time he was in St. Louis, he went to that place to see if there was an opening in the brick wall where two personages could have stopped, but there was no break in the wall at all. John felt that it had to be two of the [Three] Nephites who protected him that night.

May I take you back to our last year in Independence? In my desire to keep the story in sequence, I neglected to give a little background which I feel is quite important. At the close of Johnny's junior year at William Chrisman High School, he was chosen to be Battalion Commander of the ROTC during his senior year, and he was also chosen to represent the high school at Boys' State that summer. Both of these were among the highest honors awarded, and he was so happy about them.

Then, for several years, I had been secretary and program chairman for the city-wide women's council, and I was working with two groups of girls who sang special numbers for the different churches in Independence, besides having a fine class of piano students whom I loved to work with. And here we were being asked to give up these activities and move.

One day, when I was bemoaning my fate of having to give up my students, our women's leader, Mrs. Rosamond Smith, tried to cheer me up by saying that I would find one's reputation always traveled ahead of one, and surely enough, I have always had a group of students waiting for me each place we have been sent. But that spring of 1954, the inevitable happened—John was appointed to go to Mobile, Alabama, as pastor and district president. We all felt that we could not just pick up and go, and we spent hours and days praying about the matter. Finally, John went down ahead of us, to become acquainted with the area while the present pastor was still there to help him get acquainted and show him around.

Back in Independence one evening, I was busy packing some things in the kitchen when Johnny came in and laid his head on the table. After a while, he asked, "Mother, do I have to go?" He had been crushed, and I knew it, and had been praying to know how I could answer him, for it seemed to be tearing my heart out, and he needed a satisfying answer.

Pretty soon I began answering him, and I said, "You know, Johnny, this is your Dad's work, and I'm sure you and I can be good enough sports to go along and help him make his assignment a success, can't we?"

He paused a moment, then he straightened up, brushed away his tears, and said, "Of course we can, Mom." And from that point all negative talk was ended.

My brother, Neal, lived in Independence with his family, and several times he had said, "You know Johnny could live with us next year and finish high school training here." But, I always had to answer, "If Johnny stayed, I would have to stay too."

There were parties and sad goodbyes, but we made a beautiful transition into "life in the South." Even our little Manchester dog, Duke, who had trouble breathing as we drove into the warmer climate, soon acclimated to his new surroundings, just so he was with Johnny. The people welcomed us with open arms, and it wasn't long before Johnny as referring to our family as "we Southerners."

We moved in one week, only to have to repack our bags and go to reunion the following week, leaving our packing boxes stacked and waiting for us until we returned. In the meantime, men of the congregation came in and repainted the entire inside of our house, moving our packed boxes from one room to another. We were so glad to have it nice and clean when we returned.

Especially so since the C. A. Davies, from Australia, who were also at the Brewton Reunion, and who were also scheduled along with us to work the Memphis reunion, and we had just one week in between the two assignments. And, bless Pat, if Apostle Gleazer did not suggest that they return home with us and stay for the week, then we all could drive up to Memphis together. Imagine my embarrassment, company with my house in such turmoil, but they understood, and we all made the best of the situation.

The very night we returned from Brewton Reunion, we had hardly gotten in the door before our doorbell rang. A neighbor just across the street was dying, and they asked for John to come quickly. It was a case of "saying the last rites," for the lady passed away that night, and John conducted his first funeral before he was there a week. He was initiated in a hurry, and, although we did not know it at the time, we lived our entire five-and-a-half-years there going from one rush to another, and we loved every minute of it.

As we attended Brewton Reunion that year, we were new and unacquainted, so we sat back observing the Southerners, and learning their way of doing things. It so happened there was a feeling of rivalry between Mobile and Pensacola choirs, and since the Pensacola group sang the special numbers the first Sunday, we kept hearing members of the Mobile group commenting, "Just wait until next Sunday. Then you will hear a real choir." It concerned me very much, for I felt that combining the two groups could really produce great results. The Pensacola pastor had charge of the reunion that year, and since they alternated each year, the next year would be Mobile's time to be in charge. I called attention to that feeling of rivalry to John, and he said, "Just wait until next year. You will have charge of the choir. Then you can arrange that as you wish."

So I began planning and concentrating on building a strong rapport between the groups. As themes were chosen, I planned the anthems which I wanted to use the first two days, then asked choir directors to buy copies of certain numbers and have their folks ready to sing with the choir. Combining the two groups, plus additional singers from the district, worked out well, and Apostle Gleazer always said that we had the choir of all reunions. When I say that we had four soloists among the tenor section—that says something. I was in charge of the music the next four years we were there, and we really worked, but the results were very gratifying.

We had been in Mobile about a month when Johnny was voted in as leader of the Zion's League. It was a large group of young people, and their activities were well planned. Then, as he enrolled in school that fall, since he had been in the a cappella chorus in Independence, they put him directly in the main glee club. We were quite surprised after he began school to learn that Mobile High School was ahead of Independence High in some of the classes, so when it came to his Spanish class, they allowed him to audit the preceding semester, until he could keep up with his group. And he also was elected to be home room representative to the student council. All of this helped him to feel a part of the school he had so recently transferred to, and he was very happy. So our life in Mobile got off to a very good start, and after we were unpacked and ready to begin living again, I found there were a large number of piano students waiting for me to begin teaching.

Mobile had three hospitals, and people came in from all over the South, because the doctors had fine reputations, and when folks were ill, they wanted and expected the pastor to be at their call. When John was in town, he tried to leave our home by eight-thirty each morning to make the rounds of the hospitals before giving attention to other matters. One morning one of the men from the Alabama District called for him for administration. A nurse was attending the fellow and stayed to hear John's prayer. Following the prayer, John looked up and noted tears in the eyes of the nurse. A few weeks later, we received a call from the hospital, asking for John to come and pray for a person whose name we could not recognize. But when John entered the room, the lady explained that she was the nurse who was attending the man from the Alabama District, and she was so impressed with [John's] prayer that she wanted him to come and pray for her.

Johnny attended Graceland College two years, then knowing that Kansas University was very outstanding for its training for students interested in the field of business, we had just taken it for granted that he would want to go there for his upper-class training. However, he had heard that the University of Alabama was one of the top ten schools for business students, so he wanted to investigate before he definitely chose which school to attend. So one morning, we arose early and drove up to Tuscaloosa, so he could have a full day to roam around, talk to some of the professors, and learn something about the school. We let him out at the business building, and told him we would be back to pick him up about five o'clock that afternoon. We spent the day looking over the town, and when we picked up Johnny that evening, he was very enthusiastic and said, "This is my school."

It was a very interesting trip back to Mobile that evening, with him telling us all about the school, and after he got home, he wrote to have his transcript sent from Graceland. He was thrilled to learn, after they studied his record, that they were awarding him a scholarship to defray his enrollment, and they also appointed him monitor over his section of the dormitory, which counteracted his expenses there. We all decided he was a pretty lucky fellow to be going to the university, and his only expense would be for food. He also managed to work at Penny's on the weekends, which would help him financially. We all felt very rewarded for our day at the university.

After Johnny received his bachelor's degree, he and his little Graceland sweetheart, Melva Fears, were married. Then, while he was working on his master's degree, she also attended the University of Alabama with him and received her bachelor's the same time he received his master's.

One communion Sunday morning, a call came in from the infirmary asking for administration for a tiny baby who had been born on Thursday, yet she had not taken any nourishment nor cried at all. She was considered to be a "blue baby." John was very busy with the preparation for the communion service that morning, so I told the person who called that I was sure he would be there as soon as possible after the communion service. John chose to take with him one of the men who had recently been called to the office of elder. As they drove to the hospital, John explained that they would probably be required to put on gowns and masks before entering the quarantined section of the intensive care nursery, and how Hale should anoint and John would confirm the anointing, and that it all needed to be very short because of the situation.

Everything followed like clockwork, and after they removed their gowns and masks, as they walked toward the entrance of the room, there were members of the family with their faces pressed against the observation window in astonishment—the baby was crying to high heaven. Then it took its first nourishment soon afterwards.

There was a sequel to that story. After the church sent us back to Independence, we were working out on our lawn one Saturday evening, when a car stopped in front of our house, and a young girl about five years of age came around to where we were working. We greeted her, and then she told us that she was the "blue baby" from Escatawpa, Mississippi, all those years ago. It was a happy reunion with her folks, and so nice to know she was doing well.

One morning about ten o'clock there was a call for John. The lady told me that their daughter Sandra, who was enrolled at the Pensacola Business College, had been sent home because she was having eye trouble. Her doctor had told her that she had tuberculosis of the retina. She had had two operations, and here it was bothering her again, and tomorrow she would be back for further treatment. Of course, they were anxious to have her administered to. It so happened that John was spending the day with a man who was dying of cancer, and asked me to tell the mother that it would probably be quite late in the evening before he could be there.

When he was free, John took one of the older elders with him to administer to Sandra, and after he returned home, I noticed that he went directly into the living room and sat down very quietly. That was very unusual, so I followed him, and he said that they had had quite an experience. After the administration, he asked Brother Jernigan if he had experienced anything unusual, and he told how his arms had tingled up to his elbows during the administration. They had both experienced the same feeling, and were certain there had been an experience on Sandra's part.

The next evening, I was working on setting up the bulletin for the following Sunday, when there was a knock on the door. I asked John to answer the door, and when he opened it, Sandra bounced in and grabbed him around the neck. She was so exuberant. She said that when she went to the doctor for her examination that morning, he looked at her eyes, and could not even find the scars which had been on her eyes from the two previous operations, that she was healed and could return to Pensacola the next day. The doctor could not understand it, but what a HAPPY girl, and we were so happy for her.

For a time preceding our last reunion at Brewton, I had been almost doubled up with a side ache. The doctor could not determine the cause, and questioned if I should go to reunion at that time. However, he said I could go if I would remember that he was at the other end of the telephone line. I could not straighten up, and everyone knew I was having that terrible side ache. I had thought several times of having administration for it, but John was in charge of the reunion, and he was so busy. I hesitated to bother him until things were well in hand. I had been praying myself, but it was not like being administered to, so I kept putting it off.

Then at the prayer meeting on Tuesday morning, I had quite an experience. I was in such misery, yet, I was praying as I listened to the testimonies, and I reminded the Lord that I needed a blessing so badly. Then I was stricken with the thought, "You have not gone through the right channels." Of course I knew that, but I had excused myself because John was so busy. But after that experience, when the meeting was over, I could hardly get to the cabin fast enough to tell

John about it. He answered me with, "I have been wishing you would ask for administration."

Then, I asked him if he would make an appointment with the patriarch so that the two of them could take care of it that day. Plans were made for doing so that evening at five o'clock at the patriarch's cabin. We all had made preparation for it, and from the time the men laid their hands on my head, the side ache was gone. It seemed that it was an instantaneous blessing, and I was able to travel around through the grounds like a new person. I cannot tell you how wonderful it was, and everyone on the campus realized that I had received a great blessing. There were many blessings that year, and it raised the spiritual level of the entire reunion.

For several years, John had been collecting material with the idea of sometime working out a doctorate in theology, by correspondence from the Chicago School of Divinity. During our fourth year in Mobile, he said he would like to work it out if I would do his typing for him. And so it was decided. He did the hospital visiting in the mornings, planned his congregational and sick visiting in the afternoons, then on free evenings he began organizing and writing. Certain assignments were required every month, and both of us were challenged in meeting the assignments. Each month when John was assigned to New Orleans, he made a special effort to spend extra time at the Library at Tulane University. We both worked untiringly. Many nights my typewriter was going until wee hours of the morning, but John was working so feverishly that the least I could do was to try to keep abreast with him. Some evenings we were so tired, yet we just exchanged laughs and remarked, "We're trying hard. We'll make it."

It was in April that the last lesson was sent in, and what a RE-LIEF. Many of the church members knew we were working extra on a project, but they were really shocked when John announced that he had been working out studies for his doctorate in theology degree, and that was the reason our social life and extracurricular activities had been placed on hold during those months. Now, they all wanted to help us celebrate. So, Brother John Barlow Senior wrote to all the branches, inviting them to a reception and surprise program of "This is Your Life, John Darling," to be held in Mobile following the prayer meeting on Wednesday evening. John was in Bay Minette that evening, so he knew nothing of the fun and joy the Mobile folks were having as they assembled and anticipated John's surprise.

As John drove into the driveway that night, he wondered what all those cars were doing at the Mobile church. Anyway, he went directly into the parsonage and sat down to read the paper, but Brother Barlow, who was engineering the surprise, went over to the house after him. Imagine his surprise as he entered the church and found it was all in his honor. It was a delightful evening, and one which we shall never forget.

Mobile District extended from Bay Minette, Alabama, across the bay and down the coast to New Orleans, Louisiana, and included eleven congregations and two groups. John worked out the monthly schedule, so that he could plan to preach or meet with all of the groups each month, then reserve each communion Sunday for Mobile. That was the schedule he tried to keep the entire period he was district president. It kept him busy, but it was a schedule which he worked to maintain regularly.

After the fall conference of 1959, we were notified that John was being sent back to Independence where he was to be president of the School of the Restoration, so we made a quick trip back to Independence to plan our move. Our home had been rented during our absence, and they were lovely folks, but we did not know how they would feel about the sudden change of plans, or what could be worked out for the betterment of each family concerned. They sensed our situation and assured us that it would be convenient for them to move to another location, and the house would be ready for us in a two week period, so all was well. It also happened that on our trip to Independence, we had stopped at Tuscaloosa, where Johnny and Melva lived, to tell them of the shift in plans, so they knew we were on the move. And they had just one remaining semester at the University of Alabama before completing their degrees. Then, they would be moving back to Independence also, for Johnny had accepted a position with J. C. Penney at the Blue Ridge Mall store.

We really felt good about our trip. Our renters had been so very cooperative, and everything had fallen in order just as if they had been planned that way. But now was the part that we dreaded—telling the folks of Mobile and the district that we were being sent back to Independence.

John's priesthood schedule had him scheduled to preside at the communion service the following Sunday. Then he was to preach that evening, which would be an ideal time to break the news of our leaving. Following the service, the congregation usually spent a little while visiting outside of the church, but that night everyone went directly to their cars and went home. It seemed that everyone was so shocked that they had nothing to say. The following two weeks were filled with packing, dinners, and sad farewells.

The Christmas season was always a very special time in Mobile, but the shock of our leaving seemed to cast a shadow on all the activities. This was also the time of the year when winter begins to set in, so we found ourselves rushing to beat the change of seasons. It had been such a beautiful fall, we wondered if we could get packed and moved before winter settled in. When we think back over our years in Mobile, and the many rich experiences which we enjoyed with those good folks, we find ourselves thankful all over again that the good Lord saw fit to send us there at that time. I have told just a very few of our experiences, for the space is limited, but we hold the others as treasures to long remember, for the folks there will always hold a special place in our hearts.

John and I had put every ounce of energy into our work in Mobile, and were both so tired we thought we would never get rested. But, we quickly shifted gears and worked to orient ourselves into the jobs at hand. John had been a good pastor, concerned and caring for the people at all hours. They loved and respected him very highly, and now he was moving into an area of responsibility in advising and counseling the young appointees who would be attending the School of the Restoration.

The weather had favored us and had remained lovely during our move, but winter blew in with a blast our first evening at home. We were so thankful, and felt that our prayers had truly been answered.

During John's nine years in the department of religious education he had established a reputation as a very good speaker, so he was soon invited to speak at different churches while the change was being made at the school. In the meantime, after things were in order at the house, I lost myself in some handwork until I could get a second breath, resolving to choose carefully so as not to get involved in too many activities. But in just a short time, former piano students were at my front door, and I became very busy.

During this time, we learned that there was a lot of painting and refinishing which needed to be done around the house, so we launched into the job of refinishing the apartment upstairs. After all, Melva and John would need a place to stay while they were looking for housing. It was a big job, and we were happy to have it all nice and clean for them.

Then, in June, we went to Tuscaloosa for their graduation, helped them pack, then pulled their trailer back to Missouri, and they lived in the apartment several weeks before they found a lovely house on South Delaware. In the meantime, Melva had been busy applying for a teaching position, and was quite elated when she learned she was to teach the second grade at one of the schools. From then on, her time was taken in planning her work for the beginning of school.

It seemed that the more painting we did, the more we found to do, but we finished the entire outside the day before fall weather set in. It was a terrific job, but we were able to hire our next door neighbor, who was a good painter, and it was really a big accomplishment. I had firmly resolved to get that painting all finished before I ventured into any social life, so the surrounding neighbors were watching closely so they could set the date for their annual Thanksgiving Dinner at a time when I could be present. It was a delightful affair. As a new member, I was invited to sit at the head table, which was covered with a most beautiful net tablecloth. It was made of a brown net bordered with a five-inch strip of brown felt, which was set on with a gold-colored braid. Then, about an inch above the braid, were appliquéd flowers sewn on at four or five-inch intervals all around the cloth. I studied this very closely during the dinner. Then, I decided it would really be a conversation piece if the border were scalloped, and instead of small individual flowers around the border, possibly a basket of jonquils and various flowers on each side, an arrangement of tulips at one end and jonquils at the other end. And since the corners of the cloth hung exposed, it would be lovely to have a bouquet of roses, lilies, cosmos, and lily-of-the-valley decorating them.

The next weekend found me at the cloth shop gathering my materials. I am no artist, but thought it would be a real project to follow the patterns of flowers in the garden catalog, and enlarging them to fit my needs. It took me several months, for I finished each flower with crocheting and matching beads, and it was truly a beautiful piece of work. Of course, Melva has it now, and I sincerely hope she is enjoying it as I always did. Another friend, Gail Farnham, liked the project, so she also made one, and we really enjoyed exchanging patterns and having afternoons sewing together. After these were all finished, we launched out on Christmas cloths, using green net and Christmas decorations. It, too, was very beautiful.

Melva taught just one year, for the following October, little Stephen Rothburn joined their family. He was truly a little "Darling," and we were in the height of our glory when we were asked to babysit with him. He was a very good baby, and I shall never forget how quickly he learned the route to our house. After our car crossed [Highway 24], he always directed us with his little arm before we reached each turn.

The next two years were busy ones for all of us. John had been a good pastor and district president, concerned and caring for them at all hours. The people loved him and respected him highly, and now he would be in an advisory and counseling capacity to the young appointees who would be attending the School of the Restoration. During his years in the department of religious education, he had become well-known as a speaker in the areas where he had worked, and now he was often invited to different churches to speak. One weekend, he was invited to bring me and come over to Springfield, Missouri. Plans were for a covered dish dinner and social on Saturday evening, then he would be the speaker for Sunday morning.

That morning he went to the pastor's office to meet with the priesthood while I went directly into the sanctuary. At the door I looked around for someone I knew to sit with, and just before the service began, I noticed a young woman come and take her place in the pew beside me. I did not pay any attention as to who she might be, for we had been gone from home probably twenty-five years, and I was not expecting to find any former friends, until she reached over and put her hand over mine and said, "Hi, Bea, this is LaVerne." I quickly looked at her, and surely enough, it was one of the little girls I had in my Sunday school class before I left home to go to college. It was a real reunion. She admitted that they did not attend church regularly, but they had noticed in the paper that we were going to be there, so they acknowledged that as a reason for coming.

My own class of students had grown to where I was teaching until nine p.m. on Tuesday and Thursday evenings. John was teaching out at the school, and did not get home until around ten o'clock, so I thought I might just as well fill the hours.

Johnny was teaching two business courses two evenings a week over at the University of Missouri-Kansas City. Then one evening, he came over to our house and announced that he was going to return to school at the University of Illinois, at Champaign-Urbana. That was quite a turning point in their lives, but the "teaching bug" had gotten into his blood, and he wanted to go and work on his doctorate. He had arranged to work for the Penney company on weekends, and the university had offered him a scholarship to help defray their expenses, and he figured that he could complete the work for his doctorate in a three-year period.

By that time little Cynthia had joined their family, and she was so precious. We were thrilled with Johnny wishing to further his education, and he knew that we would help them, if they needed help. So they sold their little home, and were off to the university again.

When we first moved back to Independence, I had vowed not to repeat the experience I had in Mobile, for we had moved there at a time when the music chairman was asked to change shifts on her job. She had previously worked during the day, which allowed her freedom during the evening hours, but since she was changing to the night shift, she was unable to continue the choir, so they were looking for a director. My husband heard some of the choir members discussing the matter as to who would be able to fill that vacancy, and he said, "I believe my wife can help you out," so I inherited a job just like that. Having been a music minor student in college, I had directed song fests, congregational singing, and assisted our choir director through the years, and the years John and I attended the Presbyterian church we both sang in the choir, so I had a nice chorale repertoire to draw on. Being their director was a great challenge, and I really enjoyed it, and that opened the door for me to be music director for the district and reunions. However, after six years, I was needing a rest for a while.

During the next two or three years in Independence, I did a lot of accompanying for soloists, becoming acquainted with voices in different registers. Then three girls from the Fiske family invited me to be their regular accompanist for their family trio. I also organized a triple trio, choosing nine voices with three on each part. These girls were from among soloists for whom I had accompanied, and sang under the name of the Carolean Ensemble. Both of these groups did some lovely work, and furnished special music for the different churches in Independence. Both of these groups practiced each week, and we were kept quite busy, but we all enjoyed serving in this capacity.

I also had a group of sixty to seventy piano and organ students, and was active in the Independence Music Club, serving on the board two or three years; then treasurer; vice-president for two years; then I accepted the presidency. But when I got home that evening, my husband called me with a bit of news. He first asked me if I were sitting down, so I quickly reached for a chair, then he came right to the point. He said, "Honey, we are on the move. I have just been notified that we are being sent to Washington, DC, where I am to finish this present term as pastor. Then I will be available for the district presidency there for the next four year period."

I don't need to tell anyone that I was shocked. I was in COMPLETE SHOCK, and I finished the day in a "zombie" state, for I just could not realize that I had worked and attained a perfect set up, and was now being asked to leave it all and go into another area. However, we wives of the appointees realize that our jobs are to go and assist in the work where our husbands are sent, so with memories of our lovely farewell reception, dinners, and fond goodbyes, we were on our way to Washington, DC.

Here, again in a similar situation, the music chairman was a very qualified nurse whose schedule was being changed, so that she was no longer free for evening activities, and again my husband said, "I think my wife can help you out." So, again, I had inherited a job, but as I became acquainted with the choir personnel, I was very thrilled to find so many solo voices, which made directing a great joy, and we had some lovely programs besides our usual Sunday morning renditions.

Our parsonage was a lovely ranch-style home which had two bedrooms and a Hollywood bathroom on the first floor. The basement was a complete apartment, so we had a lot of company. It was located in Arlington, across the Potomac River about eight miles from the church. However, just recently, they have built a new parsonage on the church grounds, which has really simplified the transportation problem for the pastor and his family. When we lived there, all the appointees who came into Washington, DC, knew that the apartment was available. Then, several times different ones wrote to John asking if they could bring their family in to have a "look-see" at Washington. There were several times when I would just get the sheets changed on the beds and the apartment cleaned, only for another group to come in that evening. They usually went out for lunch and dinner, but I always served them breakfast, for they all enjoyed my Swedish coffee rings, pineapple rolls, or whatever I decided to bake.

I found quite a nice group of piano and organ students, whom I managed to work in between schedules. But I did not get to accompany John so often on his weekend trips, because there was a shortage of organists, so I had to take my turn at the organ oftentimes when I was not using the choir for special music.

While John was district president, his ministerial territory extended from Portsmouth, Virginia, up the coast to Wilmington, Delaware. However, after he was ordained patriarch-evangelist, his territory extended up the coast through the state of Maine. This part of the country is historically so very rich, with even the names of places holding secret stories of the part they played in the early history of the country. Each trip we made to the reunion grounds took us up into Pennsylvania through the Mennonite territory, and across the Delaware River which played such an important part in the navigation of troops during the Revolutionary War.

It is interesting to know that Washington, DC, is surrounded by a large highway called the Beltway. It is about sixty miles around this beltway, and it varies in width with additional lanes for the convenience of incoming and outgoing traffic. One evening, John was called for an administration at the Bethesda Naval Hospital, which was about one-fourth of the way around the Beltway from where we lived, so he called Marion Talcott to meet him at the Bethesda junction to assist him with the administration.

When he left, I figured it would take him about an hour or so, then he would be back. I watched the clock, and an hour and a half passed, two hours passed, and still no John. So, I began wondering what had happened, for in Washington, DC, anything can happen. We had heard about folks disappearing right off the streets. I picked up a magazine to read, for I could not go to bed until I knew he was safe. When he did come in, he said that he and Marion had been talking so intently that they had not noticed our exit until too late to turn, so they just continued around the Beltway again.

We had many fine experiences during the years we lived in Washington. The people were very fine, and we loved them. And their reunions were always outstanding experiences. They were held at Deer Park, which was truly sacred ground. Apostle Howard Sheehy was guest minister for our last reunion there, and he was very impressed with John's work as director of the reunion. John had a knack of working so kindly with the people, and everyone noticed it.

Apostle Sheehy went to our home for the night, intending to catch the plane home the next morning. After we had our things put away and had settled down for a nice, quiet evening, he said that there was something he wanted to talk to us about. He spoke of how impressed he was with the way John had directed the reunion, then further stated that the more he observed John, the greater was his feeling that John was prepared to receive the call to be a patriarch-evangelist, and he wanted to know our feeling about the matter.

This was no surprise to me, for several times as I was typing the material which John had prepared to present at the different services, I paused and went into the office where he was working with the comment, "John, this does not sound like a district president. These words sound like those of a patriarch." He would answer me, "Well, that is the way I feel." Then little old me would go back and continue my typing.

In just a few weeks, John received a letter from Brother Sheehy confirming the call, and inviting us to come to Independence for further instruction, and saying that the ordination would be at the following world conference.

It was following his ordination that John's ministerial territory was extended to include the state of Maine. It was a very challenging responsibility, and we started out with a recording machine taking the blessing, and me also taking it in shorthand. We had heard stories by some of the patriarchs where they had had experiences of having to restructure some of their blessings, because of different things happening to their machines, and, as a result, the blessings were not complete. And we did not want that to happen to us.

After the first blessing, John checked the recorder before he launched on to his second blessing, and the recorder seemed to be running just fine. So he continued until the cassette was filled. When we got home, we were anxious to hear how the recording sounded, so John turned it on. All went well until about half-way through it. Then, bless Pat, there was a void. The machine continued to run, but no words came through. John re-ran the tape several times, for it blanked out some two or three sentences, then was all right again. John was very upset, and held his head just wondering how he could restructure the blessing—his very first one. I quickly ran after my shorthand notebook and read that part which was omitted, and we were two relieved people.

But that taught us an important lesson, and John went directly and bought a second recorder, for I could not always go with him, and he felt that he did not dare run the risk of having just one machine taking the blessings. As he brought the recordings home, I always transcribed them in a rough form. Then, after he edited them, I typed them for the final form, always with a copy to send in to the church office. The year passed so quickly. The days melted into weeks, the weeks into months, and, bingo, the year was gone. Then, we were transferred to the Mid-central states. We could have moved to Joplin, Missouri; Springfield, Missouri; Memphis, Tennessee; Fort Scott, Kansas; or any city of our choosing. Since we had both attended college in Pittsburg, Kansas, we thought it would be nice to live where we had friends, so we moved to Pittsburg.

John was gone into the district most of the time, for it was a large territory, but I did not mind so much, for it was our home territory, and we had anticipated being back with friends. However, the first month we were there, we sensed an evil spirit among the members, and try as hard as we could, we finally decided to try to ignore it and work the best we could. The pastor who was there when we were in school, had served twenty-seven years, and even then, he was not ready to give it up. I found a large number of piano and organ students, joined the Pittsburg Music Club, and the second year I was elected music director for the church, so I kept very busy. But it was never with the freedom which we had experienced as we worked in other places.

One fall we decided to take a bus tour with the Watson Company from Erie, Kansas. We choose the trip to California, and had such a delightful time. It was during the pumpkin harvest, and I have never seen so many pumpkins. They were piled high in the fields. Cabbages and cauliflowers were also very plentiful. We were impressed the way the company regulated the changes and formation of their passengers so they all became acquainted. It was really a delightful trip.

The next year we wanted to take the Northwestern trip with the same company, but there were not enough passengers who signed up, so we took a trip around Thunder Bay, and again, we really enjoyed ourselves. It was during the fall season, and again the foliage was really beautiful. The tour took us north around Lake Superior to Sault Sainte Marie; then across the Mackinac Bridge into Michigan; visiting Mackinac Island; spending the night at Mackinac, Michigan; going through the woolen mills; then on our way home.

We only stayed in Pittsburg two years after John retired. Then, we moved to El Paso, Texas, for about eight months. Then, we decided that was too far from "home plate," so we moved to Lubbock, Texas, where our son John and his family lived. But when Johnny was elected as provost at Mississippi State University, we did not want to follow them, so we decided it was time for us to make final arrangements and turn everything over to them and find our place in Resthaven [Nursing Home].

We have been here almost two years, and we are so glad that we came in when we did, for we are both kept busy. John and Marvin Fry are on call for administrations and elder duties, and John is always helping handle residents from the third floor. I take my turn at the organ and whenever they need me. We watch new folks as they come in, and oftentimes they are much older than we were when we came in, and they have quite a time making their adjustment. It is a great step to give up one's home and belongings, and we feel for them, for we know what they are going through. But we have been blessed, and are so thankful that we came when we did. This is a great place to learn to live for others and with others.

[signed] Beatrice Deaver-Darling

End of revised text

The following material was recorded in an interview with Ruby Morgan on May 14, 1987, in Independence, Missouri. Most of the interview duplicates the material already included in the previous chapter and, for that reason, is not recorded here again. Some material, however, elaborates on the events already recorded. [Note: whoever transcribed the interview spelled the son's name as Johnnie; but I continued with Johnny since that's the way it was spelled throughout the longer narrative.]

I'm Beatrice Deaver Darling. My father and mother were Albert and Sara Jane Deaver. There were six children in the family. I was born July 23, 1910, in Carterville, Missouri. We went to church in Webb City, Missouri. We lived in Webb City. My folks lived in Webb City until they passed away.

Both Mother and Dad belonged to the church. All of us, in turn, became members of the church. We were raised in the church. In those days we walked to church. We were about a mile from the church. We had the sidewalk. We walked to church except when friends came by and it was convenient for them to pick the family up.

My dad was a teacher. Mother was director of music for years and years, until we grew up and left home, until we went off to college. All of us took piano and organ.

I don't recall that missionaries ever stayed in our home, because there was such a large family of us, but we were always having them out for meals. We had such wonderful relationships with the missionaries that came. Our parents were always very interested in our becoming exposed as much as possible to the church and the men of the church, so they always had them to dinner or to meals.

I remember that we were all very, very interested in the men that came. We had Brother Gillen. We had Apostle Hansen. The missionaries that came through were always stopping at our house, because so many people fed them rich foods. When they would come to our house, they would call [ahead] and they would say, "Janie (they called my mother Janie), may I just have something very simple tonight? I'm eating quite heavily."

Some of them just wanted mush and milk. Others wanted beans and cornbread. Whatever they wanted, why, that's what we had for the meal. They felt like they could ask mother for just something of a light nature. We had so many of the missionaries that came out, people like Amos Higdon and the district leaders always came around.

May I say before that, that it was not a large church during those days. As we progressed in our music, we took over the piano [in church], because all of us in turn helped play the piano. I started being church organist when I was twelve, and my brother sang, and my sister sang and played. We were really the music department. Mother directed the choir. The congregation was eighty or a hundred. I do not remember just how many.

I was baptized in this church, but they did not have a font [so] I was baptized in the river. They went out to Cedar Creek for the baptism. I remember so well. Brother Lee Critch baptized so many of the boys and girls in our area. He was the district missionary for so many years. And then Amos Higdon [was the district missionary]. Paul Hansen baptized me. I believe it was in the spring. I do not remember exactly [but] I was eight years old. We had been told that Apostle Curtis would be there. It was some weekend. I do not recall whether it was a weekend from reunion or just what.

Anyway, Apostle Curtis was supposed to have been there. We did not know Brother Hansen. That was before he was an apostle. That was our introduction to him. Brother Hansen was there instead of Brother Curtis, and I was a little disappointed. I knew Brother Curtis, but I did not know Brother Hansen. Brother Curtis had been to our home, and so I knew him, and I did not know Brother Hansen, but all went well.

I am the fourth generation in this church. My grandparents were members on my father's side. My grandmother and then her folks, in turn, were members. So, that makes me fourth generation. We always went to reunion. We went to reunion at Joplin. That was before Racine. I can remember when we were just in our early teens, we went to reunion. People like Mable Carlisle would direct the choir, and I got to be her accompanist. Reunion was quite an experience for us, and we were always interested in the music part. One year Evan Fry was there. He was a young man then. Mable Carlisle was there, and another time Louis Koehler. That was the year we met Brother Hayden and his brother, Bill. From then on, we were quite close to the Hayden family....

I had been teaching Johnny to play the piano. Some of his little boyfriends and girlfriends wanted to learn how, so I started teaching his little friends to play the piano, and along the same time I was helping with the girl's work. I was teaching them the songs. That year, I went to the girls' retreat at Lake Doniphan. I was taking care of the music, and we had a gay time, a delightful time. I took care of the girls' music for quite some time.

In the meantime, I was teaching some of Johnny's friends to play the piano and the more I taught those young students, the more it got in my blood. By that time, Johnny was pretty good at the piano. I took on more and more of his friends, and I found myself with a little class of youngsters. I loved that part of it. Then I started filling up my hours each evening with piano students. The first thing I knew, I had quite a group of them.

[The following material was covered earlier, but not in as great a depth or detail.]

Then it happened that during the summers we would be traveling with John in reunion work. It was the year that John was thirteen that Paul Craig asked if I would teach one of the music classes for a music institute they were having at Lamoni. I was supposed to have the last day. It just happened that day fell on the first day that we were going to be in transit. John had been teaching religious education all week in Lamoni at this institute. We planned that we would rent our house for the summer and go on this trip. I believe there were five reunions, two youth camps, and one institute, and it was supposed to cover from the latter part of May clear through to the first week of September. Our first day was the day at Lamoni.

Johnny helped me pack the car for the summer, because we were
going up to Canada, and we would have to have warm clothes for the
three weeks we would spend in Canada…. That Saturday morning,
we left for Lamoni. John and I had our appointments there on Saturday, and from there we went on to Detroit Lakes, Minnesota, for our
first reunion. We had a wonderful experience there at Detroit Lakes.
It was my first time for having the music for reunion. I had helped
at many reunions and played for them, and so forth, but that was my
first experience at having the music for reunion.

From Detroit Lakes, we had another at Minot, South Dakota. It
just happened that Z. Z. Renfroe and E. Y. Hunker were in charge
of these reunions. I believe D. T. Williams was there, too. Some place
along the way, Jouston Hobart joined the crew. We were all together
at Minot. After we had a week there, then we started up the plains of
Canada. We went to Saskatoon, Saskatchewan. When we drove onto
the grounds that day, they were putting in electric lights across the
grounds. The reunion was to be held on a school ground. They were
putting tents all around, and they had this great big tent they were
putting up, and there were no lights being strung. I asked, "How do
you expect me to have a choir without any lights for the service?"

I was on the grounds for a while that afternoon. I was supposed to
have the women's work in that reunion, and late in the evening, a lady
in a wheelchair approached me. She was the district music director,
and she said, "I hear that you are musical and that you direct music."

I answered, "Yes. I just finished over at Minot, South Dakota."

She said, "I'm in a wheel chair. Will you please take the music for
me?"

I told her that I had the women's work. She said, "Well, I think
you can take this. We have a nice choir."

So I said, "Yes."

I was one busy person with teaching the women's class and directing the choir. I had all the music for the reunion, and we had a
wonderful time.

Well, when I asked that afternoon about any lights, they said,
"The sun does not go down until ten-thirty." So, there was a reason
they did not need lights. We were up where we saw the Milky Way
right there. It was a wonderful experience. We had a great experience

there at that reunion. The Lord blessed us in so many different ways. The women were responsive to their studies and the choir was very responsive. We had a great time.

Then, after a week there, we had a week in between that assignment and our next assignment, which was over in northern Montana. There was another family, another couple, who wanted to go with us to the next reunion and spend this week in between with us. We had a nice experience. We spent a week seeing sights and there are some beautiful sights in Canada.

We had another reunion in the southern part of Montana. I had the women's work there, and I also did the accompanying for the music. Betty Mesle and her husband, Vernon, were there. She had the music, and I did the piano playing. It was a very outstanding reunion.

After that week, we had to leave on Saturday afternoon to get to our next assignment by Sunday. After our reunion, we went over to Green Bay, Wisconsin, for a religious education institute. I just vacationed, while John worked. After that assignment, we came home to Independence. Johnny's school had been going for three days, but we had made arrangements, so that the teacher knew he would be two or three days late. He was in the sixth grade at Ott School.

That finished our summer. I came back, and I was secretary and program chairman for the citywide council, and they were waiting for me to come back to begin meetings. So, I came back into a busy, busy schedule. It just so happened that I also had a full-fledged group of piano students.

Interviewer: Do you have any favorite hymns?
Oh, a book full. I think "The Old, Old Path," probably.

Interviewer: Are there any scriptures that stood out for you?
We memorized a lot of them as we went along. That's the way we spent our time.

Interviewer: Did you ever mind that you were so busy in the church like that?
I gloried in it. We just really enjoyed our work. Every summer, we were busy with reunions up until John's retirement. I went along and

had the music at many of the reunions all over the country. John was preaching and teaching. That's our life....

We have three grandchildren. Our son is provost down at Mississippi State University, and they are very busy there. [Our daughter-in-law] teaches. She has been on the women's council. I think she was on two or three years. Johnny is a bishop. He is also a high priest. He was ordained to an elder the first year, I believe, we were in Mobile. Brother Gleazer said he was the youngest elder in the church. He was in his teens.

Our grandchild, who is a lawyer, is a priesthood member. He's a priest. The other grandchild is an elder. Our daughter-in-law, their mother, is an elder. Now, Johnny and Melva go different places on assignment. My son's wife is an elder and he's a bishop. They work together. They just returned from a weekend institute in Mississippi. They work together all the time. They go different places, just like John and I used to do. In the summertime they go to reunions and work. He's the bishop, and she helps in other things. She's a worker.... She is a sister of Floyd Fears who works for the church.

Our granddaughter's name is Cynthia, and she has her master's degree in music from Illinois, and she teaches music in Boulder, Colorado. Her mother's name is Melva. Before she married our son Johnny, she was Melva Fears of Memphis, Tennessee....

[John] retired from church work, but after such wonderful experiences that we had during his missionary work, we felt as though his life had really been a fulfillment of all his wishes.

Interviewer: When he was a patriarch, did you continue with your shorthand, taking his blessings as he gave them?

After he bought his second recorder, I did not feel I needed to. After you take shorthand so much and teach it, then even when people are talking to you, you are writing their conversation in shorthand (in your mind). I guess I'll live that way always.

Every place I went, the people who were in charge always laughed. They said I had a class of piano students waiting for me. I taught piano everywhere we went and always had a delightful class. That was my life.

Dorothy Jane Pinkerton Yasaitis

BORN
May 1, 1912, Belvidere, Illinois
DIED
September 12, 1998, Janesville, Wisconsin

This is Grace Stone interviewing Dorothy Yasaitis on March 14, 1986, in Dorothy's home at Fulton, Wisconsin. Good afternoon, Dorothy.
Hello, Grace.

It's nice to have you give a little church history here for us for posterity's sake.
Well, thank you for asking me.

Would you like to give a little biographical material about your name, your place of birth, and your parents, and things?
Well, my name is Dorothy Pinkerton Yasaitis (spelled) Y-a-s-a-i-t-i-s ... I should talk probably first about my parents. My father was William Pinkerton, and he came from Scotland. He lived and worked in Hamilton, and he walked like twelve miles to Glasgow during a series to listen to the ministry of John Rushton. After the series, he decided that he needed to join [the RLDS church]. He be-

came a member and later became a deacon. His family never looked with agreement to the fact that he had joined that church, and so there were times when they would cross the street to avoid him.

My father had heard about America and emigrated in 1907. He came to DeKalb, Illinois, first, and worked for a farmer, and later went to Belvidere, Illinois, and there had a job. My mother was a member of the church in Madison, Wisconsin. She had joined as an older teenager. They were having a reunion there along one of the lakes in Madison. My father went there to attend that reunion, and this was where my parents met. They were married in 1911 and lived in Belvidere.

I was the first child in the family. I was born there. Before I put in an appearance, I am told that my father used to read from the *Ensign* and the *Herald* as my mother sat making the baby clothes, and they would sing hymns together and read scriptures. I felt this had a lot to do with my appreciation of music and reading, and, particularly, the scriptures. I am very fond of them. And then there were three other children that followed ... Earl, who was a diabetic when he was five years old, and who never had a very good life from that time, because they didn't know the things they do today about that disease. My brother Bob came when I was seven ... and we had a tremendous relationship—both [of us] interested in music and things of the church. And then a sister, Mina May, came thirteen years later.

We had a very nice home life. My parents were very kind in their discipline, and I can remember that one time I made a commotion at church. I was old enough to know better. All my father said was "You put on a fine demonstration today," and I got smaller and smaller. I could have crawled under the rug. But it didn't take long for me to understand that there were certain things that were expected of me as a member—and [one] of the things that I needed to do was to learn about the church. My father spent time on the blackboard before I was baptized—teaching and helping me to understand.

I believe your father was pastor?
My father was the pastor.

At Belvidere, [Illinois]?

At Belvidere. In fact, he was the only priesthood member there at the time. Later, there were a couple or three other men that came in who were members of the priesthood. My birthday was like on a Saturday, and I was baptized on Sunday morning. I remember that it was in the river that ran through the town, and I can remember seeing these people lined up across the bridge, wondering what was going on down there. But I was so delighted! It was an elation that I just wouldn't trade for anything, even as young as I was.

About the music that I got involved in—when I was six years old, I started piano lessons, because there was no adult to teach the music, and my father thought it was quite necessary. As I took lessons, he also sent the hymnal along, so I learned to play that. By the time I was eight years old, I was playing for the church services, because there was just no one else to do it. And I've never relinquished that particular love of that part of the service.

And you have written some music yourself and some poetry to go with it?

I have…. Yes, I have used some of those talents to serve over the years in music and theater. One thing that I do remember was that Wisconsin District and Illinois District met for reunions in a place called Epworth Camp, just outside of Belvidere, and Brother W. A. McDowell, who was the minister that married my father and mother was there as an evangelist. Although I was nearly sixteen, my mother thought perhaps that was a little young to get a patriarchal blessing; but, Brother McDowell said, "She needs it now." And I'm glad that I had it, because over the years, I've used it as a source of strength and admonition, and direction that has really been a tremendous blessing as far as I'm concerned.

There were missionaries who visited in your home, I suspect?

Yes, in those days, most of the missionaries stayed with the families of the congregations, and it was our good fortune to have them stay with us. One of the persons that I remember enjoying so much was Roscoe E. Davey. He was a seventy assigned to our district, and he came in and was, generally, our friend. My mother would clear the supper table quickly, and we sat around listening to his experiences.

He really widened and broadened our understanding of what was required of the men when they are out on assignments.

Were there others?

There were others. Yes. Some of them I don't recall very well, but I do remember that Brother Davey came one time with two young men from England—one was Arthur Oakman and the other was Charles Davies. Brother Oakman was quiet and much to himself, but he was a tremendous pianist and had a marvelous voice. I realized that he had the opportunity to take that into a professional field, but chose to do the call of the Lord in preference.

Do you remember any special prayer services or reunion experiences in your younger years?

Well, some of the reunion experiences I have had are varied. I remember that at one of the northeast Illinois–Wisconsin districts, I had been chosen to do an evening vesper, in alternate with someone—(Alma) Brookover, who represented the Wisconsin District. So, we took turns each night of having some kind of a vesper service, and it turned out to be very well received. One of the reunions that I attended, after I came to Wisconsin, was at Chetek, which is up in the further part of the state. It had very simple, beautiful grounds with cabins to live in. I remember that there were chances to meet friends that I had known over the years, and Brother Oakman was there at one time. Brother Hunker was, also, one of the visiting missionaries. [There was a] tremendous ministry from some of the Minnesota people who came to share with that particular reunion.

Then, there were times that I attended the Wisconsin District.... Ormond Kimball was able to find some property that our district bought, and we have now a very beautiful place for the present day reunions. I was there a couple of summers when I was responsible for the smaller classes, and just found it was a delight to work with the children.

Children have been important to you through all the years, haven't they?

Yes, they have and that extended far beyond the church.... The children that I had, as I said, went out beyond the confines of the church. I had worked in a woolen mill during the war, because I felt I needed to do something for the war effort. I didn't particularly like the place; then, I found a job with a dentist and I worked with him for five and a half years. He became ill and so the office had to be closed. I found a job, then, in Beloit where I had been going to church—that was with the Navy Department office.

I found it just wasn't the setup that I felt comfortable with, so I went to the employment agency and asked them if they had anything where I could be involved with children. At the moment, the only thing they had was a school for difficult children, who came from a wide area, but I would need to have transportation. I didn't have that, so I wasn't able to take that job. But I did accept something that they called "babysitting" that turned out to be much more than babysitting, as far as I was concerned. I got in to some very beautiful families, who had adequate things with which to deal and these children became almost as my children.

Because their parents were professionals, they went off on their holidays and seminars, and I was left to see that [the children] got to church, that they got their things done for school. I went to the concerts that the children were involved in. We had special parties where like—I remember one family and we had little suppers where we would say, "Now, we're going to be visiting such-and-such a country." So, the children would look up and study a little bit about that country, and ... they could dress up like someone from that particular place, and I would try to prepare meals that might be suggestive of menus from those places.

Over the years, it has been just a tremendous delight. These young people have grown up and have families of their own. We still keep in touch. I was involved in their marriages and get pictures of their own children. It has been a tremendously fulfilling thing. It was not babysitting, it was a parental thing—substitute parenting, I call it.

Shall we go back to how you happened to leave Belvidere, and where you went from Belvidere?

All right, I had worked in Belvidere, and while I was in the district at northeastern Illinois, I had written an article about education with an eye looking toward Graceland. Many people felt that you didn't need to have an education particularly to be adequate in the church. I didn't agree. I had written an article that I had sent to the *Herald* and they published it.

On the weekend I was to go to the conference that would involve elections, I found that [particular issue of] the *Herald* had already been in the houses and hands of some of those people. They decided on the strength of that article that I ought to be young people's supervisor, and I was not prepared for that. I had eleven congregations that really supported me no end, and we did a lot of exciting things. One of the things we did, which was innovative, was the world church was beginning to introduce something called the *Tenth Legion*, which was involving young people in the business of paying tithing. I wrote to … one of the people in Independence asking for more information and we developed that [program] within our own district. Later on, one of the men of the district suggested to my father that I needed to broaden my sights, and that Belvidere wasn't the place to do it. He suggested that I move into a larger community. So, I moved to Janesville and went to church in Beloit, Wisconsin—which I found had a tremendous historical background, and I was delighted to be a part of that congregation.

Do you remember who was the pastor there?
I think Brother (Ezra) Dutton was pastor.

In Beloit?
In Beloit.

Was that Jasper Dutton?
No, that was his brother.

Jasper Dutton's brother?
Yeah. Brother of Jasper Dutton. These people had known my parents when they were younger in Madison, because they came from the same congregation and the same district, but he was pastor. I got

involved in the music there and taught Sunday school classes. I lived in Janesville because at the time that this minister suggested to my father that I find something else, a family offered to have me come and stay with them. That was the Cleo Heide's—very friendly, warm, made me a part of their family. They had a little store and I helped there. I finally got jobs at another place where I was able to go to take some work at the university, and I took history and English, particularly, because I was most interested in those kinds of [studies].

You didn't stay in Beloit indefinitely, did you?

No. No, I got jobs outside … This is when I stayed in Janesville. I lived there, but I finally got a job during the war when my brother had left college (Graceland) to join in the middle of the year because there was the bombing of Pearl Harbor. His roommate was a Chinese-Hawaiian, Ed Wong. Ed came and spent Christmas with us. He was so concerned about his parents—he had heard nothing. I remember going with him to the bus station, because he had a brother who was a surgeon in Cook County Hospital, and the ticket salesman wouldn't allow him to have a ticket, because he wasn't in uniform. They thought he was Japanese, so I went in and I got the ticket and brought it out to him, and the driver let him get on [the bus]. He also had a statement from the dean at Graceland, but they ignored that. They would not accept that. My brother felt so strongly about this [incident] that, at the end of the first semester, he quit and joined the Navy.

[We all had music training] at home, because my mother felt that everybody needed at least a year of piano, and we were interested in orchestra and band. My brother, Earl, played a clarinet. Mina May played the flute. I had violin and piano, and did choral work, and Bob—he played french horn and the violin, and was the student director. He had plans when he went to Graceland to … to have his degree in music. But, as a result of the war, he lost his hearing, and when he went back to Graceland after the war was over, they found that it was almost a hopeless situation. He wouldn't be adequate in that. It really about broke his heart, but we found that the two of us, because of my music experience, could sing together. He could understand what I was singing, and we did some nice things together.

During the war, I went to the woolen mill and worked there as part of the corps that was making cloth. It was a very difficult place. I worked the afternoon and evening shifts, and we couldn't allow any moisture. It was terribly hot, and I reacted poorly to that. Finally, I decided I couldn't stand that, so I went and found a job with a doctor—a dentist. I was with him for nearly six years. He became quite ill and had to go into a sanitarium, so I went to work for the factory in Beloit. It also had a Navy Department, so I was still involved somehow in war effort. But the contacts [I had] with the church people in Beloit were tremendous.

That's where you met your husband?

Yes. Right. This is when I left [the Navy Department office]. I inquired about getting work where there were children, and I was able to be in a family where my husband came [to visit] and I met him. We were able to develop quite a nice relationship, but it was quite a while before we married, because his parents were Catholic, and my parents were concerned about that type of setup.

After a few years, we did decide to marry, and we were married in our [RLDS] church. My husband has been very supportive. He, at one time, worked in a ... Catholic school, and when there were things that were being tossed, the sisters would say, "Do what you want to with them." He would bring them home to me and say, "Can you use these for your children at church?" And many times I could.

So, I appreciated his thoughtfulness, too, and that's been true over the years. There have been times when I thought I got better treatment from my nonmember husband than some women get from husbands that are in the church. But it's because we have such a good relationship between us—that he understood some of my needs.

While you were going to Beloit you had some problems with transportation, didn't you?

Yes, for quite a while. There was a bus that went to Beloit early on Sunday morning in time for me to be there, and get in and practice whatever music the choir or something we needed, but I had trouble getting back home. A lot of times, some of the members would bring me back after I had been invited to lunch. One of the families that was very helpful was [that of] Marie and Harry Luce. They now live in Florida, and they were just very dear friends. They saw so many times when they made it easy for me to be a part of the Beloit congregation. Later, some of the people from Beloit set up a little mission in Edgerton which was —.

That was Brother Clyde Funk?

Yes, Brother Funk and his family set up a mission there. There was no connection between Janesville and Edgerton, [Wisconsin], on Sunday morning, so I continued to go to Beloit.

You mean transportation wise?

What did I say?

No connection. But you meant by transportation?

Yes, no connection in transportation. There was no bus service, and so I continued to go to Beloit. Barney Berridge was ... trying to start a mission in Janesville and he was the pastor, so he came and asked me if I would be willing to come and help with that beginning effort.

That was the Edgerton Mission?

The Edgerton Mission would become ... the Janesville Mission.

Okay.

I've been involved with that group ever since. Again, I've been involved with the music, and with the children's work, and a little bit of junior church now and then, especially with the children's choirs. We've had some really nice presentations. I think the children need to learn early that they can do something to assist in the Lord's work.

Going back a little bit ... do you remember World War I at all?

No.

You were just very young. How did World War II affect the church? We've heard a little bit about the way it affected your family, but ...

do you know of anything that you consider was the result of World War II in relation to the church?

Well, I think in some instances, from what I've read, I would think that some of our men in service felt greatly lead by the Spirit. I know … Cecil Ettinger has a marvelous testimony about God's protection and [felt] an awareness of the Deity while he was in a plane. I know that my brother was [at] … Tahiti, and they were going to have an all night session—singing and doing the things that Tahitian people do, and such warmth! He wasn't able to get permission … [to stay] overnight with them. But these people were so warm and welcoming, he said if ever he had a chance to live anywhere else besides the states, he would like to go there, back to the islands.

Now, another thing I think is very important to you is your trip to Scotland, and we would like to hear a little bit about where you went, and who you went with, and who you saw in the church, and things of this sort.

Well … after my mother and father had passed away, we sold my mother's house, and I [had] a little money … as a result of that. I knew very well that my father would like to have had me see Scotland, because … I was just brought up on his love for it, and so when someone said, "Well, what are you going to do with your money?" just off the top of my head, I said, "Oh, didn't you know I'm going to Scotland to see where my father lived and his family?"

I had kept in touch with the cousins by corresponding over the years, but I'd never met any of them. I had a few pictures, but I didn't really know anything about it, other than what my father had told me. I was so warmly received, and then I went … I was shown where my father preached his first sermon. None of his family had ever joined the church, so they just only knew fragments of things that I would really wanted to hear. I had an opportunity to go another time to Scotland, and I went with a purpose.

When was that, do you remember?

No, but it was quite a bit later. It might have been 1970…. Anyway, I went with the point of attending the British reunion, and my cousins understood that I couldn't spend all my time in Scotland or in

England, but I had to see them. So, my cousin who lived in England took me to Dunfield House and these people, again, were so warm and receiving—so welcoming! I got involved in several things there. I met some very dear people. I met Lily Oakman, Brother Oakman's sister. I met the Holmes family; they were very strong supporters of the church. Beautiful territory. This Dunfield House was a huge mansion, which houses our saints and their church activities, and it was just a very wonderful experience.

Something that I should tell you that couples up with that British reunion was I met a friend that I started corresponding with, and one time I was impressed to send someone a ticket to come to the states. I sent it to a cousin who I thought could do with [some] time away. She wrote back and said she couldn't come, so I knew that I had picked up the wrong impulse. So, I wrote to this lady I had met at the British reunion and asked her if I sent her a round-trip ticket to America, would she like to attend the world conference? She wrote back and she said, "You don't know how long I've been praying that I would have a way to once come to the world conference." And so she came, and we had a good time together.

Who was this?

Stella Wragg

What is her name?

Stella Sims Wragg. She is no longer alive.

W-r-a-g?

W-r-a-g-g. She spent ten days with us after the conference was over, and went back, and since that time Stella has gone to her reward. I knew that it was very important that I answer that impulse, but what was even stranger was I had already become a senior citizen, and about four months after she had returned to England, I got a check from the government for, supposedly, a mistake in my Social Security payment, and it covered it to the penny. So, God had some good purpose for that.

When you're talking about reunions, I remember one time that I had gotten into a little conflict with one of the people in our congregation, and the whole reunion theme was on reconciliation. A couple other friends had been involved in the same conflict, and they got their problem settled and made the reconciliation. I found it very difficult to do it, and one night in the tent, I was sleeping. The next day I would have to make a decision one way or the other, and up to that point, I had not decided [whether or not] I wanted to reconcile with anybody. But that night—it was just as if somebody was talking about me and saying that my behavior wasn't becoming to a saint. There were tears, and I recognized I had been a stiff-necked woman, and I agreed that I needed to make some reconciliation. The thing that was most marvelous was that when the birds started singing, they sang in harmony. I could hear the four parts from the various birds, and I was eager to go out and tell the person that I thought had offended me ... that I was sorry that it ever happened.

Do you remember at any time when you were struggling with a faith crisis? Have you always absolutely believed in those things that you'd been taught?

I think that probably when I was a teenager and in a very small congregation, there were times when I would say to my father, "How do you know all this is true?" Of course, his testimony was always that he had the assurance. I think that stopped when I got my patriarchal blessing, because it was saying that I needed, as a young person, to constantly keep in touch—that there were things in the offing that would take me away and change my feeling of strength in the church.

And there have been times when there have been low ebbs, but when I go back and read it, I still get the same substantial support that I always had. Another thing is, I don't question the work of the Lord—I question the people who do it. I know there are times when I could have done better, and I'm sure there are other people who feel the same. We're not condemning the Lord—we're just not adequate for the task that's given to us sometimes. We need to take a second look, and say, "He's not asking me to do this alone." He hasn't asked anyone ever to do anything alone.

Right. Shall we go back to your writing just a little bit? You still have a bit of writing here to discuss. It's the book that you put together called, *"Our Lives to His Service."*

Oh, yes. Well, I had written some poetry and things like that—just as I wanted, but, this time, the women's department of the district were having a retreat, and they wanted to do something different. Several years before, they did some material that had already been written—a monologue for Bible women, and one of the people that I thought had been sort of short-changed in that earlier experience was Rahab, the woman who lowered the people down over the wall to escape from Jericho. Her family was ... saved because of her belief in the Israeli point of view—Judaic. So, I wrote a monologue about that particular woman and included it with that [which] we took from a book.

Several years later, somebody said, "Why couldn't we do something like that about the women of the Restoration?" So, I sat down and read lots of things—church history, and other people's stories of these women. So, I chose ... this group of people ... from that particular area, covering from the time of the early church through the time of the Reorganization.

The first one I started with was Katherine Smith Salisbury, the sister of Joseph Smith Jr., and her experiences. I put it in first person—all these were done in first person. We decided that we needed to find some way of conveying their dedication to the church and the hardships which most of these people had to deal with. I chose, as I say, quite a few and then chose these six out of those.

As I began to write, I would sit down and pray about the first person and say, "Let me understand what some of her experiences were. Let me feel some of the pain." And the Lord answered that prayer. I did Katherine, and then I went on to the next person, and I said, "Lord, I need to know more about this person. Let me understand what she went through."

The second person was Caroline Booker, who was a Negro, who lived as a slave, and, even there, I sensed the desperation under which they lived. And this was true of each person. I had some feeling of their personality and the period in which they lived— the way the Lord had blessed them. There were times when I could hardly see to put the words down because the Spirit was so strong. And when these were presented at the district women's meeting, I asked several people what their reception of this was. We did it in very simple stage settings but with costumes—and, invariably, people would say, "We felt like we were in these people's homes." That's what I had prayed for—that they could somehow feel the same things I had as I wrote about these people who made such a contribution to the church.

And you have published this yourself. You have not gone through a publishing house.

No, I haven't gone through a publishing house. What I did was that there was to be an effort to create a fund for a caretaker's lodge or home. Everybody was doing something that they could do. I'm not adept at hand work. I'm not a painter, but I felt that the things I had written might satisfy my need to give a gift.

One of the people in the district came and talked with our women's department leader, who helped to set this particular project up. We talked about putting it in print, and so I was able to find a printer and a young friend, who did some of the pictures that are in there in black and white silhouettes. And we sold that to make my contribution to the caretaker's lodge.

We probably should say who did your illustrations?

Angela Miller did my pictures, and Evelyn Burke was one of those who helped, and Elaine Augenstein was one who helped to produce this for me. The booklet is called, *Our Lives to His Service*. The women that I wrote about were Katherine Smith Salisbury, Caroline Booker, Ann Newkirk Wildermuth, Emma Pilgrim, Pauline Arneson, and Jessie Ward LeBaron.

And so you still have some of these available?

Some of these are still available, but one that I was very anxious to work on was Ann Newkirk Wildermuth, who was part of the Reorganization. It was in the Yellowstone Mission.

In Wisconsin?

In Wisconsin. I contacted … where I could, I contacted relatives of that particular person. But as I say, I did a lot of research on each of them, and felt that it was something the Lord helped me to do.

There is one person that I'm—a man and his wife—I am sure were very important to you in your early married years—patriarch-evangelist Harry Wasson and his wife, Gertrude. Do you want to say a few words about them?

Well, when I first came to Janesville, I lived with a lady and took care of her child. Her husband was in a veteran's hospital, and so she had to kind of go it alone as far as earning a living, but, after while, I was invited to come over and stay with the Wassons. I went there a lot, even while I was on the other particular job. They were like my extra parents and were very supportive of me—saw that I got to Beloit, and became very dear. We had a relationship, as I say, that was almost parental for me.

I may have been wrong in saying that you were married at the time you were living in that house.

Yes. Mr. Wasson—Papa Wasson, as I called him—married my husband and me in the Beloit congregation, and his [Joseph Yasaitis's] family did not come to the service. But, I was challenged to prove to them that we could have a good marriage, and this has been very true. It has been a good marriage.

Just a couple more questions, I know you're getting tired. Do you remember any stressful situations when you received the support of the Saints, who helped you through some difficult area?

Well, I think probably the loss of my parents, both my father and mother. People were very kind. My father had an asthmatic heart, and he meant so much to me that I found his loss very difficult to deal with. Yet, I told my mother that I felt him so close that if I could put my hand through the wall, I could almost touch him. He was this close. And there have been times through my years, since that time, I felt he has been close enough to minister to me somehow. I've been aware of this.

Another thing is ... my brother died six weeks after my father, and he was the one who was diabetic. That was hard for our family, because we had already gone through one grief, and then to have to deal with this other. But again, I saw that God, in his kindness, took Earl because he was not in a position to take care of himself anymore, and my mother certainly wasn't alone. It seemed as if people were there. I felt kindnesses in outreach that might have been there, but I was never aware of the extent that I was at this particular time.

Till you were in need of it. In the context of the gospel or the Restoration, as you understand it, what issues, and/or beliefs, have really spoken to you—then and now?

I think the same things stick through. I was always interested in anything that was Indian ... probably because of my love for the Book of Mormon. I remember that my father one time brought a young Indian family (the Indian father was speaking at another church at the time—not ours—and ... in this service we went to, he wore his Indian headdress and everything)—so my father invited him to come and have supper with us some night. His wife wasn't feeling well, so she didn't come, but he brought the little children ... [we told] him about our belief in the Book of Mormon, and Dad gave him a copy. We never heard from him after that, but at least an inroad was made.

I have collected books about Indians, and there are some that our church has put out. I bought the children's ones that Biloine Whiting Young wrote and her friend illustrated, and I have a real urgency to somehow tell that story. And I'm sure that I make openings every chance I can to people who don't understand.

And you have a real hope for the church, for the people in it and for those who are yet to come into it?

Right. There isn't anything that would take its place.

Nowhere else to go?

Not in my life there isn't. I wouldn't consider anything else. Right. I think this is why there have been times when I've had to make decisions that weren't particularly happy for somebody else, but for me they were the thing that I needed to do. And in most cases, I think I've had support to be firm in the decisions I've made.

Well, Dorothy, I think this has been a very rewarding experience, and I'm sure a very tiring one. I very much thank you for it, and I'm sure generations from now will read this and marvel at the things that happened during your lifetime.

Well, one thing I've found that when there is need, God always answers that need, and if it isn't Him, He's put it in the mind of someone else. So, I've been served by other people, and I hope to some extent I can—what do you say—?

Pass it on.

Pass it on.

Dorothy Harriet Elkins Wixom

BORN
August 2, 1912, Highland, California
DIED
April 27, 1991, Sacramento, California

Interviewed by Sheila C. Weidling

My father met my mother in Highland, California. Highland was a small town of about two hundred people. It was an orange-growing, packing, shipping town. The town was nestled in the midst of several thousand acres of orange groves. The town was divided into East Main Street and West Main Street. On the east side were the four orange packinghouses, the railroad station, the blacksmith shop, one hotel, the livery stable, my grandmother's boarding and rooming house, and various and sundry mismatched houses, including the strange house of Chung the Chinese man and his brother, who did everyone's laundry and grew green vegetables for sale.

Chung the Chinese was a very friendly, lonely, strange man. He was a good friend of my grandmother and others who lived at the boarding house my grandmother ran. The boarding house had a large screened-in front porch with a seating bench and several old rockers for the comfort of the boarders, as well as the roomers. It was always breakfast, dinner, and supper—lunch went on picnics.

After supper, almost everyone congregated [on the porch] to sit and talk. Very interesting talk to me as a child. These men were all transient to this area and most were former sailors, soldiers, tramps, pioneers, etc. And the stories they could tell about hangings from yardarms on old sailing ships, scalpings and torture by Indians, shooting and getting shot by Mexicans, and old General Santa Anna and President Teddy Roosevelt! (Most of the time they forgot I was there listening.)

This talk session was joined in on many occasions by Chung the Chinaman—he looking strange in his oriental clothing, including the little cap covering his head with his hair done in a queue down his back. Chung took great delight in tormenting me. He liked me, no doubt about that, but he would take a little knife out, which he always carried in his sleeve, and start to chase me. He said he wanted to cut my hair off. I always had long hair, and my mother took great care of it, and it hung in long black curls.

Well, we two had many a merry chase around the boarding house porch and adjoining rooms—me in front, and he right behind. I really knew he was teasing me, but it worried me, too. Chung outlasted my grandmother by several years, so it was many years later I read in the paper that he had died and had saved enough money that his body could be taken by ship back to China, so that he could be properly buried according to his own instructions. Funny thing about the brother of Chung—he lived and worked along with Chung in the same house all those years, but we never saw him.

On the west side of Main Street were the bank, the church, the post office, the library, the telephone office, the doctor's house and office, several owners of orchards and packinghouses, schoolteachers, and the clubhouse where we regularly put on home-talent dramas and, later, black-and-white movies with lots of reels to change.

When he first met my mother, my father was a "horse skinner" in that he was driving a big wagon loaded with lumber pulled by a six-horse team. He drove down the old Daley Road with many switch-backs (a sharp turn in the road). My father was a young man, but he sure "chawed tobacky," and when he was driving around one of those switchbacks, he could spit on his leaders. They say he was an expert. The loads on the wagon were being taken from the old Swartout Mill at the top of the San Bernardino Mountains down into the San Bernardino Valley. This old mill land finally, years later, became the famous Lake Arrowhead. The old Daley Road was so dusty that one driver died from suffocation. Some loads overturned, some horses died. All in all, it was a rough line of work. My father survived.

My mother, meanwhile, worked in the telephone office in Highland. In the good old days, you picked up the receiver, and someone said, "Number, please." If no one answered when the operator rang the number, she would tell you the person you wanted probably was at the drugstore or grocery, or whatever. Only about two hundred people lived in Highland, and everyone knew everyone, and everyone knew everything about everyone—good or bad.

When my father wasn't working, he hung out at the telephone office. My mother was beautiful. My father asked her and asked her to marry him, but she considered him a little too rough for her. But she finally said, "Yes," thinking he was so handsome, and what a wonderful man he would be when she got through reforming him and got him to join her Reorganized Church of Jesus Christ of Latter Day Saints. She thought he would be just perfect then—not realizing that he and all his family belonged to the Methodist Episcopal Church. They were, in fact, charter members—not that he ever went to church, anyhow. Well, in 1909, they did get married, but she didn't ever reform him.

I was born August 2, 1912, at 6:20 a.m., in Highland, California. I was delivered in a small, two-room house (kitchen and bedroom—no bathroom) by a rather inept doctor, assisted by my father's sister and a fifteen-year-old niece of my mother. Due to complications, I was an only child. Both my mother and my father were thirty-one years old at the time. My mother's name was Dora E. Dustin Elkins. She was born in California. My father's name was Charles Henry Elkins, better known as Harry. He was born in Kansas City, Kansas, in 1881.

My father had no profession. He only went through the third grade. In fact, he was expelled from school and told never to return. You see, he knew all about guns and shells, etc., so not unduly liking the teacher—who didn't like him—one night, he put some live shotgun shells in the heating stove in the schoolroom. When the teacher put a match to the stove the next morning, it was terrible! My father didn't care. He got what he wanted—freedom! All the rest of his life, we just existed on the odd jobs he could find, and when we couldn't pay rent, back we went to Grandma's little two-room house.

When I was born in 1912, I was thirty years younger than my grandmother's next-youngest grandchild. I was sure a latecomer in the family, so that made me lonelier than ever. I was growing into a regular adult and hadn't even made it to kindergarten, yet. My grandfather, Sam the Cherokee, saved me. He thought I was the greatest thing that ever happened. When he went, I went. He let me ride in front of him horseback riding. We took walks. He told me stories, taught me to walk, carried me in his arms or on his shoulders. He even let me ring the dinner bell to summon the boarders to eat. He loved me, and I adored him. When he died, when I was four years old, I was devastated. I kept asking for him, and everyone said that he was gone. I couldn't believe he would go without taking me. No one would tell me he was dead—they thought I was too young to understand. Nothing could have been worse than my feeling of being abandoned. I've never forgotten him and often see someone on the street who reminds me of him.

We moved a lot in those days. We went to Saugus, California, and worked in the oil fields. We went to Fullerton, where my father drove a trash truck for the city. We went to Whittier, where he took care of some horses for an orange ranch. We went to Delano, and worked in the grapes. We went to Modesto, and worked drying apricots. We went to the mountains and cooked for road gangs making new roads. We went to San Pedro, and worked in a fish cannery. We returned to Highland, and my father worked in a garage as a mechanic, then drove a passenger bus between San Bernardino and Highland. After this, his most permanent job was as a motorman on a streetcar trolley. In between all these jobs, my mother and father both worked in the orange packinghouse, but this was only seasonal work, due to the time the oranges were ripe, like November to March. Well, we really got around. When I had to start school, we tried to settle down.

I started school in the same school my father went to until he left in a hurry in the third grade. At the time I started school, we lived in the best area a child could ever find to live in—if he or she had the choice. We lived about halfway between the railroad depot and the empty land where the circus put up its tents every year. In those days, when the circus arrived on the train, they formed a parade from the depot to the circus location. The calliope was first in line, playing all the way, followed by horses, elephants, clowns, and all the cages filled with their animals. And all I had to do was sit on my front step and listen, watch, and adore.

This same ground also housed gypsies when they came to town—not at the same time as the circus, however. They sent chills up and down my back. They were so strange and dressed so differently than anyone I'd ever seen before—gay, long dresses; long, flowing hair; long, gold, dangling earrings; flashy black eyes that didn't miss a thing. Well, everyone was afraid. We locked our houses—both windows and doors—kept our horses, chickens, pigs, cats, and dogs—everything of value, out of their sight. They came to our doors wanting odd jobs, to tell our fortunes, and to beg or steal. They came in a caravan of odd little wagons pulled by horses (good horses, too—probably stolen) and they lived in these little house wagons. Undoubtedly, they were the very first trailer houses of which we see so many today.

Just around the corner from where we lived then, was old Chinatown. I wasn't permitted to go near the place at all. It wasn't until later that I found out the men who lived there sold opium and delivered it on the spot, and these little houses had beds in them where the Chinamen could go and have long, sweet dreams—for a price, of course.

I made good grades in school. My mother and father, and all the rest of the adults surrounding me insisted that was what was expected of me. After school, I stayed with my grandmother in the boarding house and did odd jobs for her—setting tables, running errands, etc. My grandmother never nagged me about good grades. She could neither read nor write, and had never gone one day to school. She spoke an odd sort of English called "the Queen's English." Her family came into the Appalachian Mountains about 1760 from England, and to her dying day she spoke the language. If you didn't know her well, you couldn't understand her. She told me lots of stories about Missouri during the Civil War and how cruel the Union soldiers were to the

Southern people. She, being Southern to her dying day, really hated Abraham Lincoln with a passion.

I must say that all the moving around was hard on me as young as I was—always with adults, never any children—me an only child. My family didn't really know what to do with me—that included my parents as well as the various other relatives. I was always around, restless, and with nothing to do. They must have finally got their heads together, for soon there was a deluge of projects for me to accomplish. My aunt's husband was an ex-lumberjack, and, before that, he had been a cardshark. Well, he did his duty and taught me many finger and hand exercises to make me deft enough to be able to cheat at playing cards. He taught me how to play poker, but my mother put a stop to that.

My aunts, in turn, had me sit on a low stool while they taught me the intricacies of delicate hand sewing. I learned to hand hem so you couldn't even see the stitches. I had to sew many a hem before I got good enough to suit them. I'm glad now, though, because I use my knowledge in craft work. They taught me the ancient art of making lace by using one or more thread-filled shuttles and by making millions of tiny knots that turned out pretty credible lace called tatting. I still do that today, and it is a cause of much curiosity.

My father taught me to clean his guns. My mother taught me how to cook a few simple things. For her, that meant if she had to work late at night, I could have the table set and some fried hamburger, boiled potatoes, and a vegetable ready. My father loved chocolate cake, so she taught me that recipe, too. Before he died, my Cherokee grandfather taught me about the birds we saw, and the trees, and to be kind to animals, especially horses. He also kept me in kittens.

In later years, my cardshark uncle, maybe regretting his former teachings, began buying me books. They were not junky books, either, but good authors, beautiful binds and pictures. I still have several: *The Little Lame Prince*, *Little Women*, etc. Due to this change, I began going to the small library we had in Highland and before I left Highland, I had read almost everything they had.

The one constant in my life at that time was, as I have mentioned, my father's father. He was a Cherokee whose people were from North Carolina. My grandfather was born in Kentucky during the flight of many Cherokees to get away from the troubles brewing, such as the Trail of Tears. His family settled in Napoleon, Missouri. His name was Samuel Loren Elkins. In due time, Sam met my grandmother, Elvira Ragan Watson, and they were married by the Reverend Laws in Pink Hill, Missouri.

Elvira's family did not approve of this marriage, and caused my grandfather to renounce his Indian heritage and pretend to be a white man. Sam never told his children about his parents. By the time they left Missouri for California, the older children were ten and eleven years old, and they knew nothing about Sam's heritage, and had never met their Cherokee grandparents or any of the other family members.

At this time, the Watsons and Elkins lived in Liberty, Missouri. Elvira's father, James Watson, made a living by being an overseer of slaves on some plantation in what was called "Little Dixie." He worked with slaves, probably not treating them too kindly, and was a close neighbor of Jesse James and family, so probably incurred some enemies. In 1860, somebody—we never knew who—shot my great-grandfather in the back and fled. This left my great-grandmother, Rebecah Ragan Watson, a widow with ten children, some of them old enough to try to replace their father in providing for the family. Rebecah smoked a corncob pipe!

In 1881, Elvira and Sam with their children: William; Lucy; Hattie; Dollie; and (my father) Harry, aged six months; Elvira's mother, Rebecah; Elvira's sister, Ellen Henderson and her husband, all left for California by train on a land promotion deal which made the train fare one dollar each. Cheap, but not comfortable. Waiting for them in Messina, California, were three of Elvira's brothers, who had gone ahead to look at land to buy. They were gone three years and finally sent word that now was the time to come. They had bought a portion of a Spanish Royal Land Grant on a foothill of the San Bernardino Mountains at the foot of Mount Gorgonio. They all settled there and planted orange orchards—all except my grandfather, who went several miles away by some running water and built his own house, Cherokee style, and went into the cement business—sidewalks, walls, cesspools—whatever came his way.

My grandfather and my father did lots of hunting: rabbits, quail, pigeons, etc. They also rode all over the area on horseback exploring.

Where my grandfather lived was called Messina, and it was a very small town, with a church, of course. Then along came the railroad. It didn't come near Messina, so they moved Messina two or three miles up to where the railroad was and changed the [town's] name to Highland. They even put the church on rollers, and, with enough horses pulling and tugging, got the church moved to Highland, too. My grandfather and others built a frame two-story house in the town. It became a boarding and rooming house. From then on, my grandmother became the main wage earner, with grandfather the helper. She was a good cook.

Eventually, the orange trees grew and produced, and four packinghouses were built, which provided the mainstay jobs for the area. My whole family was involved. My uncles provided oranges from their groves, my grandfather and others picked them. Horse-drawn wagons brought the oranges to the packinghouse, where two of my aunts sorted out culls. Then, the oranges went on down to bins graded as to size, where my mother and others packed them in boxes. Next, they went down to the uncle who worked as the pressman, who stamped a lid down with a wire bale and put the boxes into a waiting freight car to be shipped to Chicago, New York, or even overseas.

I didn't mean to leave out my father and my championship box-making uncle Otto, for they made boxes to pack the oranges in. They ordered up the "shook," which was the ends, middle, and sides of wood to make those lovely packing boxes so many of us later got for free from the grocery stores and made shelves, cupboards, bedside tables, and much more from them. No more—now the oranges are just dumped into cardboard boxes and sent off. No pride any more.

Back to my father and uncle—the boxes were either made outdoors under a tree, if the weather was good, or down in the "hole," as they called it. You went down through a trapdoor from the packinghouse room, down a ladder into a rude room with dirt walls and floor, and there made boxes day after day, and some nights too, if you couldn't keep up with the packers.

When the boxes were made (and this is where I came in), a logo-like label had to be pasted on the front end of the box—usually a pretty girl holding an orange or a picture of an orange grove, etc., along with the name of the packinghouse that sent these oranges out to be sold. Hour after hour, I was handed a big can of paste, a good-sized paint brush, and was half-begged, half-ordered to paste on labels because "we won't be able to come home tonight if we don't fill our quota of new boxes." They never paid me either—just another effort to keep me busy, maybe.

We had a real catastrophe when all four of the packinghouses caught fire and burned to the ground. No one ever knew how it happened, but at one a.m., it sure caused a commotion. All we could do was watch. Our hose and reel fire equipment was not adequate for the situation. We rebuilt the houses, but it took a long time to get back into production.

When I was ten years old, I started taking violin lessons from the doctor's daughter. I was in the school orchestra and that brought a lot of joy and experiences. I still play the violin and find great satisfaction in it. In junior high school, several of the boys formed a dance band, and they invited me to join them. I felt I had reached a high point in my life, being the only girl in their band.

About this time, my father, who was a great hunter (fisherman, no—hunter, yes) decided, since I was all he had—just me, a girl, and no son—he would teach me to shoot a gun. In fact, he taught me to shoot all his guns, including his handgun. I was an apt pupil, and my father was very proud of me. One gun I failed at, though—it was a German Craig from World War I, and it kicked like a mule. The first time I tried shooting it, it knocked me flat on my back. My father didn't like it too well, either, and sold it.

My father was always a part-time or volunteer deputy sheriff. He was called out in emergencies, and had a permanent badge, and permission to carry a gun any place, anytime, anywhere. He even wore it to church on Sundays. One day, when I was about ten years old, he and I were in the car together going someplace and we went by the old County Hospital and saw that their barn was on fire. (The hospital had their own vegetable garden and their own milk cows in those days.) He ordered me to remain in the car with his "I really mean it" look in his eyes that I never ignored. He was one of the first men to arrive, and as the cattle happened to be where the fire got to them, they were bellowing in pain, with their hides in flames. My father, without hesitation, pulled out his trusty gun and began killing the suffering cattle, including the prize bull. My father was a little worried about having to kill the prize bull, but nothing ever happened over it. Well, I sure had a long wait, but I never left that car.

My father also taught me to ride horseback. I got a very thorough training there, and became a good rider. He and I took an overnight ride once—no trail, just over the mountain. We took in a big party at the old Box S Ranch and came home the next night. The horse I'm most proud of riding was a beautiful Morgan stallion down in Claremore, Oklahoma. That was quality and twenty years after Box S!

My father taught me how to hike and not get lost, and all about snakes, particularly rattlesnakes, which were in great abundance. He bought me a strong pair of leather boots that laced from the toes to the knees and turned me loose. We were in mountain country then, and I walked and walked—I never got lost and never got bit by a rattlesnake.

In Highland, where I grew up, we were on the famous, or infamous, San Andreas earthquake fault. I've certainly been in my share of earthquakes. I was in so many that I really never had much fear of them. The middle-westerners all say it must be terrible to live in a country like that, and I just love to remind them that the worst earthquake ever known was in 1812, in Missouri. It even made the Mississippi River run backward for a while.

I think I have one distinction—my diet has been a little offbeat. I've eaten mule meat, horse meat, buffalo, antelope, ground squirrels, jack rabbit, elk, quail, pheasant, crows, and rattlesnakes.

All the time I was growing up in Highland, my mother talked to me constantly about the [RLDS] church. She read to me from *Autumn Leaves* and the Book of Mormon. At my father's request, I did try to attend the Elkins's and Watsons's choice of church, the southern Methodist one, but my mother prevailed. My father's people came from Missouri and, having lived there for so long, took a dim view of the Reorganized Church of Jesus Christ of Latter Day Saints and of all who belonged. My father's people probably helped run our people out of Missouri, and were glad to see them gone, and regretted no end that a member of their family had the audacity to marry one! However, while my husband, Herald, was pastor in San Bernardino after World War II, my father, long after most of his family was dead, did join the RLDS church at age seventy-two.

After my family moved to San Bernardino from Highland, and I got to attend church regularly, I was baptized at the age of fifteen by Evangelist John Martin. I met Herald G. Wixom and in due time, in 1934, we were married. From the age of fifteen on, I was very active in the church: Temple Builders, Religio, Oriole Girls, as a choir member, church secretary, and church auditor. Temple Builders were before Oriole Girls, so this was quite some time ago. All the girls in the church at 5th and G [streets] belonged to this group of Temple Builders (all aged around sixteen).

Sister Rose Bussey was our leader, and she had a beach house down at the ocean. My uncle had a cabin in the mountains that we could go to, so we girls wanted to take advantage of that. As there weren't too many girls, we could all fit into Sister Bussey's big car. Well, the boys knew we were going, but all unsuspectingly, as we were on the way to the beach in Sister Bussey's big car, who did we see following close behind us but four boys in their cut-down stripped car. We were suspicious, so we stopped the car, and they stopped their car, and we had a little talk. They introduced themselves as the "Barn Builders," and they respectfully requested that they might join in on this little Temple Builder trip. Being the lovely lady she was, Sister Bussey said, "Okay, come on." From then on, where we went it was a Temple Builders-Barn Builders trip.

I was the oldest girl in the Temple Builders, so she worked me in as an assistant, and not too long after that Oriole Girls began, she resigned and I took over Oriole Girls. I was working for the state of California then and had bought an old secondhand Willys Knight that was still big enough to pick up the girls. I had a wonderful association with those girls. Helen Draper Lentz was one of my most faithful Orioles and Beatrice Teagarden, too. I served very faithfully for several years until Herald and I decided to get married. I still see the girls, though, after all these years—mostly at world conferences.

As secretary, I sat in on two elders' courts to take notes at the request of Apostle Gleasor about two very scandalous affairs which today would hardly cause a stir. Brother Gleasor took me aside, partly because I was so young and he wasn't sure he could trust me, and gave me a strict talking-to, almost a threat, that I should never, never reveal what I heard and took notes on. Well, I've never to this day ever revealed anything I heard there to anyone, so help me. He scared me to no end!

My mother and father never had any traveling ministers stay in their home. My father was not too receptive; he thought my mother was just trying to convert him. Herald and I were blessed by having many stay in our home. Elbert Smith was a very good friend of Herald's father, George Wixom, who was himself a missionary in the church, so Elbert Smith was in our home several times. We've also had as guests: Albert Carmichael, John W. Rushton, Frederick A. Smith, President William W. Smith and Rosemund, Brother Njeim, Brother Hield, Apostle Paul Hansen, F. Henry Edwards, Apostle Gleazer, Brother Weaver, John Darling, Brother McDowell, Patriarch William Patterson, Duane Couey, Maurice Draper, Brother Neff, Reed Holmes, James Kemp, Charles and Lita Vreeland, Apostle Serig, Apostle Spencer, Paul Edwards, Aleah Koury, Paul Lucero, Lee Pfohl, Larry Pool, Frank Weddle, William (Bill) Williams, Brother and Sister Jacka from Australia, Eddie Butterworth, J. C. Stuart, Gene Theys, Glen Johnson, Frank Hunter, Lew Zonker, John G. Wight, and Wayne Simmons.

I never was within walking distance of a church. I've taken a streetcar, ridden a bicycle, rode with my sons in their car when they were trying to get a driver's license (nerve-racking, to say the least)! But we made it to church. I've ridden in a surrey with a fringe on top pulled by a horse. When I was seven years old, Herald's folks picked me up and took me to church in the surrey.

I think my most stressful time was when I was diagnosed as having cancer. That diagnosis, and the following distress and chemotherapy made me feel, "why me?" But, through the prayers of church members all over, which I'm sure contributed to my cure, my last CAT scan was clean. I am most thankful and grateful.

I was only six years old at the end of World War I. I remember the whistles blowing and standing on the side of the street watching our soldiers come home. Little more than ten years later, the Great Depression hit us. That meant no work for my family, food lines, etc. When I graduated from high school I was very fortunate. Several years before, I was working towards a college experience—I had my language, Latin, and geometry, etc. But one day, my mother made me face up to the fact that I didn't have and couldn't get the money to go to college. Our family situation was so moneyless that what she thought I should do was shift to a business course and that way help out with the finances at home.

That was hard for me to do, but I did, and [I] became the number one business student, so that even before I graduated fully from high school, the school had me a job that I could move right into. So, I did both at once—finished high school and went to work for the division of highways, state of California. I worked faithfully for four years, supporting my parents and trying to save a little. At the end of the four years, I had three hundred dollars.

Herald, also, had been going to junior college and [was] working nights for Hunter Ferguson at his gas station, so he had some money saved. So, it being 1934, we decided it was time to get married. Herald had this idea ... about some church-owned property down in the Ozarks that church people were buying land adjacent to and planning to run sheep on the church land. It was permissible to the church, but as it turned out, improbable. Well, we got all caught up in this getting married, etc., and we sent for some log cabin plans. The people where I had been working wanted to know what I wanted for a wedding present, and I said, "A BIG pressure cooker," so I could can what we grew back in the Ozarks. I got my hope chest all up to date, etc.

Well, Herald and his brother-in-law went to see this Ozarks [property] and took off while I waited back at home. They arrived, found the place, talked to the man who had all this property to sell for one hundred dollars, and talked to the Curtis family who had already done what we intended to do. But, somewhere along the line, Herald caught a slight drift that the church wanted to sell the land we were going to depend on for sheep grazing. He is a very practical man, so he stalled on the deal and said he wanted to go to Independence and talk to Bishop DeLapp. He went. He saw Bishop DeLapp, and DeLapp said that was not going to be too permanent down there, the land might be sold, etc. He gave Herald such a lecture on the value of education that Herald returned home to tell me the news and offer an alternative: "Let's go to college."

So, we decided to get with it, and try to better ourselves, and go to college. The wedding date was getting near, but we shifted gears and counted our money. We didn't have any money, but with the optimism of youth, we left California and took off for Kansas State College, Manhattan, Kansas, the same night we got married. It had been thought about before, so it wasn't a complete surprise. Herald majored in veterinary medicine, and I began studying home economics and journalism.

One semester was all it took to see that only one of us could make it, so I quit school and went to work for thirteen and one-third cents an hour. I had worked four years and thought it would be no trouble to get a job, but for a year I had my application in all over town and school to no avail. So, I babysat, cleaned houses, pulled weeds from lawns, and much more.

One day, I took Herald some lunch, and we were in the anatomy room, sitting on the edge of the enormous formaldehyde tank where a dead horse was being embalmed to be used for anatomy work. The dean of veterinary medicine happened into the anatomy room where we were eating, looked at me, and said, "Mrs. Wixom, if it is possible for you to sit where you are sitting and eat lunch, I think I have just the job you want."

So, that's how I finally got a steady job with the college and worked the rest of our years for the dean. I became the first woman ever to work in the clinic where the smells were terrible and the blood profuse, and a lot of actions crude, but we made it.

I was quite a hit with the clinic boys, because I typed and mimeographed all the exams—but I never snitched, not even to Herald. One professor refused to let me do his exams for a while, but Herald made such good grades he finally gave in and let me do his typing, too. The second year we were at Manhattan, we lived in a very small, homemade trailer that you couldn't stand up in, in order to save paying rent. Nobody in Manhattan had ever seen a house trailer before, so people came driving out by where we lived on Sundays, instead of going to the zoo. The newspaper wrote us up, too, which added to the interest.

We had a little added income also. Herald took such good notes in his surgery class that had no textbook but was all lecture, that the other students started asking Herald for copies of his notes. We went one step further. With the permission of the surgery professor, we made up books of that class's notes and drawings, and sold it to classes ahead of and behind us. When we left, the surgery professor took the same book of notes we put out and had it printed nicely. Of course, he had to change his style of lecture, but they put out that book for ten or more years after we left.

Well, we made it. We ate lots of oatmeal and beans, and since we had a gun, we practically lived on wild rabbits. By the way, we didn't owe anybody a thing when we left. We had good friends at Kansas State College in Gene and Ruby Connell, and Frank and Fern Parsons, and our dear friend Sister King and her daughter Nellie Bryces King. We met at Ruby and Gene's house for church on Sunday nights. Ruby would fix us waffles. After so much oatmeal and beans, waffles were a delight!

After Herald graduated and we returned to California, it was no time until World War II caught up with us. As Herald was in the reserves, off we went. He was in the Air Corps, as it was called then. We first went to Wendover Field in Utah, out on the salt flats, and, after two years, we went to Rapid City to the air base. It was much nicer for us there. Many church people lived there, and had had no church since the one in Spearfish closed, maybe twenty years before. We got them all together and had church in our house. We had some baptisms in a creek running through a cattle yard, had some marriages, a few funerals, some blessings, and, all-in-all, hated to leave Rapid City. We came back to California and Herald went to work for the Department of Agriculture for which he worked for thirty-four years, ending up in Sacramento as state veterinarian and assistant director of agriculture. Herald has been retired for fourteen years, and if you think you won't be busy in retirement, think again!

Zion and the outreach necessary to bring it about is my strong point. I think ordination of women is okay. I think we, the members of the church, have been coasting along, spending too much time on ourselves, and forgetting the mission that has been before us for over one hundred fifty years—to get out and follow Christ into the world. I'm all for it!

I've been teaching English to a Hmong group for over two years and have been accepted by them. They call me "Mother." I try in many ways to help them adjust to our culture, which is very hard for them to accept. I talked to Don Ewing at length at world conference, and he is sending me some material that will help me tell the Hmongs about Christ, which has been difficult until they knew some English.

My husband has been in the priesthood since before we got married. We knew what it would be like. Herald grew up with his father in the missionary field. In his church work, I could go with him and assist. I was always the recorder, or church secretary, so I had a few talents that could assist him. Working for the department of agriculture took him away a lot. Since we had three children, two sons and a daughter, I found plenty to do at home to keep the home fires burning. I didn't resent it. He had a job to do, and I had a job to do.

I feel that I owe a lot to my mother's sister, Ida Dustin Dexter. She had eight children. When we moved from Highland to San Bernardino, we lived close to them. They became my brothers and sisters, and I lived at their house more than at my own. That's when I began going to church. That was the first time I lived close enough to really belong to and be a part of our church. My mother's family had been members of the RLDS church for years. Some I know of were members in 1836.

I love to travel. I've sailed on six of the seven seas and been seasick only once. I've traveled on most of the continents: North and South America (including Canada and Alaska), Europe, Africa, Asia, Mexico, the Yucatan, Quintana Roo, Japan, Korea, China, Malaysia, Thailand, Singapore, Hong Kong, Central America; also to Jamaica, Aruba, Cozumel, Curacao, Panama, Venezuela, Colombia, and Vancouver Island. I'm glad to have already been to Israel and Egypt, Jordan, Greece, etc. I'd hate to go now. It was dangerous enough when we went, now it's much worse.

Herald and I have three children: son, Lynn Wixom; son, Willard Wixom; and daughter, Susan Wixom Stodden. We have eight grandchildren: boys, Grenden, Chris, Chad, Colby, and Todd; girls, Robin, Wilynda, and Kelli; plus, one great-granddaughter, Cheyenne Rose.

Herald and I have been attending church a long time—every time the church door was open, we've been there. We are still going strong. In fact, we went to Graceland last fall to attend the maturing conference. We were thrilled with the facts and figures, and talks and associations we had there. We were at world conference again this year (1986). We thought we wouldn't go if they had enough delegates, otherwise. We were sadly short of enough delegates this year, so off we went again!

I have done a lot of genealogy work and have all my family background worked out, except for my Cherokee grandfather. His parents lived in Napoleon, Missouri, but I know nothing more, nor ever met them. As Will Rogers once said, "I never worried about coming on the Mayflower. My folks were standing on the shore to greet them."

The first Dustin came to America with the Trelawny expedition in 1630. His name was Thomas, and he had a son named Thomas. The second Thomas married Hannah Webster in 1657. In 1676, Thomas is listed as a private in Lieutenant Swett's Haverhill Company in King Philip's War. In 1697, Hannah presented Thomas with their twelfth child. About a week later, when Thomas was working in the field, and Hannah was with the new baby, Indians came. Thomas came in to get Hannah and the baby, but she sent him on to go to the fort and take the other eleven children. She said the Indians wouldn't bother her. Thomas gathered the other eleven children together and escaped to the fort. The Indians came into the house, turned it upside down looking for things they could use, roused Hannah in an undressed situation from her bed, and told her to come with them. They burned the house down. Right away the baby started to cry, and one of the Indians took it from Hannah and killed it. They started walking to get from Haverhill, Massachusetts, to Canada, where they planned to sell Hannah as a slave.

To make the story short, when they reached New Hampshire, they camped on an island in the middle of the Merrimac River, now known as Dustin's Island. That night, Hannah, with the help of a young boy taken captive some years before, killed twelve of the Indians, escaping in a canoe. They bashed holes in the rest of the canoes and took off for Haverhill, after scalping the twelve Indians, because Hannah knew she could get money for the scalps.

They made it to Haverhill without mishap, and rejoined the eleven children and Thomas. They made their new house a garrison after that, which entitled them to have several soldiers to guard them, as they were outside the fort in order to grow food. Hannah had one more child. She was awarded twelve pounds, eleven shillings for the scalps, and Reverend Cotton Mather wrote about her experience in his *Magnalia Christi Americana*. She was the first woman in America to have a statue made in her honor.

Lineage of Dustins in America

Thomas (1) came to America in 1630, and had a son named Thomas Dustin (2), who married Hannah and had a son Timothy (3), who had a son James (4), who served in the Revolutionary War along with his (James's) son Ebenezer (5). No harm came to either of them, and Ebenezer had a son Bechias (6), who was at Kirtland, 1836–38. On page 27, volume two of *Church History*, it tells of a Kirtland elders' quorum [meeting] held February 24, 1836, concerning the ordination of official members of the Church of [Jesus] Christ of Latter-Day Saints and also to ordain the following men to the office of elder. Seven of the men were received, and they are listed. Nineteen were rejected. Among those nineteen was my great-grandfather Bechias.

But six months later, he did receive his elder's license—August 6, 1836. Bechias was at the dedication of Kirtland Temple on Sunday, March 27, 1836. He was also a shareholder in the Kirtland Safety Society in 1837. A later note in the records shows he was a high priest in Nauvoo in 1846. Bechias was washed and anointed in the Nauvoo Temple January 5, 1846, and endowed in the temple on the same date. The record also shows he did not get rebaptized in the temple at Salt Lake; someone in 1967 got baptized for him. He seemed to stay at Nauvoo and left for Salt Lake with Brigham Young, taking his family with him.

Bechias had a son Joseph Dustin (7), who was at Nauvoo. His job was as a fence viewer. I never heard any more about Bechias, but Joseph and his son Hiram (8) came to California over the Mormon Trail in 1852. They subsequently had to be rebaptized in San Ber-

nardino in the RLDS church. Hiram was my grandfather and my
mother, Dora, was his daughter.

Lineage of Leffingwells in America

Thomas Leffingwell came to America in 1637. He was a Lieutenant in the British Army. He was gifted with unusual physical strength
and was on friendly terms with the Mohegan (NOT Mohican—even
Cooper erred!) Indians. He was endowed with courage and held important positions of honor and trust. In 1637, he became acquainted
with Uncas. He was threatened by his superiors for not wearing his
British uniform and leather stockings, but Thomas was strong-mind-
ed and went on his way. Finally, his superiors found his friendship
with the Indians was a benefit to the army and created a new position
for him.

To make a long story short, James Fenimore Cooper was intrigued
by Thomas and wrote his Hawkeye, Leatherstocking, etc., books using
Thomas Leffingwell as a prototype. Uncas gave Thomas a big share
of land in Connecticut and also allowed him to marry either a sister
or a daughter. Our history is not clear on that. Lieutenant Thomas
Leffingwell lived a long life, dying in 1714 at age seventy-seven. This
lineage continued down until, in Texas, my grandmother was born to
Ira Leffingwell, and at eight years of age, she came to California and
became the mother of my mother, Dora Dustin Elkins.

Ira Leffingwell and his wife, Sarah Jane Scott Leffingwell, came
to California in 1865, via the old Spanish Trail from Williams, Texas,
in a covered wagon drawn by oxen. Their daughter was Melissa Jane
Leffingwell (Dustin).

This is all the lineage I have on my great-grandmother Sarah who
was Grandfather Dustin's mother. She married Joseph Dustin. Sarah Jane Littlefield was born January 12, 1830, in Palmyra, New York.
Sarah Janes's mother's name I don't know, except that her maiden
name was Shaw. Her brother's name was Lyman Shaw, and she had a
cousin named Henry Shaw.

When Sarah Jane Littlefield was five years old, her mother took
the oldest son and ran away from home. Neither were ever heard
from again. She left because of polygamy. In New York state at that

time, many communes developed that believed in polygamy, which had nothing to do with Nauvoo. They seemed to be entirely separate from any experiences we have encountered since.

When Sarah Jane grew older (thirteen years old) she was dissatisfied with the situation at home and hated the woman or women who replaced her defiant mother. Joseph Dustin (fourteen years old) came along about this time, and they eloped on horseback. They were later married in Quincy, Illinois.

Lyman Shaw took Sarah Jane's two younger brothers and raised them. They offered to take her, also, but she refused. Lyman Shaw went to Nauvoo and later to Utah where I suppose he stayed. (I'm working on that through the Mormon church.)

Sarah Jane and Joseph soon had a son (my grandfather Hiram) born to them when she was fourteen and Joseph was fifteen.

Many years went by. In later years, Sarah divorced Joseph and took back the name Leffingwell. Joseph shortly married a much younger woman who had one son; they had nine more children of their own.

Our family was very stubborn and refused to recognize these nine new children. In fact, if they happened to walk down the road on a Sunday afternoon, we all went and hid in the barn, so we wouldn't be home if they called. In later years, I tracked them all down, because, after all, they were related to me. Maybe I wasn't as stubborn as some of my pioneer-spirited relatives that couldn't face facts.

Something I meant to say about my grandfather Hiram Dustin, son of the above Sarah. He was a very rough man, drove horse teams, drove a horse car (early street car), had a dairy and milked cows, cleaned barns, and had a long beard, and chewed tobacco. At church on communion Sundays they passed a single cup (all partook from the same cup). No one would partake after my grandfather. He always had to be last. I guess no one wanted even to sit by him, either. Those were the days.

Enid Irene Stubbart DeBarthe

BORN
October 5, 1912, Missouri
DIED
July 9, 2005, Lamoni, Iowa

Interviewed by Sandra J. Ogier on March 11, 1986

Just start in and tell me about some of your growing up years, and who your parents were, and all that good stuff.

Well, my parents were Audrey Morford and John Perry Stubbart. They met here in Lamoni. My [maternal] grandmother [Etta Lyon Morford] was a widow with five children. She took her family and went to the Ozarks, because she couldn't support them here, and had a chance to go down there and farm. She raised five children, plowed corn barefoot in order to feed them. My father came down there to help out. He and my mother were married, and I was born October 5, 1912. My mother was seventeen. Daddy was five years older.

Were you the oldest?

I was the oldest child. I was born a perfectly normal child, but I did have long, sharp fingernails. [I] weighed seven pounds. I started scratching my face, and Mother begged them to cut my fingernails. She had had a lengthy, twenty-four-hour delivery and was too weak to do it herself. She begged the midwife and my grandmother to cut them. But the midwife, who was also the pastor's wife, insisted that if they cut my fingernails before I was two weeks old, I'd be a thief. So, I scratched the corner of my eye. Infection set in and went to the lachrymal glands, and collapsed my left nostril. By the time I was six weeks old, I was so frail they had to carry me on a pillow. They couldn't even handle me. They finally got a doctor. Down there in the Ozarks at that time, you didn't get doctors very easily, nor anyone else, climbing those mountains.... He said, "She won't live—too much infection. You'd better hope she doesn't live, because, with all the fever she's had, she'll probably be retarded. She will be blind in the left eye and probably in the right eye."

My folks wouldn't take that verdict. They finally got an elder to come. He administered to me, and while his hands were on my head, he said, "She will live, because she has a work to do." Immediately, the fever broke. Grandmother took the pillow I was on and laid it across her lap, took a toothpick, and lifted from my left eye, a membrane like the lining of a chicken gizzard, all wrinkled, rubbery, and tough. I did not have any eye problems—didn't wear glasses until I was forty-five years old.

My parents moved to Wyoming when I was three. By then, my left nostril had collapsed. I had no other problems. Then, the adenoids grew until I could not breathe with my mouth shut. I had to have my mouth open to breathe. Because of that, people thought I was retarded. I remember when adults would come—strangers would say, "Well, what happened to her?" Mother would explain.

When children were around, they made fun of me, told me, "Go on home to your mother, Stubnose." I became so shy, I didn't want to be with anyone outside my family. If strangers would come, I would crawl into a corner and hide.

When I was about eight or nine years old, I was sitting on the kitchen floor one day, feeling sorry for myself, not wanting to live. I was vomiting much of the time. My parents didn't know what was the matter. I remember, while I was praying, a man came in and sat down in my grandfather's black rocking chair. My father's father was a missionary, and he was gone at the time. This man beckoned to me, and though I was afraid, his kind brown eyes made me feel like I could trust him. He had dark hair, brown eyes, was dressed in the type of clothes which the farmers and ranchers wore—which I was used to seeing.

I finally got up and went over to him. He put his arm around my waist and drew me to his knee, and said, "Honey, don't you know God loves you? Don't you know he wants you to be happy? Remember, you have a work to do." After he talked to me a little bit, he put, in the palm of my hand, some packets of seeds. He said, "Now, these are seeds of kindness and love and good deeds. You plant these in your life, and you'll grow up to be a happy woman and have many friends."

After he talked some more, he stood up and disappeared. I turned around to my mother who was in the back of the kitchen with her back to us, kneading the bread on the old zinc-top work table. I said, "Mama, who was that man?"

She turned around and asked, "Honey, what man?"

I said, "That man who was just here."

She said, "Honey, there hasn't been anyone here."

"Yes, there was. See?"

I held out my hand. There was nothing there, but I could still feel the packets.

She said, "Honey, you just had a daydream," and went back to her bread baking. I cannot remember how Grandfather found out, but I have a faint recollection of his patting me on the head and saying, "Bless you, child. You've been visited by one of the Three Nephites."

I cannot remember a time when I did not read. I started to school when I was four years old. When I was in the fifth grade, I got a teacher who took one look at me, decided I was an idiot, and put me in a seat by myself at the end of the schoolroom to entertain myself. I read all the books I could get my hands on and listened to the other classes recite. It turned out to be a good thing, because she reported me to the state department to be institutionalized.

One day that spring, a woman came to the door, asked for me, and took me out to her car. It was a Model T. I think it was the first car I'd ever seen. I think she was one of the first adults outside the family who treated me as though I were a normal human being. She would say a word and then say, "Now, you say as many words as you can, as fast as you can think of them." We played games and had a wonderful time.

In a short while, a report came back telling [my parents], that with my intelligence, if they couldn't get medical care for me, the state would take over. My parents didn't want me to be a ward of the state, so they sent me to my maternal grandmother in Independence, and she took me to the Children's Mercy Hospital in Kansas City. They thought that because I had no bridge, to speak of, in my nose, I was a victim of syphilis. So, for three years, I was given shots to cure a condition I did not have. My brother's wife did part of her nursing in Children's Mercy Hospital. She [later] looked up the records and found there had never been any positive tests indicating any kind of a disease condition.

I had five surgeries. Only one of them, the first one which removed the adenoids, was a success. The doctor took cartilage from my ribs, slit the end of my nose, and ran [the pieces of cartilage] up [my nose] to try to make a new bridge. It didn't work. Finally, my mother complained, after I had four operations without any success. The head of the hospital fired the man, because he had not been qualified. She [the head of the hospital] was a plastic surgeon, and she tried the fifth time. I'd had so much anesthetic, and had already been a victim of rheumatic fever and had a damaged heart. The heart specialist said I was not able to endure another operation. But Doctor Richardson decided that I didn't want to go on through life the way I was. She risked it.

I remember sitting in the bathroom, weeping and praying. I just didn't see how I could face any more, because the last operation I had, I had heard them call for the last can of ether. The doctor was worried I wouldn't be able to stand any more. I remember while I was praying, a hand took hold of my hand, and a calmness came over me. And I went through surgery with no problem. I awoke to my grandmother's smiling face, and told her what I had experienced. She wept, and said, "Honey, I prayed Jesus would hold your hand." I still wanted a straight nose, but there was nothing that could be done. By the time I was sixteen, I was no longer eligible for the [Children's] Hospital.

I graduated in 1932, most definitely not retarded, because I was next to the top out of 217 students. I tried to get a school [to teach in]. I was qualified, but there were no schools [in Missouri] on account of the Depression. So, my folks asked me to come back to Wyoming. They were needing teachers, and they thought I could get a school. When I got there, I found that one had to be a graduate of a high school in Wyoming in order to teach in Wyoming.

So, I took my last year of high school over again. My brother and I moved to the town thirty-two miles from home, a little railroad town. [We]lived in the basement of the parsonage and got along on five dollars a month. We lived on flour and water pancakes baked on a coal oil stove. The only heat we had was what would come through the asbestos-covered furnace. I collapsed with malnutrition toward the end of the year, six weeks before school was out. Because my grades were high, they told me I could go on home. I went home and helped my father's mother with the lambing.

I taught that winter and then went to summer school, the next summer, in Spearfish, [South Dakota]. Clifford Cole and his girl-friend, Lucille Hartsorn, came to South Dakota and got me, and we stopped at the Devil's Tower reunion on our way home. A young man by the name of Joe DeBarthe came running down. He knew Clifford, jumped on the running board, stuck his head in the car, and began to talk to me. I thought, "What kind of a monkey is this?"

That evening, he brought lemonade to me while we ate supper, and tried to talk to me about going to Graceland. I knew it was financially impossible for me to go. He had gone for two years, graduated, and taught one year. He was hired to teach our home school, and I was teaching twenty-five miles away at the Hartsorn school. We began seeing each other, because he was staying at my parents' home. When I came home for the weekend, we would visit.

During that Devil's Tower reunion, I had chummed somewhat with a church boy that I knew and thought a lot of. He was a good boy, but I had promised the Lord that I would not go with anyone who smoked or drank, danced, or did not belong to the church. This young man belonged to the church, but he smoked and drank, and went to the dances. There really wasn't anything else for the young people to do out there in Wyoming. There were not enough young people to have church activities just for young people.

When I was sitting with him on Sunday morning, after we had had a moonlit walk around the tower, to my left, Joe DeBarthe was sitting taking notes on the sermon. I was impressed by this young man. In the early morning prayer service, Joe had said in his testimony, "I want to grow as straight and tall as these pine trees." And he had committed his life to the service of Christ.

While I was thinking about that, a light suddenly appeared over my right shoulder. In front of me, appeared a book with blank pages. It was held out open, with no hands. I saw no pen. But, the writing began to appear on the left, and said, indicating the young man I was thinking about and watching, "This is the only man you have met who is worthy to be the father of your children." On the next page, it said he would soon be called to the Aaronic priesthood and, in due time, to the Melchizedek priesthood. That was August. That November, he was called to be a deacon. A year from that, November [1935], he was called to the office of elder.

The next May we were married. We came back to Lamoni on our honeymoon. Joe worked at Graceland College, painting to earn the money for our tuition for school that fall. He had told me I could have either an engagement ring or a year of college, and I chose a year of college. It was wonderful to be in college. I thoroughly enjoyed the classes. I rated very high on the entrance exam—they told me I was in the top of the top ten.

But at Christmastime, when it was discovered that I was expecting, the dean of students told me I'd have to drop out. I didn't want to, and Roy Cheville tried to go to bat for me, but he couldn't get anywhere. They were adamant. He said, "Well, you come to my classes and audit them. You can't get credit, but you can come to my classes. I know how much you want to learn." So I did. But in January, the dean of students caught me on campus, took me by the shoulder, and said, "Young lady, you know you don't belong on this campus. You're a bad influence. Now, you get off and stay off."

I went home and cried, wrote to my mother in Wyoming and told her about it. She wrote back, and said, "Honey, don't you remember that Apostle Paul says, 'If it offends your brother to eat meat, don't eat it?'" So, I had to conclude that's the way it is, and make the best of it.

Who was the dean of students at that time?

Dear old Brother Johannes Burgman. I can understand now, having learned that under his culture in the old country, no woman was allowed to be seen out in public when she was pregnant. No woman had rights of any kind—they were subject to their husbands. They did what they were told. They didn't own property—they couldn't even keep their own wages, which was true here in the United States until the early 1900s.

You were married?

In 1936—May 20, 1936. Our David was born April 20, 1937. He was a month early. That fall, Joe had tried to work all summer up in northern Iowa trying to earn the money to go on to Iowa State to get his bachelor's degree. Roy and Nell Cheville invited me to stay in their house to take care of it, and take care of the garden, and do the canning, while she was visiting her parents in California, and Roy was in Chicago working on his doctor's degree. She was a Weldon. They were very, very good to me.

That fall we went back to Wyoming. Joe decided to try to improve on his homestead, because his aunt promised him a thousand dollars if he would improve it, so they could add it to their holdings out there. Joe taught school for seven years. Then, World War II made it hard to get a school, because school boards were afraid to hire a young man who might be drafted in the middle of the year. So, Joe went to work on the ranch. We lived there a year with our two little boys. Jerry had been born seventeen months after David in Gillette, Wyoming. We saved every penny we could save to [go] back to Lamoni. Joe had fallen in love with the Lamoni area. We thought about it, because we didn't even have that—just sagebrush and cactus and hardpan flats.

We [finally] came back [to Lamoni], tried to comply with the stewardship law, filed our papers, got recommendations from the district president and the missionary in charge, and so on. Bishop Ted Beck did all he could to help us. I remember him telling us that if we had waited two more years, we probably couldn't have accomplished it. We started out with a thousand dollars, paid six hundred dollars down, and had the rest of the money for our first horses, first cows, walking plows, and so on. We managed to pay for that farm, and then came to this farm, owned by the church. We rented it for five years, and then bought it from the church. We have it paid for now [in 1986]. We have done without, but we got it done. Joe has been active in trying to visit the sick and shut-ins, especially in the nursing home and hospitals.

When our oldest children were about eight-years-old, I developed a physical condition which required surgery or another pregnancy. Of course, we chose a pregnancy, even though the doctors said that my heart would not stand it. Since the choice had to be made ... it wasn't hard to decide. We had Paul, and then twenty-two or twenty-three months later, we had little Joy, our first daughter. Joy was the joy of our lives, the apple of her daddy's eye. She got poisoned, when she lacked one week of being eighteen-months old, and she died in our arms. It was one of the most traumatic experiences of our lives.

Our neighbors were very good to us. They organized themselves to see that there was someone here with us every night for two weeks. We were having a stressful time financially, and our church friends furnished the money to help with the funeral expenses, and to help us get clothes for our baby. I remember, after the funeral, lying on the bed crying, and thinking, "She was so tiny, she'll never know she had parents or little brothers." I thought of Alma [chapter] 19, where Alma tells his son that immediately upon death, every soul goes back to God, who gave it life. I got up and got my Book of Mormon, opened it, and started reading. A little below that [verse], I read, "And they shall forget not their own." I could never find that again.

I remember the stake president, Robert Farnum, said that he started for Independence the day that Joy died. He heard about it somehow, and the Lord told him to go back. "Enid and Joe need you." He was a lifesaver to us, because we didn't have transportation at the time. Our car was not working right. He helped us through the whole thing. Someone told him about my reading, "And they forget not their own." He said, "But it's there. I know it is. I've read it." But neither he nor I could ever find it again. He, too, had known grief. And no one could have been better to us.

Shortly after that, I bottled up my grief until I had a heart attack. In fact, I had several of them, with three hospitalizations in one
summer—one of them for six weeks. I was given up to die on one
occasion, and I was sinking down, down. I thought I really was dying,
and I was too tired to care any longer. But, through the experience
underneath, were the everlasting arms that sent me back, and I knew
I could not be afraid. That's not God's way for us to be afraid. We are
to trust him. I had to learn that, maybe, what I thought was my will
... was not to be his will for my will to be done, but I had to learn that
his will was best. I've come to believe that whatever man can do, or
whatever Satan can do, God can bring good out of it, eventually.

About two years after the heart attack, I wasn't able to do farm
work. I was being drugged with the medicines they were giving me
and couldn't think straight. I finally got disgusted and threw the
medicine away—threw it down the toilet hole. I decided to go back
to college. My boys were going to Lamoni to school by then, and I
could ride back and forth with them. It wasn't easy, because I was out
of practice, and I was still numb with grief.

I remember sitting in the library one day, praying, because I wanted to study. I wanted to learn. I'd always been a student. It seemed as
though a hand peeled a membrane back off of my brain, and it was
released, all of a sudden, so that I could think again. I had to do it a
little at a time, and finally got my bachelor's degree in English education in 1964. It was a long while after 1936 and 1942. I got my associate's degree in 1955, and my bachelor's in 1964.

I began teaching English in Mount Ayr High School and was
high school librarian. I taught there for eight years. At the end of
that eighth year, I was told I was not being given a contract, although
they could find nothing wrong with my work. It was cheaper to get
someone out of college than it was to keep someone with a master's
degree. There were four hundred teachers that year in Iowa, who were
released on that basis. There was no law at that time giving tenure or
seniority, but one was passed shortly after that.

The Iowa State Education Association wanted me to sue the
school board. They said that though there was nothing wrong with
my work, I had the seniority and had all of the qualifications. After
all, I had a husband to take care of me. On the way home, weep-

ing, this verse came to me that I didn't remember having memorized, "Vengeance is mine, saith the Lord. I will repay." I was so exhausted, that I decided that was my answer and I did not sue. I dropped the matter. I came home, and my husband and I became very involved in church work. He already was [involved], but I joined him in it.

Tell me about the missionaries—who they were, and something about the ones who stayed in your home.

I remember missionaries had a lot of impact in my life (my grand-father [James Mitchel Stubbart] being one), and when missionaries came to Wyoming, they usually stayed in my parents' home. There were the two Curtisses, Brother J. F. (I took down patriarchal bless-ings for him when I was older), and Brother Ella Wildermuth [who] helped get Joe and me together. Brother P. T. Anderson—I remember him at a reunion, when I was young, saying, "One who takes offense is as guilty as one who gives it." And I adopted that for my life com-mandment. I would not give offense, and I would not take offense, no matter what people said about my appearance or anything else. I was just not going to take offense.

But, I have learned that there are times when a life command-ment needs to be broken. Some life commandments are good—thou shalt not drink, thou shalt not smoke. But, there are times when one can't help giving offense or can't help taking offense. I remember how near tears I was for so much of the time after section 156 [which dealt with the priesthood ordination of women] was incorporated into the Doctrine and Covenants. I had no trouble accepting it mentally, but emotionally, I found myself near tears a lot, because so many of my friends were offended. My life commandment was, "Thou shalt not be offended or give offense," and I didn't like to see anybody offended.

Do you have memories of special prayer services or reunions, other than the one where you met Joe?

I remember the time when Clifford Cole was called to the priest-hood—my brother had his first call. Joe had gone back to Lamoni for the summer. I rather anticipated he would be called because of the experience I'd had, but his name was not mentioned. I went out among the trees and the rocks to pray, very early in the morning, and had such an outpouring of the Spirit—it seemed to me, the trees were bowing in adoration, and the rocks seemed to be vibrating, crying out in praise. I was given to know that God still loved me—that I was still accepted of him, and Joe's and my relation was good, and he would take care of things, and he would give me my answer.

I went back to the reunion and the minister in charge spoke to me in prophecy, reminding me that I had been told, several times, I was to study and write for the church, and my husband's name was given as one being called to the priesthood. Joe didn't know how church policies worked. He wondered why he wasn't called when his friends were being called here in Lamoni. Then, he got my letter saying his call had been announced out there and discovered, because he was a member out there, that's where it had to be processed and so forth.

When you were growing up, and later on, you were close to the church.

We were close to the church when I was a child. My parents helped establish the first church in the little schoolhouse about a mile away. They kept the congregation going as long as they lived out there. There were several families that came out of the Oshotso, Wyoming, group—Clifford Cole and his family; Mable and Fayette Cole and his parents; my parents and I. Some of the families went on west. While we were married and living in Wyoming, we were isolated. The year that we lived on the ranch, we were twenty miles from the nearest post office, [and] the store; sixty miles from the nearest doctor; and one hundred twenty miles from our church. There wasn't even a Catholic Church within commuting distance. I'd have gone to any church, regardless of what denomination it was. Our little boys were going to have to go to school three miles from home—ride a horse—and there were only two other children in the school.

Joe and I did a lot of praying about it. We decided that was not the condition we were going to raise our family in, and we made our move to Iowa to get them where they could go to school.

What are your favorite hymns and scriptures?

One of my favorite hymns has always been, "Dear Lord and Father of Mankind." As I would walk to school when I was teaching,

I would memorize hymns or memorize scriptures. I remember my mother would require we memorize one scripture a week, and I've always been grateful, because so many times, one of those scriptures I don't remember having memorized, pops back into my mind when I need it.

Do you remember a time when you were struggling with a faith crisis?

I remember one when my brother had lost two children by drowning—just two months before the twins were born. A very dear friend, a Seventh-day Adventist lady was trying to convince me that Joseph Smith just copied Protestant beliefs, and there was no consciousness after death—that our ideas of consciousness after death were pagan, that they sleep in the grave. I was called out of that funeral. I had been studying and studying, and I thought it would be easy to disprove this woman's philosophy, but when I sat down with our scriptures, it was not easy to do, because the Old Testament is full of that kind of philosophy—the dead know nothing at all, they're as grass to be burned.

I said to her, "But Jesus said to the thief on the cross, 'This day thou shalt be with me in paradise.'"

She said, "That's easy. The punctuation was put in later. Jesus said, 'This day, thou shalt be with me in paradise.' He didn't say when."

I said, "Well, if you're going to do that, and if it's just the punctuation, it would read, 'Jesus said, "This day, Jesus said thou shalt be with me in paradise."'" But, I didn't get anywhere.

I don't know why I became so disturbed over it. I really wanted to know if Joseph Smith really knew what he was talking about. I had to go to this funeral, and here were the two little caskets in the corner. I had to sit on the front row with my brother and his wife. The funeral home was shaped like an L and we were facing one wing, with the audience and the congregation in front of us. One of my high school friends sang, "Sleep, Little Lamb, Sleep," and I thought, "I just can't take it." I was going to go into hysterics, and I just don't do that.

So, I said to myself, "Lord, you've got to help me." Immediately, that congregation disappeared. It was as though a curtain had been pulled open, and I saw my grandfather who died at eighty-three, a very ill man—he died with cancer. Grandpa was sitting in the most beautiful meadow. The grass was so green and perfect, and the trees were beautiful. There was soft, white light, the birds sang, flowers bloomed. The little children were with him. The little boy was five, and the little girl was three when they broke through the ice and drowned. The little girl was sitting on his lap, leaning on his shoulder, looking up at him so adoring and so happy. The little boy was facing him, with his knee on Grandpa's elbow, his chin cupped in his hand, looking up at Grandpa and asking questions.

Grandpa answered the questions and looked back at me. There was just as much eye contact as any of us can have. His hair was still white, but his skin was firm—there were no wrinkles. He was in the prime of health. After the eye contact, the curtain closed, and the people were back in their places, and I knew that Joseph Smith knew what he was talking about. Those children had only gone through a door to another condition. They were not asleep in the grave.

When I got home, I started typing my grandfather's autobiography and discovered he had worked in the Lincoln, Nebraska, area among Seventh-day Adventists. His autobiography told about the trouble he, too, had, and the vision he had which helped him come to the same conclusion I had reached. That was one of those many highlights.

Probably the next most critical session has been the conference of 1984 [which allowed for the ordination of women to the priesthood]. I remember, when the document was read on Tuesday morning, not knowing how to respond, because I thought intellectually, "Someday it will happen." But, since a survey had been taken, and only a third were in favor, and a third were opposed, and a third hadn't made up their minds, "Well, that takes care of that for now. There won't be anything done with that for a while."

Then the document was read, and I saw some of my friends so thrilled and elated, and I saw others so shocked and hurt, and almost distraught. I went home that night. My mother works at the *Independence Examiner*. She's ninety-years-old, and she still works full time. She wept until she could hardly talk. She cried herself to sleep that night. She was convinced it was wrong, wrong, wrong. She still feels that way. I got up and walked the floor, got out the *Interpreter's Bible*, read and studied and prayed. We all did for all the hours until the day of the voting—Thursday afternoon, April 6.

That afternoon, Garland Tickameyer stood, and said that one afternoon Fred M. Smith had said, "The day will come in the Reorganized Church of Jesus Christ of Latter Day Saints when women will be ordained." Garland T. was a close associate of Fred M. Smith, and I did not doubt his testimony.

At the beginning of that business meeting, President Smith gave awards to a man and a woman, who had done much work in families where there has been violence, trying to counteract the abuse of children. The woman who received her award, stepped forward, with her emotions creeping up her face, and mentioned the sweet spirit she felt there. As I recall, she was not a church member.

As we sat there, there was such a sweet spirit that swept through the whole congregation, it seemed to me. I felt it vibrating around me. When the meeting was over, I went out and got in the car with my sister-in-law, who was a delegate for the first time. She is a very accomplished musician. She plays for soloists and orchestral groups, and all kinds of musical productions in Columbus, Ohio.

She said, "Enid, did you hear that rush of the Spirit?"

And I said, "No, but I felt it."

My sister-in-law, up in the balcony, and her aunt turned to each other and asked simultaneously, "Do you feel that?"

Since that time, I've had letters from several parts of the country and one from Australia. That dear friend said she had been sitting there with her hands clenched so tense because of what she was afraid people would say—the hurts that were being expressed. Her district president reached over and touched her hands, and said, "Vera, relax. Feel the Spirit in this place." She said, "I relaxed and I felt such a breeze. I looked both ways, at both doors, to see if somebody had opened them, and they were both closed."

Many people have borne testimony to me of that "rush of the Spirit" that they experienced, and the vote was approximately seventy percent in favor.

I still didn't have a conclusive answer of my own. Finally, the Lord told me, "You go search for the pieces of the puzzle, and, when you get them put together, you'll have your answer." So, I was started on a year of research, and the things I discovered about the condition of women and the laws that were operative at the time of Christ, the more meaning there is in the Scriptures.

I learned that in Greece, no woman was allowed to attend any religious activity, no deliberating session. They were killed if they tried. One woman, Pharaniece of Rhodes, tried to go to the Olympics, because her son was competing. Her husband died while training. She dressed as a male contestant, and when her son won, she ran to hug him. Her garment slipped and betrayed her sex. Ordinarily, such women were taken to a cliff and thrust to their death, but popular opinion would not allow her death because her father had been a champion, her brothers were champions, and her son was a champion. So, they passed a new law that all contestants had to compete in the nude. That's why you see many statues and pictures on Greek vases of nude contestants.

When Rome conquered and took over Greece, she adopted the Greek rules, and her women were kept in gynoecia with eunuchs for guards. No man, other than an authorized father, husband, or brother, could go to those quarters. If they did, they were killed. So, when Jesus began his ministry in Nazareth and started giving his liberating gospel message, quoting from Isaiah, the people said that his words were gracious. But, when he rebuked them for the way they were treating their widows, they rose up and tried to kill him.

In the early days, there had been temple funds provided to care for widows and orphans. Even in the time of the Maccabees, that was still the case. But under seven hundred fifty years of subjugation to the Assyrians, Persians, Greek-Syrians, Egyptians, Babylonians, and then the Romans, the Hebrews had adopted the same cultural patterns about women. At the time of Jesus, no woman could approach a rabbi, or a leader, unless attended by her husband or father or an older son or brother.

When Jesus allowed the woman with the alabaster box of ointment to anoint his head while he ate meat, three taboos were broken. No woman could approach a rabbi unattended or where there were men gathered, especially if the men were eating. Not even a wife could be in the room when a group of men were eating. I've found

Enid DeBarthe visiting ruins in Meso-America. Used with permission of Paul DeBarthe.

there was even another taboo broken, because it was in the house of a leper.

We read that many followed Jesus from Galilee to Jerusalem. They ministered to him for his burial. They stood afar off. All of this was against Roman law, because women weren't out in public like that. Only slaves who had to go to the market for supplies, or a freed woman, who had been a slave who purchased her freedom, were allowed in public. I found documentation that men killed their wives for appearing in public without being accompanied or having their faces covered with a veil. A woman could be killed for adultery, without any proof—just the accusation of a husband or father or guardian. Throughout a woman's lifetime, she had no freedom. She was somebody's property—a father, or a father's brother.

You remember the Levitical law, where the widow had to marry the husband's brother? I learned when I was in Israel in 1983, that it is still a problem, because women whose husbands' brothers are in Poland, or wherever, still have to get permission if they follow the old traditional teachings from those people. Some of them write back and say they won't have any part of that monkey business—they're through with that, they don't want to believe that any more. Religion is not well accepted in Israel any more. There are a few of the fundamentalists, who still stone people for adultery and so on, or just for religious prejudice.

Those were some of the problems that Jesus was facing. But when Jesus was resurrected, the angels commissioned women to bear testimony—to go and tell the disciples. Jesus gave them that commission. And no woman under Greek, Roman, or Hebrew law was allowed to testify. [Jesus] made his first, his outstanding commission for women.

Then, I finally discovered in the *New Catholic Encyclopedia*, about a week ago, that women were ordained in the apostolic church and in the early Christian church, because they needed women to go to the Roman gentiles and convert women who were not able to receive the ministry of any man. The *Catholic Encyclopedia* said they did baptize. They did exorcise evil spirits. They did teach and preach. And women were needed up into the third century when baptism by immersion was superseded by sprinkling. They called it infusion, and the women were not needed so much.

The last record I have found for a woman having been ordained, is in the eleventh century—an abyss, one who is in charge of a convent. I found in the *Catholic Encyclopedia* that abbots and abysses were comparable to bishops, and that they could officiate in these ecclesiastical rights. Several writers claim that some of the words that are translated in the New Testament, such as the word for apostle is also translated "witness" and "minister."

Some believe that when the King James version was translated—because these were men of the Middle Ages who could not believe that a woman could be a minister—they changed the word "diaconia," the feminine ending of Greek for deaconess, in relation to Phoebe, to "diaconius" without realizing they didn't agree any longer. In no other manuscripts, did Paul address the apostles and name Junia, but in the King James version where Junia was changed to the male form "Junius," because of the belief that that just could not have been.

So now, my reasoning and my faith are united together. I cannot see how we can deny it, but my heart aches for those who still reject it, and I've had to take my share of the condemnations, even to a nine-page letter, chastising me recently.

After the hours and hours of research, in about a year (April 1985), I was standing by my kitchen stove, and, suddenly, the Spirit rested on me, and I knew God does not want discrimination. I hadn't thought so much of the discriminatory times in my life until after that, and then they began to come up out of my subconscious. I remember when I first came to Lamoni, just after we were married. In the summer of 1936, we were having a severe drought, and Arthur Oakman was preaching a series.

Early in the morning, the women who could, and what few men could, would meet for early morning prayer service, praying for rain and praying for the series. One morning, not a man showed up—there were about twelve of us women. I was the youngest, just out of isolation and didn't know church policy. I asked, "Why can't we go ahead and have prayer any way? There are about twelve of us here."

About six of the dear, little old ladies said, "Oh, no, women can't have prayer meetings unless there's a Melchizedek priesthood member present."

I asked, "Why?"

"Well, they don't think women can be trusted, because they get emotional, and they might get carried away, so we just don't do it—it's not allowed."

I couldn't understand it, but I just decided that was just another one of those things—just the way it is. Then, I found while doing this research, that that was policy for a long time, and the women had a real struggle, all through our reorganization, trying to have their own women's association without having a man present.

Finally, Audentia Smith Anderson, when they were trying to organize the Daughters of Zion and were to have their organizational meeting in Independence, wrote to her father, Joseph Smith III, complaining about it. He wrote back and said, "You go ahead and have your meeting, and don't let a man say a peep. If you do go down, go down with your flags flying, everybody at the helm; but don't let an elder or the son of an elder, have a thing to do with it from A to Izzard. That's my opinion." And still they kept on having their problems.

When I began going to conferences, I was aware that they were still having some stress, because no elder wanted to miss his quorum meeting in order to sit with a group of women while they had their meetings, but they couldn't let the women go ahead on their own, because it just wasn't tradition.

That's what a lot of it is—tradition.

Well, I'm hopeful. I'm really hopeful. I lived in Independence back in 1925. Fred M. Smith was a close friend of my grandmother's. Their birthdays were the same day. They would quite often have birthday supper together at my grandmother's. So, I knew him as a tender, loving man—brusque at times—[because] he knew what he wanted. He did like to have some decorum and reverence at church. In Larry Hunt's book about it, he says that Fred M. liked having worshipful music, and he wanted people to meditate through it. He wanted to enjoy it himself. He wished we would learn to be more worshipful between our services. I really loved that man. I remember, I was there for the 1925 conference. I remember T. W. Williams saying, "Fred M. always was that way. If he couldn't play first base, he wouldn't play at all."

I remember that I thought so much of one of the elders in our congregation. He was supposed to be such a spiritual man, frequently speaking in prophecy. Just a few weeks after that conference, he came up out of a basement room on the square—drunk. I was just shattered. I just didn't see how anyone could do such a thing. But, he was shattered, too, because he just could not accept the idea of having what he called *supreme directional control.*

Apostles had told me about those out in the field, that each one was a law unto himself. He set the policies, he told the people what they could do, and what they couldn't do. Fred M. was trying to get them to realize that there had to be some sense of a final authority. I think the battle's still going on. I think that's the problem in the church even today. Those people who don't want to have a final authority. They want to be an authority unto themselves.

Jessie Marie Carter Gamet

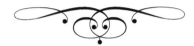

BORN
April 8, 1914, Little Rock, Arkansas
DIED
July 16, 1994, Independence, Missouri

This is Irene Waite. I'm sitting in the kitchen of Marie Gamet, at 605 Orchard Road, in Berryville, Arkansas. This interview will be by me ... asking the questions. Marie has been a member of this church for many years, has been very active here in Berryville and in Independence, Missouri. At this time, I would like to ask ... where you were born, Marie?

I was born in Little Rock, Arkansas. My grandfather was from the eastern United States. My grandmother believed we came out of that "Trail of Tears."... I look just like my mother. She was short and stout, and all Indian. I was always really proud of coming from Arkansas. Sometimes, I get pretty provoked when people want to call it Ar-Kansas. They tried, but they didn't get it done. When someone comes up and starts talking, and the occasion permits, they say something about Arkansas—if they say "We Arkansaers do this and do that," [then]I know they're from Arkansas, because everyone else says "Ar-Kansas," and I just don't like that.

Okay, then. Your early life was spent in Arkansas?
Yes!

Where did you go then after you left Arkansas?
We went to Harrison, Arkansas. There was a call for workers of the railroad there. It was going to fail unless they got some employees. People were afraid to go there, because they had a strike and they hung a Negro from one of the trestles. That upset us, and we didn't know whether to go or not, but Dad decided that he'd try. So we moved to Harrison in 1922 and left in 1929, for there was still trouble on the railroad, and they were talking about closing it.

Dad had always wanted to go to St. Louis or Kansas City, so when all this trouble kept going on, he decided to move out. He left us at home.... He still didn't have his mind made up ... but when he was traveling north, he decided on Kansas City, and that's where he landed. He got a job, and that's where we moved to ... in August of 1929.

In the meantime, one thing led to another. Clarence came along. Clarence is from Mondamnen [Mondamin] in northwest Iowa. That's an Indian name and the closest we ever got to being an Indian. His mother was of the church and joined against her mother's orders. Her mother told her, "Don't ever darken my door again, Minnie, if you're going to go to that church." Well they went anyway, and I think a funeral got them back together. Clarence's mother and father really, really fell for the church—I mean hard. Now, to have a mother tell you never to darken their door — !

[Back] then there was a fever to go to Independence—the Center Place, Zion—and they moved to Cameron, Missouri. Clarence went into the service before they came down. He was stationed in Salt Lake City, Utah, and it was there that he was baptized. That's because the regiment he was with was about to go overseas, so his mother wrote and told him to be baptized before [hand] because there weren't any [RLDS] churches over in France. He had to go down a stream that was really hot.

Do you think he had any doubts at that time about the church?

I'm not sure. I don't think that he would have been baptized then, if it weren't for his mother. He had been attending church … but he hadn't been baptized. Why, I don't know, because his other brothers and sisters were baptized. There were nine of them. At one time there were two high priests and an elder in the family. They're all gone [now] except one. That's David, who's a high priest at Lamoni, Iowa. He's in a retirement center. It's the [Crown] Colony [Retirement Center], there in Lamoni.

Most of them who live there [in the Colony] are church members, but some of them aren't. There David met a sweet lady named Emily, from Hawaii, who had been living in Hawaii for forty-two years. She had come back and was on the board of this Colony. She and David fell in love and got married. They've only been married about two years. They were down here last year, and she told our class all about Hawaii. They're just dying for them to come back down here. They ask me if they are going to come back. I don't know whether they are or not. I hope they do.

Okay. So Clarence was baptized in Salt Lake City, Utah, in a hot river. They had to go a long way to cool down enough to [hold the baptism]. The further they went, the cooler it got. When they came out, it was really hot—you couldn't even put your finger in it. Anyway, they got to New York, and they didn't have to go overseas because the war had ended.

What war are you talking about?

World War I. Clarence was the first-class bugler and bugler of the regiment. He was a good one, too. Almost everyone in their family was musical. I don't think they took lessons, it was just one of their gifts. They would just gather together and play. They were just like an orchestra. That's the way our family is. Clarence would play the trumpet. But somewhere or another, his trumpet got mislaid, and he never got it back—after the service anyway. He did get a flag. I think we gave it to his family.

We got married in 1934, and we came down [to Arkansas] on a vacation.

Where did you get married?

At Kansas City, Missouri. That's where I met Clarence. He came from Cameron. His brother, Carl, was already at Kansas City. Clarence didn't have a calling, because all he'd ever been was a farmer and a soldier—that's all he knew. His brother said, "You get behind that block, and you act like you know all there is to know about meat." Clarence said, "Well, that's hard to do, because I don't know anything about it."

But that's where he learned [butchering]. He went in just like that. One day … the boss's wife came in and threw a cleaver at him. He quit that job and went and looked for another one. They were very excitable people. He said it was fun sometimes, but then other times it wasn't.

We came down to Arkansas. We started up at the corner and started down this way, and didn't know exactly where we were going. In the meantime, my folks had moved from Kansas City to Butler, Missouri, and that was where Clarence's brother Everett was. He was a high priest, an evangelical patriarch. He wanted us to stay there awfully bad, but we just stayed from August until the first of the new year.

In fact, that's when Clarence started working in Independence, Missouri—January 1, 1954. We liked it at Butler and just loved the people and everything, but Clarence didn't feel that that was where we should be. Besides, it was a job where the man running the place wanted both a man and a wife to work. That was the first year when they started putting meat in open cases. And they wanted man and wife teams to work: the man to cut and the woman to wrap the meat. Clarence didn't want me to work, and the man couldn't decide whether he was going to keep the store open or not.

Butler wasn't but about fifty miles from Independence, and we'd go back and forth to visit Clarence's cousin. Charles wanted to know if sometime when we were visiting, Clarence would talk to some people there about working. Clarence said, "Anytime you want me to."

So, it just happened that we went up there, and they got together, and they hired Clarence, and he started right at it. They were good people to work for. They were good Baptists, and we had a lot of talks with them. The wife was the strongest willed. She didn't want to listen. But his man boss would listen. One thing that he was really

crazy about was our tithing law. Of course it was during this stay ....
[garbled].... We moved to Grand View, Arkansas, and the church
was formed there.... Sister Nellie Smalley will tell you all about that.

We went to our first reunion, and it was one of the grandest things
in the world—to live in that kind of a condition, and spirit, and everything. It was wonderful. It was there at our first reunion in 1950, I
think it was. Or in 1952. I believe it was when the great flood was up
in Kansas City, Kansas. That area up there. The reunion was at Racine,
Missouri. At that time, it was the Spring River District, not the new
name of Springfield District.

During that reunion, someone at the reunion discovered a dog
near one of the pools of water where they had dug out coal and left
just big holes. It was filled up with the most gorgeous blue water, just
beautifully clear. They found this dog sitting there, and no one could
coax him out, in any shape or form. They never did. I think they just
took him away bodily, but that was something for the Saints to go
over and see, and compare with the love that he had for his master.
They never did find a body, as no one was missing. It is still a puzzle,
because they never found any dead dog or cats or anything. The only
thing that they could think of, was that maybe he floated off and
into those caverns and [went] way down to another one in another
place, and got caught on something, and didn't get out—whoever or
whatever it was.

I'll never forget that reunion, because Clarence and I were like
two kids who couldn't get enough candy at one time. We just ate and
ate and ate, and loved the love everybody gave us and everything. One
day, I think it was one Monday (it was very early in the reunion), the
man from Butler, Missouri (I think he was in charge of elder LeRoy
Beckam) was in charge of the children's classes. He came up the next
day and asked if he could have the floor a minute. They said "Yes," and
he announced that they needed help in the children's department.
"Would some of you offer to help?" Well, without thinking, up went
my hand. I didn't know what he was asking for, really, and I went and
followed him. There weren't very many of us, I'll tell you. I followed
him and I got—.

About how old were you at that time?

I was … thirty-six years old—never had a thought about getting old. I thought I was going to stay young forever. I knew I'd have to if I kept riding in the rocky car.

So, I went down there, and there were all those little faces looking up at me, a whole tent full of them. I thought, "Oh, my golly! What am I going to do? I don't know a thing about what to do." So, he introduced me and told them where I came from, that I was new at the work, and that he surely was proud of me, because I stepped right up without thinking.

I told him that when we were walking down to the tent from the hill, the one who was in charge in that tent was giving a flannel-graph presentation. I just ate it up with my eyes. Oh, I just wanted to do it so badly.

So, after the class was dismissed until the next day, I talked with her and asked, "Is that hard to do?"

"Oh, it's easy as pie," she said, "You can do it just as easy as pie. In fact, tomorrow you're going to give a lesson."

Boy, listen, let me tell you something. I've had butterflies in my stomach ever since then, but I did it, and they thought I had practiced for hours—but I hadn't. She gave me the figures that I had to have, and told me what background to use, and that was it.

The most wonderful part of it was that … a young girl (I think she was twelve or thirteen) made up the figures and everything, and it was from the Book of Mormon. I had never had too much to do with the Book of Mormon. I'd been in the church just that short time. Of course, I knew it, and when it was supposed to be about Indians, of course, I was more interested than ever.

Anyway, before the reunion was over, I asked if I could borrow those figures and take them home and draw them off. Of course, they didn't belong to the woman. They belonged to someone else. They were going to go within a week or two to another reunion and use those figures. Well, I didn't dream I could ever do anything like that in that length of time, because you have to mail them, too, and get them there before they leave. I took them home, anyway.

The next Sunday, our district president came, and they stayed with us, because we had moved to town [by] then. When the apostle told us to choose between the farm and the ministry, he [Clarence?]

naturally took the ministry. Everybody lived out at the edge of town, away from the town of Berryville.

Anyway, I was drawing when he [the district president] came, and he said, "What are you doing, Marie?"

I said, "Just tell me what I'm not doing!"

He looked at me and said, "I don't see anything wrong with it."

Now I did good on the background, because I drew the background of where I was living, and I did real good on those. I did a little bit of tracing, not much, just a little—a faint outline once in a while.

"Oh, those are beautiful, Marie!" he said, "Have you done this before?"

I said, "No!"

He said, "Well, boy, you are sure good!"

I said, "Well, these figures, I don't know about them."

Before he left, he and Clarence would go out and visit people and everything…. The district president would get Clarence in a corner, and talk to him a lot about this and that, and ask if there were any needs that Clarence wanted. When he came back, the first day I had some figures drawn, and he said, "Who said you couldn't draw?"

I said, "Me! You don't call that drawing! That's just something to take the place of something that ought to be there."

He said, "I don't see anything wrong with that. I think you're going to be all right."

From that day forth, I have not stopped being a church school teacher. I have not had to attend adult classes or anything, and people won't believe this—but, just add up thirty-two years and see how many hours that is. I have spent thousands of hours drawing and cutting. There's a lot of drawing and cutting if you want to give your pupils something that they can see, because I'm a very devoted believer in audio-visual for any age—old or young—for them to understand a lot more than if you speak it. Especially if you use large words. Everybody loses the thought that the person is trying to give, because they're trying to figure out what that word means, and they lose their place. That's right! I spend a lot of time at it. I stay up late to work.

When we moved to Independence in 1954, I got a half-day job working for a member of the church who had a State Farm Insurance office.... I just fell in love with them. They were the sweetest people. They came from where Clarence had—they came from Iowa. Clarence always teased her, "You wild Iowaian, you."

One day, their daughter got married, and they were crazy about children. I'm crazy about children. Clarence was crazy about children. They hadn't been married very long, and she found out that she couldn't have children, because she was going to have to have surgery that would prevent her from having children. It came up sooner than you thought. There was no preparation. There just is no preparation for insurance offices to get a helper, because it has to be someone who knows insurance, really. You can get almost anyone to answer the telephone and everything like that, but they need somebody every once in a while to do a little bit of something, because they don't have to know what the others do.

I called one day, and I said, "Floyd, is there something that I can do that can help you guys down there, so that you can go and see your daughter?" He said, "Marie, God bless you, yes! Would you just come down here and answer the phone, so I can go see my daughter?" I said, "Of course, I will. But you'll have to come after me because Clarence has the car." I wasn't driving then, so he came after me, and I started working for him.

We got along just fine. I worked there just half days. She would work in the morning, and then he and she would go out calling for insurance, and I would stay in the office in the afternoons. That's where he found out that I'm an organizer. At that time, I didn't know what an organizer was, outside of reunions, but I was always one to keep things in their place and keep them straight. I'd write notes here, there, and everywhere.

They decided to go on their first vacation since I began working for them.... Usually they take a long one, but this time they were going to take a short one because of no one being in the office. So he left me with it. Well, I got a notebook and kept track of everything that was done, everyday—except for me filing things. Each day, I kept notes about people who came in, what they said, their dispositions, and everything. When he came back and read it, he said, "Marie, I haven't been out of the office at all. It's all right here."

If anyone talked rough to me, he really told them about it. I was always in the office when he bawled them out. He didn't bawl them out mean. He was a gentle person, a very gentle person. He told them, "Don't ever, ever talk to my secretary like that again. Ever!" And, listen, no one ever talked rough to me after that.

So what was Clarence doing when you were working for the insurance company?

He was a meat cutter up the street three doors. It worked out just fine. Of course, I had to work a lot more hours, but I had to wait until Clarence got off work, because he had to close the office before the grocery store did, you see.

But you, at this time, were still not a member of the church?

Oh, no! I was a member before we left to come down here from Grand View, when we were on the farm—when the apostle told us. And Clarence, deep in his heart, didn't realize that that farm was a place for us, even though he had accepted the priesthood. It just wasn't a place for us to do church work. We stayed there our ten years, and one of the things that helped me was that I wasn't quite sure about the gift of the Holy Spirit. I didn't know. I thought, I've been told that when you're baptized you get the gift of the Holy Spirit with the laying on of the hands. I didn't know just quite what that was.

I soon found out, but not until 1954, when we had our first conference at Independence, Missouri. We were living in Independence then, and when we moved there, we found it difficult to find a place to buy. Housing was pretty high, and houses weren't to be found exactly where we wanted to be. My husband always liked to live close to where he worked, so that he didn't have to drive in bumper-to-bumper traffic. We always tried to get near the store, and we just couldn't find anything.

One day, we went to a real estate office, and they were church members—D. O. Cato. I imagine a lot of people know him. He was in Independence. He had a man working for him named Wakeman. He was certainly a wonderful lecturer on the Book of Mormon, and he took us around. Finally, we found a place, but we decided that we wouldn't take it. He said, "Why? It's just what you want, a nice neigh-borhood and everything."

Clarence said, "Well, it's not near where we want to be."

He asked, "Where do you want to be?" [Clarence] told him that we wanted to be over there by Clarence's cousin, by the Englewood Branch, and go to church with them, because her husband had just joined the church. We wanted to study together. He said, "Well, I don't see anything wrong with that. But, after all, there's a [house] down at South Chrysler that just fits you."

Clarence said, "Oh, you think so?"

He said, "I'm certain it would. Go on down there and try. If any-one doesn't come up to you and talk to you, you go and talk to them."

I didn't have to worry about that, because I do that. I couldn't work in an office if I didn't do that. So that's what we did.

We made friends with the Saints, and we fell in love with each other. I was talking to the district president one time, and he came and stayed at our house during the 1954 conference. He was then district president in Hawaii, and we were talking one morning before breakfast.

I said, "Brother Black, you tell me something."

He said, "Sure, if I can. What?"

I said, "When you and Brother Doubledee laid your hands on me, in that little nondenominational church not far from Grand View, Arkansas, from Berryville, I just felt the strangest sensation."

He said, "Well, what kind?"

I said, "Just as soon as your hands touched my head, I felt a burn-ing. I mean a real burning, and it just kept going on down further and further, till it got to the tip of my toes. I don't know where it went, but I just felt like I wasn't exactly there."

He said, "You then received the gift of the Holy Spirit. There's no doubt about it. You did."

He added, "Marie, the Spirit of God is like a fire burning in you. Keep it up. I'm not worried about you at all."

Of course, Clarence was working hard and had few hours to study. We weren't having a very active priesthood as far as home ministry was concerned. Clarence made up his mind that he wasn't going to be one of those who didn't go out, because he was selected as the pastor of one of the groups up there. I think there were five groups in South Chrysler, and now I think there are a whole lot of them. He found one man who would go with him, and another time he would go with another. One man was Eldon Oliver who was from Canada. The other one was Marion Turrentine. They were both wonderful to go visiting with. Most of his visiting was with Eldon.

Sometimes, it was just Eldon, and Clarence, and the pastor there when they'd start out on their nights of visiting. It was something that they did. They got along real fine. They got into two homes that they didn't think they were going to get into. I finagled that idea. I saw their names were in the sanitarian admittees, so I said to Clarence, "Two of our members who won't let you come to their houses are in the hospital. When you call to make an appointment, they won't let you come, so how about you going up there to visit them now, because they can't run away."

That's right.

"Oh, that's wonderful," he said. So, he called up Eldon and away they went. One of them was a young woman with two little boys. She had polio and was in the iron lung, but she had the sweetest smile. Of course, she wanted a visit, but her husband didn't. So it ended up that Clarence and Eldon could visit [her], but nobody else. They wouldn't accept anybody else. We picked up the two little boys the whole time we were up there and took them to church every Sunday. Do you know that man was a scout leader, a worker in the scouts? He worked the whole time, and still works in the scouts, and he will not join the church.

Now the other couple, whose names were Charles and Mary Smith, were really wonderful. The other couple (with the wife in the iron lung) were Elsie and Roscoe Robinson who lived just three blocks from us. There was a terrace between the two couples, and they could visit there anytime they wanted to. We just loved those two kids. She got out of the iron lung, but from her waist down, she was tiny. Well, mostly from her thighs down didn't come back like her top did. The polio didn't bother the upper part of her body; she could use her hands and everything. Her mind was quick, and she was always full of laughter.

I kept her with help. Sometimes the help would stay a long time. The first one I think I got to stay quite a while, and the rest of them didn't stay so very long, especially the young ones. Someone else would get her, but I couldn't get them to stay. I would try to get older people who were more stable, to give her exercise and everything.

One day, when I went up there, she had the most beautiful thing in her lap—a head dress that her son was making in the scouts. He needed some help from her. She could do it if it was something like that. Oh, it was gorgeous! I had hoped that we'd get to see the other one, but we didn't get to stay long enough. We were just there ten years. She just loved to do things like that.

She said, "Marie, I wish I could be down there and help you." And I said, "Well, you're raising two boys. That's enough for you. You just live like you're supposed to, and just see what will happen to Roscoe." I just hope and pray that Roscoe ... I think he believed in the church. It was just some of the people—he saw their actions and everything. That was what he said anyway—that they weren't living their religion.

We said, "Well, that doesn't make any difference." I said, "If you join the church and live yours, then you might bring others into the church. Who knows?" But he still wouldn't do it. You know, he never asked anybody to help him with his wife. He picked her up to take her to the tub and bathroom. He washed clothes, and he cooked. And he never moaned, not once. Elsie said, "He did not once complain. Wouldn't he have made a wonderful Saint?" Anyway, our ten years were kind 'a short there.

We never had any difficulty getting to the church. Wherever we have lived, we have tried to pick a place so that we were as close to the church as possible, because we believed in that—you should choose your church home first, and then choose your home. That's what we planned on ahead. I've always been a planner. I plan ahead. I don't wait until the last minute, unless it's an emergency, so that's what we always tried to do.

We were grateful for them, the ministry, all the men who came to Berryville when we were here and still here, and for the ministry of our own priesthood, for the counseling that we received from the higher officers of the church. They have truly loved us, and we love them. It's a heavenly love that everybody has for each other.

There was one time I thought was pretty heavenly. I have had quite a few surgeries in my life, eleven as a matter of fact. One of them was just a year ago, a year ago last May—two years ago this May of 1986. My husband had heart trouble and had had it quite a few years. Every time he'd have an attack, he just got worse and worse. So he was always afraid that I would go first and leave him by himself. He thought of it as terrifying. When it came time for this surgery, he was scared to death. The doctor terrified me even some [when he said] that Clarence shouldn't be alone. The doctor tried to find someone, we tried to find someone, everybody tried to find someone to stay with Clarence at night. He'd be all right in the daytime. We just couldn't. Finally, our sweet congregation solved the problem. The men said they would come, and sit with him, and stay at night, and the women said they would come in the daytime and fix his meals.

Both of us asked for administration and we were administered to out in front of the congregation. I had no idea of being fearful of anything. I had faith that everything was going to be all right and everything. But I was worried about Clarence, and I knew there wouldn't be any beds for him to stay up there at the hospital and be in the same room with me. This testimony happened before the offer from the congregation to take care of Clarence. Both of us were administered to.

Right away, people started testifying that they were given the assurance that I was going to be all right. My husband's fear was gone from the moment that the hand was taken off of him, and he got up. He didn't have any fear at all. But the Saints weren't so sure, because Clarence wasn't a young man, and they loved him so much and were so concerned about him, that they just weren't going to take any chance. They were going to come to our house and take care of him anyway. They were glad, because they had some wonderful times together. They really talked, deep thoughts. It was good for Clarence, because Clarence was pastor of this group for eleven years.

[Note: the following date of 1970 doesn't mesh with the paragraph just above which supposedly was in 1984.]

That was just when we were having the celebration in 1970 of the mission becoming a branch, and our twentieth anniversary, and receiving a set of flags—the church flag and the American flag. [They were gifts] from Brother and Sister Hunt, now living in Berryville, but formerly from Iowa, where Clarence was their boyhood friend in the service and living in the same area.

One of our district presidents was from Clarence's area in Iowa, also. Down through the years, I have wondered what the congregation thinks when a lot of people come in [to visit us], and [they are] people we knew from Independence. It seems there have been hundreds of them that we knew in the past, who have come to visit us here. Yet, we didn't move out very much in Independence, because, when you get a job in one of the congregations and are really a consecrated and dedicated person, you don't get away from that congregation except on vacation. Then you have to hurry up, and shut the door and run, because you just don't go away from your job. That's what we did.

Several times, I was chosen to go out and teach. Other congregations would have classes. Especially, during vacation church school, they would have series of classes and would ask me to come take lessons for that. I was given the privilege to be a teacher one time when Sister Parker from the Herald book shop came and gave a slide lesson about the story of the caterpillar. I had given that story in class and mine surely wasn't like hers.

Our church superintendent, Brother Jimmy Pimblot, told them that I was to give a lesson, also, about whatever I wanted to do. I thought, "Oh, she was before me." I thought, "There it goes." I just went over and told them, "No, she gave the story that I was going to give, so I'll just go on."

He said, "No, you're not. You're going to get up there and tell what you are supposed to tell. Do it."

Well, I did. I told the story of the caterpillar, and there was such silence afterward that I felt so silly. Sister Parker got up right then, and she says, "Now that's what I want you to do—what Marie is doing. That's what I'm here to show you—that it can be done. She did it and she wasn't taught. You can do the same thing ... that's what this was for." So, that's the way it was.

Then it was that Clarence said, "You're not going to use any more of the church's material. From now on, you spend so much time on them that you will keep them for yourself, because we're not going to stay here forever."

So, that's what I did. I've got an attic almost full of Sunday school material. I have two large rooms up there that are equivalent to three rooms long. If they spread everything out wall to wall, it wouldn't hold them. I've got Sunday school materials on hanging shelves on one side of part of it. I have an antique chest there that's full, and I have boxes everywhere. Downstairs, everywhere that you go, there's stuff. I'm trying to condense it more and more, because I feel that my time isn't much longer at the work. I surely hope that the Lord sends someone younger who will take over like I did, and go from there. They won't have to worry about the audio-visual part because it will be there. All they'll have to do is study and learn how to use the materials. You've got to use it with love. You don't just slap it on, you caress it.

Is there any testimony over the years that stands out more than any other?

Well, this one (above) about the administration, and the one about Brother Black, and nearly every time I've been administered to—now, like the other night when Terry was administered to—I received. I wanted to be administered to, but I didn't want them to have to do two that night. I knew that I was going to receive one, too, because every time that someone is administered to, I am, too. Even though I'm not ready to ask for administration, I receive administration, too. I thought I was going to have to go to the doctor the other night, and I didn't. I always receive a blessing....

Well, I don't know, when we first started here, we were told that we couldn't stay in the little house or the little church anymore. There was a group trying to undermine all the rest of them. They tried to make it into a Baptist church. I was once a Baptist, too, so that was why they thought we were going to get a hold there, and they would lose out. They persuaded the man who owned the building to ask us to leave. We hadn't done anything, anything at all.

Even the preaching we had wouldn't hurt anybody, so that's the part that really reassured me that it was the work, was that first communion service that we had at Nellie's house. Clarence was spoken to, and [told] that he should study for the ministry, that he had wasted time enough already, and not to be concerned about the things in the past that he wished he hadn't done. Then I was spoken to, and told that I was not a member, but would be. That's really the most outstanding one, but also the one when Clarence's fear was taken away from him.

I really wasn't exaggerating to myself that I had the spirit in me. Some people you know don't really know if they have it or not. It sometimes confuses you. I have never denied that this is the church. I've been kind of disgusted sometimes with the action of some of our people, and I've wondered how many I have turned away by my own actions. I tried hard not to do them anymore.

But, in this world of today, it is rather hard to overcome some of your actions. You see it all around you, as the harder you try, while Satan is right there tempting you more and more, you really have to fight hard to keep him out of your life. When you think of so many who need God's help and Jesus's help, so many who are wasting their time with foolish things that they ask for, knowing that if you ask for that which is necessary that God will give you what you need, and give you peace of mind. We sure need peace of mind nowadays. This forthcoming world conference is really strong on my mind, and I surely hope our people won't be foolish as the ten virgins were.

I'm so happy that I've been permitted to have the ten pictures. There are not very many pictures of the ten virgins. There are always just five. Everybody that comes, wants me to will it to them. Well, I can't will it to all of them, but I wish there was a way that they could be taken off. I'm going to talk to a man here about that. He's in painting and everything.

I would just like to leave you with this thought. Don't give up. The scripture says that you will be tossed to-and-fro by every wind and doctrine. It's up to us to have faith in God that he won't let us fail if we will just not fail him. That's right.

You mentioned prayer service. Are there any prayer services that stand out more than any others over the years?

Was that a prayer service when Brother Ben told about his experience? Was that a prayer service when he told about the girl? Yes, it was a prayer service on a Sunday morning. That was very outstanding. One of our younger families had just moved here, Ben and Terry

McKinney, and their teen-aged children: Benjamin Jr. and Dawn. He recently went northeast to chaplain's school. He wanted to be a chaplain with the National Guard.

He told a story of his ministry to a colored girl who was there. She was pretty near the breaking point, and he brought her out of it. The sergeant who was drilling them reprimanded him very hard for what he was doing. The sergeant told him that he couldn't do it, and had them both get up there and do what they were supposed to do.

Ben said, "This girl isn't able to do anything. I'm going to take care of her."

The person over the sergeant came along and asked, "What's the matter, sergeant?"

He said, "This Private McKinney ...." He gave him permission to stay with the girl, and he got permission to keep on administering to her. The girl got better, and even after he came back home, she called. I think she's called for him, and now even his wife is involved in it. I know Terry has talked to her on the phone. I say that's really wonderful.

There are other's testimonies, but at this time, I just can't bring them out, because there have been so many. I'd like to tell who the charter members are: me, Larry Hunt (he's a son of Lester and Hazel Hunt. Brother Hunt was our pastor for a while). The other charter members are: Nellie Smalley, Shirley Hudson, Virginia Pritchard, Jack Farmer, and Jackie Farmer. Now, those were all baptized in 1950. There's a long list since then, so I won't give you that.

Larry is a handicapped boy, but he's really smart. They attended a nondenominational Bible study. Donnie, one of our members, goes. None of them knows where the lessons are, Larry always tells them. That tickled me, because Larry is at the nursing home in Rogers, Arkansas. He is just grand over there. Everyone likes him and he helps them. The lady who has the recreation, she is the activity chairman, and he won one time for the best decorated door. Last year or the year before, he won something over here when they came over here at Eureka Springs. I didn't know he was coming. He didn't know he was coming, or I'd have been over there. So he's just really good, and he helps her a lot.

She and the lady over here that I work under are friends. I volunteer two afternoons a week at the rest home here. I write letters, and visit them, and read the Bible one day, and the next day, I work in hand crafts. This lady here and the lady over there at Rogers where Larry is, are very close friends. When they have to go away on meetings or anything, they go together. So, when I bring up something different that she doesn't have, Mae gives it to her.

Is there anyone you know in this congregation who celebrated their fiftieth wedding anniversary?

Just two couples, Lester and Hazel Hunt in 1970, and us (Clarence and Marie Gamet) in 1984. Lester and Hazel were originally from Walthill, Nebraska, but they were born in Iowa. He was a pastor up there before he came down here. They were very close to us because of being acquainted up there in Iowa.

Louise Minor Murdock

BORN
September 2, 1916, Heppner, Oregon
DIED
March 26, 2009, Santa Barbara, California

Written by Louise Minor Murdock

Ozark Zionic Journey: In the Beginning

INTRODUCTION TO THE ZIONIC MESSAGE

"Hearken ye my People! Thus saith the Lord!" These phrases have been the clarion call of humankind as the people seek to reinstate the stewardship of Mother Earth. Through the ages, there have been people who answered this call as they understood it. In the Bible, the Book of Mormon, and the Doctrine and Covenants, one word that conveys the meaning of this stewardship is *Zion.*

A study of the Bible reveals thirty-two references to Zion as a city, ten references as a people, ten as a mountain, and ten other references. The Book of Mormon contains fifteen references to Zion as a place, two as a people, four references to the Daughters of Zion, and two to the Mount of Zion. Many references are to "Zion of the Latter Days." One-third of the references in the Doctrine and Covenants are about Zion as a people, a cause, and a city. Therefore, in reading the scriptures, one [can] conclude that Zion has been an important concept in past history, as well as in present times.[1]

Zion has both historical and sectarian definitions. Historically, the dictionary defines Zion as the "Holy Hill of Ancient Jerusalem," the "Jewish People," the "Jewish homeland as a symbol of Judaism," and the "Kingdom of Heaven."[2] Zionism is defined as "A movement begun in 1897 that sought and achieved the founding and development of a Jewish land (Israel) in Palestine."[3] The Latter Day Saint movement would define Zion more broadly, for Zion would be complete stewardship of all the Earth.

Genesis 7:23 states, "And the Lord called his people Zion, because they were of one heart and one mind, and dwelt in righteousness, and there were no poor among them."[4] These verses in the beginning of the [Bible] define the desire of mankind to achieve the ideal community, although this particular city ascended to Heaven, many have continued to pray, "They Kingdom come."[5]

With these ideas in mind, we find that before the church was organized on April 6, 1830, Joseph Smith gave, in April, 1829, a revelation stating, "Now as you have asked me, behold I say unto you, keep my commandments, and seek to bring forth the cause of Zion."[6] Further revelations determined the place and cause of Zion in church doctrine.[7] Even though the distances and travel proved difficult in those pioneer times, Joseph Smith moved quickly and was determined to develop a people who would answer the call to Zion as a place and a people in Independence, Missouri.

The Minors, for whom this memoir is written, grew up in the little town of Heppner, [Oregon], where the public school teachers had to promise to teach in a local Sunday school if hired by the district. The church-going Minors would have considered the concept of Zion as the Sunday school classes would have read from Genesis, Isaiah, Psalms, Samuel, Kings, Jeremiah, Joel, Amos, Obadiah, Zechariah, Micah, Romans, Hebrews, and Revelations.[8]

In the Minor home, the Book of Mormon was taught, discussing Zion in the latter days. Grandmother Rush taught from the books of First, Second, and Third Nephi, plus Mosiah.[9] She would add the testimonies of Joseph Smith as she had heard them in Ohio. She was always anxious to tell the stories of Zion to any who would listen in the Condon and Heppner areas. Her love of Zion led her to return to Independence, Missouri, often supporting students to Graceland College, and spending the final years of her life near to the Stone church.

Ozark Zionic Journey: In Preparing
PREPARATION FOR THE ZIONIC JOURNEY

The grandmother of Ellis Minor, for whom this paper is written, was Mrs. Celestine Rush. While living in Ohio near the Kirtland Temple, she heard the message of Joseph Smith and became vitally interested in the cause of Zion. William Rush had traveled to Oregon and established a freight line that serviced the gold fields of John Day, Oregon, from an office in Portland, Oregon. Ten years later, he returned to Ohio for Celestine and his family, for he had said that when he became successful in the West, he would return for them. He immediately returned to Oregon with Celestine; Willa May, the oldest daughter; and Carrie May. After settling in Oregon, Grandmother Rush sent east for elders of the RLDS church who were able to establish a church in Condon and Portland, Oregon. Later, Carrie May contracted tuberculosis. Grandmother called for the elders to administer to her, and as a result, [Carrie Mae] was completely healed of the dreaded disease. She was convinced of the truths of the gospel story.

Ellis Minor (the grandfather of Ellis Minor), and his father, Arthur Charles Minor, were early founders of Heppner, Oregon. The town was founded at the confluence of three creeks, and the creeks are lined with beautiful trees. It is like an oasis in a valley with high barren hills surrounding the area. The founders laid out wide streets, so it is a delightful little western pioneer town.

Heppner was a center of the wars between the sheep and the cattlemen. Arthur Minor and his son Ellis [Rush] Minor, named after his grandfather, found it necessary to arrest and convict a close friend for stealing cattle and shooting the noses of the sheep, because he did not approve of sheep on the range of the Blue Mountains. Those were rough times.

Sam Van Vactor, a lawyer, lived next door to the Minors, and later, Grace Van Vactor, the daughter of Sam, and Ellis Rush Minor were married in 1915. Grace spoke of the ten saloons passed each morning on her way to school. Chinese labored in the mines nearby, and she often felt that justice was not adequately dispensed in the Morrow County courts. Heppner had become the county seat of Morrow County ... her father often presided as judge, and she heard the stories of the trials. She loved her childhood in this little town, but was always aware of the need for a better life for all.

Grace and Ellis were married and honeymooned for a year in Oakland, California. They returned to Heppner to run a sheep ranch. They often invited the elders of the RLDS church to come to Heppner and tell the story. Grace was an Episcopalian, but Ellis had been instilled with the stories of Zion from his grandmother and mother. He prayed for Grace to listen to the cause of Zion. The elders talked far into the night and after being sent upstairs to bed, I would creep down to the bottom step to listen as they talked. Grace listened with great interest to the revelations of this dream of an ideal community, for she remembered the inadequacies of her home town.

Excited elders were talking to excited listeners. Grace and Ellis started a Sunday school in Morgan, Oregon, where they sang the songs of Zion. As they had never been in an RLDS congregation, they used Union Sunday school material. The traditions or forms of worship were their own, and they were interested in working on their vision of the ideal community. They had many friends in and around Morgan.

Father had tax-deductible eyesight, so that with the sale of the lambs, we would go to Portland to checkups and for reunion at Gladstone on the banks of the Clackamas River. It seemed to the Minors that the focus of the dynamic meetings was Zion, as elders Burton, Carmichael McDowell, John F. Garver, E. J. Gleaser, and Fred M. Smith excited the people to their mission. Ellis and Grace would often spend hours at the tents of the representatives who came to reunion discussing Zionic concepts.

In volume eight of the *History of the Church* is the statement, "Interest in the gathering and the building of the kingdom mounted in the administration of President Frederick M. Smith, and especially keen after Bishop Carmichael became presiding bishop in 1925."[10] At reunion, suggestions were made that one could become a steward, and the rules governing stewards were studied by Ellis and Grace along with the New Maddens, isolated Saints in Hermiston, Oregon. Ellis and Grace decided to move with their sheep to Hermiston where they could learn more of the church.

Madden was an elder and studied the stewardship plan. At a reunion, previous to the conference of 1928, the New Maddens and the Minors met with the bishops concerning a sheep program in Missouri. Volume eight of the *Church History* states that the church had purchased ten thousand acres of land in the Ozarks in eastern Taney County.[11]

In 1928, the Minors and the Maddens traveled to Independence to attend the general conference, after which they went with President Smith and Bishop Carmichael to Taney County to view the land and discuss the possibility of bringing sheep to the land. The land was situated on Long Creek, which flowed the length of the land and entered Beaver Creek at Old Hilda. Beaver Creek borders the land and is a meandering clear stream. The group stopped at the spot where the creek made a graceful bend with a small hill above the plain. This overlooked the beautiful valley.

My parents never forgot the vision of President Smith as he described a church at the crown of the hill, with the home of the Saints along the stream, and the development of agriculture which would bring growth and security to the area. To the Minors and the Maddens, listening to Fred M. was like listening to a voice from heaven.

The *Saints' Herald* of May 19, 1926, published "An epitome of a sermon by Bishop Koehler of what was attempted in group stewardship enterprises."[12] Shortly afterward the *Herald* carried "An official Call for Agricultural Stewards to locate in the Holden Stake."[13] Bishop Koehler had many letters from many places, all parts of the United States and Canada.

In 1926, the standing high council had agreed on the laws governing stewardship, which were: 1) membership in good standing; 2) filing a financial statement; 3) payment of the tithe; 4) payment of surplus, if any; 5) setting apart; 6) management of the stewardship in harmony with the laws of the land and of the church; and, 7) an annual accounting."[14]

With these ideas in mind, the Minors and the Maddens returned to Oregon to study the implementation of these ideas, and with the help of the elders from Portland, Oregon, they began to prepare for a move to the church land in Taney County, [Missouri].

M. H. Siegfried had reported that in September 1928, there was a total of 12,818.66 acres of land at a cost of $27,341.84, which did not seem to any one like an exorbitant amount, for times seemed to have good portents for the future.[15] The reports also give the amount paid for a sawmill and the purchase of a truck. I was surprised when I read this report, as I remembered that it had been purchased after we were on the land, but such is not the case. President Smith envisioned many of the Saints settling in the area and wished to be prepared to help them in their stewardship. I remember my Father murmuring that a sawmill to build a house, some fences, and a barn [would be] expensive, but President Smith's voice disallowed all doubt, when he said, "Where is your faith?"

My father, having never lived in a congregation of the church, believed that all elders spoke the word of God, and, as he was only a layman, his thoughts were not sacred.

In one of the preserved letters concerning the move to Missouri, J. A. Becker, bishop, states, "We look with favor upon your effort to plan coming through next season and shall be glad to have you keep in touch with the progress you are making in completing your arrangements for such a move."[16]

He also said that they had traded some land, and they had 3,120 acres of land in one block. Long Creek passes through the entire length of the land which would give plenty of water, although the past season was dry. In March, Bishop Becker wrote, "I do think that you should bend every effort to make it possible to bring some of your stock through at least by fall." He also stated, "If necessary, we would help by advancing the money needed to ship the stock."[17]

The land was lying idle in the Ozarks, and, as bishops, they were anxious that there be some income from it. Other letters were written, and, with this encouragement, Father contacted sheep men friends in Morrow County to ship the sheep to Montana for the summer, which would put us one step on the way to Missouri. Near the first of June, we herded our sheep by ferry across the Columbia at Patterson, Washington, and joined the through train that took the sheep directly to the Blackfoot Reservation at Browning, Montana. One of the herders, a friend of the Krebs Brothers, agreed to take care of our sheep until the family arrived on the range.

Over the two years that we were in preparation for this move, we had many gatherings with the Maddens, and my mother, always enthusiastic and theatrical, planned many a skit and play about "Going to Zion." Hope for the future and anticipation of joyful living were the trademarks of my mother, which edified those about her.

From a small town with many friends, she had received beautiful linens, Haviland China, [and] doilies, but, because we lived on a ranch and cooked for the lambing and haying crews, she always kept those beautiful things in a trunk along with her wedding dresses of the 1915s. I spent many delightful hours in that old trunk. She decided that these were not of much use in Taney County and, with some sadness, stored the trunk in a Seventh-day Adventist school. She was not sad for long, as she prepared her poem of the bright Zion before and her hopes for a place where everyone would have their just needs and wants.

> *Westward, westward they journeyed*
> *Those men and women of old*
> *Onward and onward they hurried*
> *Looking for home or gold*
> *They came in the covered wagon*
> *Over the dreary plain leaving*
> *Homes and loved ones*
> *To give us freedom, they came.*
> . . . . .
> *Who are they that go down immortal*
> *As time in its course takes its flight?*
> *Who are they that have lifted humanity*
> *From the realm of blister and blight?*

Greater love hath no man than lay down his life
for a friend.
Here we find Marcus Whitman who
preached, fought and died.
Father McLoughlin stands as a beacon
light, guiding men on their journey, westward.
Guiding to where home fires burned bright
Where but for him they would have perished,
And so we go on through the pages
Naming the countless number who have
Stood like the Rock of Ages.
All these winters and summers they stood.
Their sons and daughters have the
Heritage of health in body and mind
To lead us in search of freedom,
That will leave to all others behind.
Of course there were others
Who made up these caravans.
The sons of many mothers
Became cowboys.
They drank their whiskey undiluted
And gloried in shooting up the town.
They gave parades quite denuded
And would have been a chase for the greyhound.
They too have left a heritage
To their sons and daughters now
The weakened mind and broken bodies
of their age
We can trace to many a cowboy row.
What so a man soweth
That shall he also reap
And behind those piles of rubbish
The beacon lights still cast a
Ray of hope to the scattered parade.
And we press onward
The lights we see at last
Zion the Beautiful Beckons Us On.[18]

On June 4, 1930, with a letter off to the bishops and President Smith, we drove off in the 1929 Pontiac for Montana. Grandfather Minor was sad to see us on our way, for he had been ill with heart problems, but he wished us well, for he was a real Oregon pioneer and understood the visions of the future. The Montgomeries, who were friends of the Maddens, wished us well, but Grandfather Van Vactor, a lawyer and a conservative, had made it plain that he had no use for this venture, for it was too close to Arkansas, and he had heard many stories of Hatfields and McCoys. He informed Mother that he would not write to her while she was there and, if by chance she would want to come home, he would send her the money to do so. He had never been happy, because she joined the Mormon church, and this was the last straw.

Our first night was at a beautiful motel at the foot of Camels Hump along a trout stream. The next day, we (and that means Father, Mother, Mary Van, Arthur, and myself) climbed the Rockies and over the Continental Divide. The valleys were deep and the road graveled and narrow, so the passing was made in absolute silence for driving a car was not my father's favorite activity.

We stayed in Helena, Montana, at a hot springs, but spent the night listening to our next door neighbors talk about coming down the Rockies with no brakes on the Model T. One woman passenger had jumped and was quite bruised, but the others had made the ride intact.

On the sixth of June, we arrived at the Blackfeet Reservation to live for the summer in a covered wagon, which was a forerunner of our mobile home of this day. Our neighbors were Doggone and Mrs. Many Whitehorses. We rented horses from them, but they did not trust us with anything but "plug alongs." The summer was delightful in Montana, for the fish were good solid trout, and Father could even kill a quail with a rock. Arthur, Mary Van, and I determined to go swimming on the Fourth of July, but the mountain stream was a good refrigerator, but not good for swimming.

Arthur and I made spending money by gathering old buffalo skulls and selling [them] to the Many Glaciers Hotel where so many tourists came on the Great Northern Railroad. No more buffalo heads are found in 1991. Each Sunday, Arthur and I walked to the Glacier Park to buy the Sunday paper and the *Saturday Evening Post* for the detective stories that were serialized at that time.

About the middle of the summer, Mr. Krebs took the lambs to market in Omaha, and they brought a little less than six dollars a head. This would not be enough to transport the sheep to Missouri, but after conferring with Bishop Becker, the church was able to secure the services of the Missouri Pacific Railroad Company, as they were anxious to have a new industry in the Ozarks.

The growing of corn on the corn ground and the growing of cane on the cane ground for the last hundred years had not been profitable to the railroad. Bishop Becker wrote that he had been to the land and that, even in the dry summer, there was plenty of water and the grass was in good condition for grazing. With characteristic optimism, my Mother states, "It is God's work, if it is for worse it will be our fault not God's. We must live and be more worthy of His Great Love."[19]

Henry Krebs returned from Omaha after selling the late lambs, and reported that the depression in stock prices had even gone lower than on the first trip to market. Mother, worrying about the trip to Missouri, decided to sell World Book sets. She sold some to people near Glacier Park and then took the bus to Kalispell, Montana. She did sell some, and I do not know the amount, but I am certain that it was not enough to transport the sheep and the family, but one cannot fault her for trying.

Grandfather Arthur had given Grandson Arthur quite a sizable Liberty Bond from World War I, and Arthur was agreeable to applying that to the trip to Zion. I do not think that he was too happy in surrendering his college future, but "Zion the Beautiful" beckoned the Minor family onward.

Finally, with the money from the lambs and other sources, plus the cooperation of the Missouri Pacific with the Great Northern Railway, the sheep were on their way from the mountains of the Great Northwest to the Ozarks.

As soon as the one thousand head of sheep were on their way from Browning, Montana, to Branson, Missouri, with Billy Lowe to take care of them until their arrival in Branson, the family said goodbye to the Krebs family and began their journey to Taney County.

Louise Murdock. From Jorgensen Collection.

As I write this, I am listening to a journey of a people from Ethiopia who are being airlifted from their land to their Zion or Israel. When some Jews left Yemen across the desert to be airlifted into Zion, an old man was asked if he were not afraid to fly. He answered by quoting from Isaiah 40:30, "But they that wait on the Lord shall renew their strength: they shall mount on wings as the eagles; and they shall walk and not be faint."

These people dared to be ready when the time came that they should return to Zion. Grace and Ellis were anxious to be on their way to Zion as had been prophesied in these latter days by the elders in Portland, Oregon, and they were hoping to fulfill the words of the Doctrine and Covenants.

The journey to Missouri was not as difficult as the crossing of the Rockies. Louise wanted to stop and check out the Custer Battlefield in Montana, and, as we passed Leavenworth, Kansas, Arthur was indignant that we did not let him check out the information that he had been reading about guards in penitentiaries. But the car knew only one place to go, and that was Independence, Missouri.

We finally reached Independence, and Ellis and Grace went into the unfinished Auditorium to meet with President Smith and the bishops. Arthur, Mary Van, and I remained in the car and watched a man across the road plowing in the field. Bishop Carmichael came out to the car to bid us on our way. I did not know exactly why tears were running down his face, and we were all crying, but I did feel that we were on our way to do something worthwhile for the church and the development of a Zionic endeavor.

The Minors drove to the church cottages at Rockaway Beach and unpacked. Arthur and Dad drove to Branson where the sheep would be unloaded. I researched the papers of Taney County, but could find no reference to the sheep. The pages were full of the capture of a gangster, Jake Fleagle, and his gang, who had been hiding in a cabin near Branson and had come to the train to pick up some supplies.[20] This was on October 16, 1930, and such was the day of the arrival of the sheep at the railroad station.

Arthur, Billy Lowe, and Dad drove the sheep to eastern Taney County, and, on their way, had many conversations with the local people, for they were certain that sheep, in numbers like we were herding, would not live in the Ozarks. With the help of Dr. Corlis, agricultural agent for the Missouri Pacific Railroad, it was determined that sheep eat close to the ground, and, in this warmer climate, would pick up worms. So, a mixture of blue vitriol was given to the sheep by mouth. The sheep were also dipped in creosote, which we called sheep dip. Thus the problems were solved.

An article at the same time, in the *Independence Examiner*, is incorrect, for it mentions three carloads of sheep going through Kansas City at the time that ours went through, I believe.[21] These carloads are credited to New Madden, who was never able to come to the Ozarks because of problems of the Depression. Later, he bought a farm near Davis City, Iowa, which his grandson has at present. Mrs. Madden spent her last years at Resthaven [Nursing Home] in Independence. He did make a payment on a Scott Ranch on Beaver Creek, but was not able to make further payments.

Soon after the sheep arrived at the church land, Bishop Becker arrived with the Nichols boys of Rich Hill and a young man from Kirtland. The young man from Kirkland had read of the feuding in the hills and was afraid to leave the ranch without someone with him. Bishop Becker brought a large circus tent which Mother separated into living quarters. I imagine this was one of those tents used for reunions in the early days. Mother went to the ranch, but Arthur and I remained for the winter in Rockaway Beach for school. Mother remembered the difficulty of carrying water up a steep hill from Long Creek, and, sometimes, there was not too much water remaining as they stumbled over the many rocks along the path.

The work of Zion had begun.

Ozark Zionic Journey: In Progressing and Regressing

PROGRESSION OF THE ZIONIC JOURNEY
REGRESSION OF THE ZIONIC JOURNEY

One of the first plans of work was to construct about three miles of road into the ranch headquarters. The selected place for the ranch was on cleared ground where a former resident had lived. This was on a bald knob, and the road was built around the edge of the bald knob. Bishop Becker, Father, and the men hired by the church grubbed out the road. I am certain that none had been road builders, although Father had driven many rough miles to sheep camps in the Blue Mountains. As to building a road—that was hard work!

They also began cutting the timber for building a house, and the steam engine was finally used to run the wheels of the sawmill. Father had no idea about machinery—in fact, Father bought a new model-T each year, for the sheep camp roads were hard on a car, and if he should break down, he would not have the faintest notion as to what to do. Therefore, when someone asked him to come learn about the sawmill, he stated that he would not mind learning to blow the whistle—otherwise, he was not interested, because it would probably break down.

The first winter was spent in the tent, but everyone was excited about the work that they were doing, and, though quite uncomfortable, no one seemed to be unhappy. Our neighbors were quite interested in these "furriners" [foreigners] as they called us, and we could look frequently from the house to see someone observing our activities. It was like living in a glass house.

On my first trip to the ranch, I was sent to herd the sheep at the top of the bald knob. People had tried to scare me about the Ozarks by telling about the many dangerous snakes, and I was not comfortable on that bald knob. But, as I observed the sheep, they, too, were jumping with fright at every bug or grasshopper. I was not sure that they were not afraid of this new country.

I have no letters to or from the church at this period of time, but I am certain there were many. I did find reference to the time that Arthur and I attended school in Rockaway Beach. The *Taney County Republican* of Forsyth states that Louise Minor and Arthur Minor, in November 1930, were learning to cook in the 4-H Club, which the school had formed to make hot lunches at noon.[22] On February 13, 1931, the Minors from Hilda had attended a carnival at the school, and one of the workers had won the raffle of a quilt.[23] On March 5, 1931, Mrs. Minor had entertained the local women's club, and they had worked on a quilt. So, it is obvious that from time to time, Mother would stay a few days with Arthur and me in civilization.[24]

Bishop Becker and Father built a three-room house with an attic. Bishop Becker, a banker, and father, a rancher, managed to get the roofing on wrong, and so with every rain, it was necessary to use buckets to catch the rain. The green lumber did not fit together too well, so the rain came through the cracks.

In the year 1931, the Stogsdills, who had worked for Madden in Oregon and had studied the stewardship plans with us, came to live at the ranch. Myra, their daughter, and Earl Grigg left Oregon in 1929 to go to Graceland College, and her parents drove on to Independence, or Zion, as we would have said in those days. Earl and Myra had been married. Earl was a good carpenter, so the building proceeded with more ease.

As lambing is in February, it was necessary to get the sheep barns built also. Bishop Becker was busy planning everything, locating supplies, so no one had time to listen to the radio or to read a paper, which would have been old by the time they went to the post office.

In the spring of 1931, because of the Depression, the church had to stop work on the Auditorium.[25] The church began to estimate the church debt, so they sent for Bishop Becker to return to Independence, but, as this project was important to him, he continued to stay in the Ozarks. Finally, a telegram was delivered to him, and he sadly left the project with all intentions to return soon. When he returned to Independence, new bishops had been called. No one ever worked a shard and believed in Zion as much as J. A. Becker. L. F. P. Curry was called to make an assessment of the debt, and Bishop Delapp replaced Becker, who continued to work at the Auditorium to help with the financial problems.

Birch Whiting of Rich Hill was interested in the sheep project and came to visit us while [we were] living at the church cabins in Rockaway, and then, as a friend of the church officials, studied the program. Because the value of the lambs was so low and wool price low, as well, Whiting decided to buy some of the sheep, for he thought that he might send his son from Kansas City to the ranch, which he was never able to do. This helped the program to continue.

The Depression had contributed to the loss of jobs, and small businesses failed, thus, some people moved to the land, or near the land, to get away from the city. The Ed Curtis family moved onto the Scott Ranch, part of the church property. The three Nichols boys, who had worked for the ranch, settled near Hilda, and Ellis Murdock and family, [and] a cousin of Birch Whiting moved to New Hilda. The Joe Curtis family lived on Long Creek. Among others were the Christiansons and the Hansons near Hilda. Many had heard about the ranch and came to look over the land, and were hoping to find a place to live. So many came that it was difficult to feed them. Father wrote to the bishops to discourage the people from coming down, as most did not have any money to make a move. The hotel stopped.

The Missouri Pacific had secured a place for me at the School of the Ozarks, a Presbyterian boarding school for the children of the Ozarks. Dr. Corlis took me to meet Mr. Good, president of the school, and I was so frightened I about forgot my name when Mr. Good asked me. Nevertheless, they took the "Mormon Girl," as they called me, and the Missouri Pacific donated to the school. I do not know just all that followed at this time, for I was away at school. There was no high school near Hilda for me to attend. The summer times were spent at the School of the Ozarks to pay for my room and board, clothes and books, by working in the canning factory and the kitchen.

My brother and Mary Van lived at the ranch and went to school at Three John, the local one-room school. At that time, the school had a four-month-term, which my father did not approve. He asked for a hearing of the school board and the county superintendent, and, after much talk, they agreed to an eight-month-school. Arthur was in the sixth grade and Mary Van in the first. At the end of the four months, the teacher became ill and school was dismissed. The following year, the county superintendent did insist on an eight-month school year. Arthur did not know how to hunt raccoons or tree opossums or go barefooted, so he was surely a "furriner" in a foreign country.

Soon after Birch Whiting bought the sheep, he and J. F. Garver came to look over the church land. As they started to cross a small stream, Garver took off his shoes, and the astonished people asked why. He said, "If it is as far across this stream as it has been from the house to that Pilot Knob that looks so close, I want to be prepared." He had seen enough of the ranch and sheep. The sheep did not need to be herded, as they would rest in little bunches in the middle of the day and then congregate at evening to graze back to the ranch.

Finding them sometimes was a task, and Garver was not up to that. The spring had been rainy, and the work in caring for the men had been difficult for Mother, although they had drilled a well. Mother had not had time to plant grass or flowers, nor neither had Father the time. As Garver came in, he said, "Always lived in a place like this?" My mother changed her mind about the infallibility of the priesthood at that moment. At home in Oregon, Father's place had always been a show place for its landscaping. Also, Garver informed her that he did not eat mutton. After eating, he stated that it looked like, from bones in his plate, he had eaten a cow, but mother informed him that he had eaten a sheep unknowingly.

August 14, 1931, we had a letter from Bishop Delapp concerning the Taney County project and the tone of things began to change from Bishop Becker, Bishop Carmichael, and President Smith, who had deep feeling for the ranch and for the stewardship of the land. But to Bishop Delapp, there were more headaches in the settling of the financial problems.[26]

Church History states, "Some members of the General Conference, particularly among the Twelve, felt that one adverse factor in the financial situation had been the pressure from the First Presidency on the Bishopric to purchase land in Taney County, Missouri, and elsewhere in connection with the gathering."[27] The twelve then presented the following resolution to the floor of the conference and the resolution was adopted:

> That the Presiding Bishopric shall assume and [is] hereby directed to assume full responsibility to see that the finances of the Church are used strictly in accordance with the laws and the enactments of the Church, and with faithful responsibility they shall be held answerable to the Church in General Conference.[28]

Thus any further correspondence, other than letters of encouragement from President Smith, was with the office of the bishopric.

On August 14, 1931, Bishop Delapp forwarded a letter to Bishop Curry stating the program for the use of the land in the Ozarks.[29] I have found no letter stating the status of the people on the land previous to this time. I have believed, and others have stated, that the forms that Father and Mother signed at the Auditorium before leaving for the ranch indicated that they were stewards as set forth for the church in previous meetings. My brother states that this certainly was the intention of all the participants of the program at the beginning.

From the evidence of letters and memories, I believe this was a stewardship program. The church secured the help of the Missouri Pacific Railroad to bring the sheep to Missouri. They secured a loan at the Jackson County Bank to finance some of the program. They hired the men who worked at the beginning of the program. The church bought much of the materials needed for building and caring for the sheep when the program began. My parents were anxious for the project to be of worth for the church and the community, and I do not believe that they would receive any profit for themselves. All income would be part of the annual inventory. Birch Whiting and

J. F. Garver went over the books carefully. In a letter of August 21, 1931, Delapp states about the land, "That those leasing should do so as the stewards, but this cannot be made a strict rule."[30]

At this time, a decision had not been made to sell the land. As I remember, it was thought that the sinking fund for Graceland College needed to be backed with cash and not land as the Church had thought permissible prior to the Depression. They also considered renting some of the pasture to cattlemen from the states in the dust bowl for the dust in the air was harmful to the cattle.

There are three letters of August 14, 21, and 26, 1931, prepared by Bishop Delapp, in consultation with Bishop Becker, to Bishop Curry, outlining probable use of the land in Taney County. The bishops wished to consolidate the land and sell off outlying tracts of land that had been purchased by Bishop Carmichael since 1928. The program would consist of the following points:

> Organize a holding or management group, having in mind a five-year-test period during which the feasibility of retaining possession of this land for the purpose of stewardships will be proved or disproved. If disproved, sell the entire acreage as quickly as possible.
>
> Abandon the idea of establishing a central town or village, until such a time as the necessary expense involved in the development thereof is justified by our policy relating to expansion, the number of people to be served, or the decision to proceed over a long time period with this territory as a stewardship project.
>
> Lease only to those who are found self sustaining, emphasizing to them that the church is unable to contribute further than it has done, except as pointed out under the terms below.
>
> Utilization:
> (a) By leasing to approved applicants as above. Examples, Minor and Whiting;
> (b) By encouraging those interested to put sheep or cattle in charge of Minor or other lessees under contracts concerning care, rental and sale;
> (c) By putting into effect, if careful study indicates feasibility, the pasturing of cattle on this central tract, and fattening with Atherton grain;
> (d) By selling selected acreages of timber when and as a satisfactory market develops....

As far as possible, those leasing should do so as stewards, but this cannot be made strict rule for stewards because the possibility of men like Dr. Baldwin being used to bring this property more quickly to a paying basis. The present financial condition of the church does not favor the waiting period probably needed to secure favorable stewards."[31]

Other points of the letters have to do with the amount that probable lessees would have to pay for the rental of the land. I do not know if Father ever saw the material in these letters, but Mr. Whiting visited and consulted with him often. It appears that the church in 1931 was continuing the stewardship endeavors.

President Smith had been anxious that the project be a model for agriculture in the region, so lespedeza, a legume, was planted on the hills and the deserted farming land was planted to alfalfa and corn for the use of the sheep. Dr. Corlis went to the ranch quite often to bring agricultural improvement ideas from his office in Hollister, Missouri.

The neighbors, the Hiram Davids, were anxious that we become members of the socially-accepted church goers at Johnson Schoolhouse at Hilda. They would drive by with their wagon on Sunday morning to take us to church where Mrs. A. C. Sturgis or Frankie Stewart, from Kissee Mills, would hold forth with an hour or more sermon in a high-pitched voice. The first time that the Minors attended, they were unable to quite comprehend this different experience, but, as Mother sat in wonderment, she felt that the Spirit of Christ entered this humble meeting. The people were sincere and desired friendship, so the Minors accepted the traditions for this is their country and their worship.

Ed and Joe Curtis, RLDS elders, preached at the little school house. The people loved to hear them preach. The local preachers developed a larger vocabulary, especially about the last dispensations of time. This subject was especially interesting to them. In the evening, the young people would walk to Johnson school again.... Children of the owners of the moonshine stills on Caney Creek would only come into the service to drink from the common dipper in the water pail at the back of the room.

In January 1932, Mr. Minor wrote a letter to Bishop Delapp as to whether he should fill out a tithing report or needed an inventory. No bishops were in the area, so no report instructions were available. He states that they had finished a barn about three hundred feet long, built a cellar, a summer kitchen, two bedrooms on another house twenty-six by thirty-two feet. They built feeding troughs and plowed land for the next year's crop.[32] I do not know if Bishop Delapp answered, but as there was plenty of work to continue in the preparation of the ranch, every one stayed busy and their progress was duly discussed by those sitting on the barrels in Robert's General Store in New Hilda, built on the new highway.

A letter of September 6 from a church member, Vernon Reese, speaks of the Stogdills who were living at the ranch, whose son-in-law, Earl Griggs, was the good carpenter and sawmill operator.[33] It appears, from the letter, that Mr. Stogdill wanted to rent a portion of the ranch which had formerly been farmland on which most of the crops were being grown. I do not know the result of this letter, but it is certain that he did not have the money or the livestock to qualify for any of the requirements as set forth in the letters of the bishops. Myra Grigg, the Stogdill's daughter, had a baby at this time, and I stayed with her in Branson until the baby arrived, and, because of the ineptness of the doctor, the baby did not live. The baby was buried on the farm, and the grave is unmarked, as Arthur noted when he visited the farm in 1989.

Three letters concern the Stogdill request for land, but the part of interest is that Bishop Delapp states, "It would appear that this is another one of those problems concerning group stewardships."[34] I do not know of other problems to which he refers, but he does indicate that Taney County land was a stewardship program, and he desired that no problems arise. In September and October of 1932, letters about Whiting and the Stogdills state that they wished to move to the Scott Ranch and care for the portion of the sheep belonging to Whiting. I do not know the result of the plan but I remember that Garver, Whiting, and my dad spent time reviewing the program and the books. My mother, who could never stand a disagreement, saddled Old Nellie and rode off to spend some time with Mrs. Ed Curtis who was living at the Scott Ranch. On her return, Garver said, "Figures do not lie, but liars do figure." My Mother expected trouble from that remark, but that was one of Garver's conversation quibbles and all was decided peacefully. Dad continued to run Whiting's sheep as he had previously.

Evidently Garver and Whiting realized that Dad had some problems that he did not voice to them. He was, at this point, still in awe of an apostle. On returning to Richill, Whiting wrote a letter pointing out some things that bothered him about the care of the sheep. Father may not have known too much about church policy, but he did know about the care of sheep, so he fired a letter to Whiting covering everything that had troubled him from the beginning of the program. Immediately, Whiting brought his family and came to see us. He had written the letter for the purpose of getting Father to explode, for he knew of no other way to understand the problems. I will never forget the great relief that it was to Father and to Mother, for they had thought a great deal of Whiting and trusted him as an elder. Mrs. Whiting was especially helpful and understanding, and it was such a relief to Father that this friend was really a friend and understood him.

Culturally, the Minors were not the typical sheep ranchers. Father was talented at the piano. His instructor, during the year in Oakland, had wanted Ellis to become a concert pianist, and in our days in Oregon, he would waken us by playing the piano. Mother took classes in speech and storytelling. Her instructor encouraged her to become a member of a chautauqua group. These days in eastern Taney County were difficult for them, and, as the bishops were no longer able to support the Zionic program, Mother and Dad were discouraged, but not without vision.

Father wrote to C. L. Olson in the office of the bishop in February of 1934, that Taney County might build a road to Caney Creek which would make the church land more accessible. The road was built by the labor of the local people in place of payment of the poll tax that Missouri had imposed for voting.[35]

On March 12, 1934, C. L. Olson wrote a letter saying that the church had given an option to the government for a tract of land. The church was interested in having the government accept 2,120 acres of land which was still mortgaged to Mr. Serat. The sale was made in 1934, with the church still owing eight thousand dollars, but the owner of the mortgage discounted two thousand dollars.[36] The land is now Mark Twain National Forest.

In two letters of February and June, Bishop Curry says he would sell the improvements on the church land to Mr. Minor, but he would hope that Minor would not buy in that country, but go somewhere that would have more culture for his wife and children.[37]

Later, Bishop Curry states that the settlement for Minors leaving the church land was "fair and should forestall any contention later that the Church took advantage getting him to Taney County. We had nothing to do with his going there, but I see no way in which your adjustment could be fairer in the sale of the property."[38] I do not understand the statement that they had nothing to do with the Minors going there, but perhaps he is speaking of the change in the responsibility of the different bishops. I do not assign the total responsibility to the bishops for the program, for certainly the Minors chose to go to Taney County, but I believe that it was a cooperative movement.

Volume eight of the *Church History* has the following paragraph. "On the Sunday following the close of the Conference of April 17, 1932, Elder L. F. P. Curry was set apart a Presiding Bishop and G. Leslie Delapp to serve as his counselor."[39] I do not believe that the bishopric felt that they had no part of the program, for to Bishop Delapp's credit, he told me to have Father come to Resthaven, and it would not cost him anything. Father had Parkinson's disease and finally lost his eyesight. Father was home in Oregon, and he did not want to leave home again. Bishop Curry visited us at every opportunity and Apostle Ellis was especially helpful to the family.

President Smith wrote a letter to New Madden in February of 1935, in response to a letter of Madden inquiring about the land. "Brother Minor worked very hard to make this project a success, but was extremely handicapped because of the lack of capital. We have not heard definitely what his plans are for the future, but expect to cooperate with him to the best of our ability to secure a new location."[40] He further states that "I have been intensely interested in the development along sheep raising lines and deeply regret that we started our experiment when changing conditions made it so difficult to give the matter the test that I should like to see given."[41]

One of the families who lived adjacent to the church land was baptized by Ed Curtis, who had come down to live on the Scott place. We learned from him before we left Missouri that the many neighbors who lived near the ranch had met at the Big Spring, the source of Long Creek, to discuss the fate of the Minor family on their arrival at that land. Government agricultural agents and Missouri Pacific agents had been forcefully forced from the area. All these neighbors had been using the land for cattle, hogs, and produce from the land for many years. The families making moonshine or whiskey did not want people on the land, and, especially, on Long Creek where they had their stills. Tommy Stafford spoke up for the "Furriners," for it seemed to him that as members of some church, they might prove to be helpful to the poor community. Thus we were given a period to prove ourselves. The Roberts finally confined their whiskey-making activities to Caney Creek and left the area of Long Creek for the sheep. The fact that Tommy Stafford and his family were the first in the area to understand and accept the gospel is interesting to me.

Louise graduated from the School of the Ozarks in 1934. Grace had sold her diamond ring for supplies needed to care for the family and the sheep. They had sold the Pontiac car, for the price of gas and any items that would need fixing on the car were expensive. In order to travel to the ranch, it was necessary to ford Beaver Creek. My Father could ford easily going downstream on the way to town, but could never be able to return without flooding the engine. Our neighbor, who lived on the creek, by the name of Mel Davidson, would have his team of horses ready to pull Father through on the return trip. My parents had no way of attending my graduation, but the Ellis Murdocks had come to live at Hilda. They brought Mother, Dad, Mary Van, and Arthur to the School of the Ozarks riding on the back of a truck. My Mother was so dusty and ashamed that she would not come into graduation, but Father would not be deterred, for he was anxious to be there when I received some honors. My brother and Orison Murdock came also, but they were fascinated with the campus and spent their time looking.

I returned to the ranch with my parents, for I did not know that Dr. Good had written that he would see to it that I could go to college if it took his last dime. Shortly, we received a letter from Dr.

Good, president of the School of the Ozarks, to report to him to take the bus to Central Missouri State Teachers College. I had a place to work for room and board. Luckily, Mr. Whiting was at the ranch, and he took me to town and gave me enough money for the bus fare. Mr. Good gave me the money for tuition and books. Fearfully and thankfully, I was off to begin my college education.

I mentioned the Davidsons. During the first year, Father would take the fence wire that was standing on the abandoned farms. He had prepared the wire to use at the Scott place. He went to town, and, on return, it was gone. Dad followed the tracks of a wagon that had driving into Davidson's yard. The wire was not there, so he asked Davidson about the wire. Davidson said he knew nothing of it. Father believed Davidson had taken it, so he wrote the bishop's office to write for him to return it. The next time that we went to town, all of the wire was piled in front of the house driveway. Neither family ever mentioned the wire, and Davidson continued to help the car across Beaver Creek. A letter to the bishop in September of 1934, [Father] asked if the bishops needed an inventory of the year and states that it has been the hardest time of all and states that "At times it looks very discouraging but we hope that our work here, some time, will be of benefit to the Church." Besides the inventory of the ranch, he wishes to trade some outlying land rather than have the Church let it go for non-payment of taxes.[42]

By the letter, one feels that he is disappointed, because he has not accomplished much. He reminds the church of the difficulty of trying to develop a ranch, such as he had in Oregon, for the Depression did not allow him to have the capital needed to do all he had planned.[43]

In May of 1933, President Smith visited the ranch, and when he returned to Independence, he was concerned about the family, and about Mary Van in that lonely place. He wrote a nice letter and sent her two books that belonged to his daughter, Lois Blair. That is one letter that has been a keepsake.[44]

The letters from the bishop in early 1935 to Father are concerned about the land that was being sold to the government and several disclaimers were needed in order to clear the titles of the land, so the government could develop what is now the Mark Twain National Forest.[45]

President Smith was disappointed that his vision of a Zion in the Ozarks did not become a reality, but he was interested in the development of the country, and I am certain that there were benefits to the area that he would have been justly proud of. The people became aware of the necessity of rotation of crops, the use of irrigation on the land, the necessity for developing the grazing land with better grasses. Several developed the idea that education in these times is a real necessity, and developed their schools to promote the welfare of their children. I am certain that the neighbors received a positive attitude toward the Reorganized Church of Jesus Christ of Latter Day Saints, even if they still wondered about the long name. These days in the Ozarks gave me an understanding of the value of all people, and prepared me for twelve years of living in Sao Gabriel, de Goias, of Brazil. I imagine that it was a memory that Arthur could use in the five long years on the islands of the South Pacific in World War II.

A letter to Bishop Curry from C. L. Olson speaks of the use of the sawmill by Mr. Crandall who had purchased the right to cut the white oak on the land. Crandall had paid five dollars, and had maintained the steam engine and the sawmill so that it would be possible to move it out to the main highway at Hilda where it could be more readily sold. He also writes that the government wanted the improvements moved by the time that they received the land deed. They had decided to sell the improvements to Father, in order for him to build on the land he had purchased on Caney Creek, adjacent to church land. He would be allowed to make time payments.[46]

March 1, 1928, President Smith wrote [in] a letter to Ellis, "That you have a definite impression not to go back to Oregon. I cannot but feel, I am at least still strongly hoping, that the way will open yet for you and Brother Madden to accomplish what we have so long desired to see accomplished, either in the Ozarks or in some place which we term the 'regions round about.'"[47]

He also refers to the eighty acres that Father had been able to buy with twenty acres of bottomland for crops for winter months. Father, also, had put a pump and a ram in Caney Creek to irrigate a large garden and the fields. The neighbors, as usual, wondered how this "furriner" thought that he could keep a garden growing after July, for everyone knows that the August drought destroys the garden. They were watchful of the program, and, as the experiment was successful, they asked to be helped in preparing their gardens. Father had built a screened-in porch around the house, and most neighbors decided that was a good idea and followed suit.

President Smith also writes, "I have no doubt that with the right kind of work where you are, a branch can be soon organized, and I feel that we can become quite a strong religious factor, as well as a strong civic factor in that part of the country, and I am really happy that you do not feel whipped as yet."[48] One can see that though, by this time, the problems of the church were many and difficult, that President Smith remained optimistic, and this, of course, was reassuring to the Minor family.

September 30, 1935, an agreement was signed by L. Bishop Curry that absolved any obligations of the Minors, and their heirs, and the church to obligations incurred during the transaction of the project.[49] This was a very sad day for my parents for, although they knew the needs of the church, that final signing was more or less shattering.

Father built a house on Caney Creek and a barn. At this time, I received a contract to teach at Three John where Arthur had gone to school, and Mary Van was in grade six. The PWA had come into existence, and Father received the job as supervisor of building a road at Hercules. This road was on the eastern edge of the church land and was quite a horseback ride each morning to get to work on time. Therefore, I was left with the task of milking Heifferetta before I walked the two miles to Three John. The school board president could neither read nor write, so I had difficulty explaining to him and other board members, why I put more of my lessons on the board for the students to copy. The geography text in the school was dated about the time of World War I. The health book spoke of discovering proteins and, of course, had nothing of vitamins. I could use the spelling books for words do not change much. I was rather appalled that my brother had attended this school for three years before [going] to the School of the Ozarks.

Most of the students at the School of the Ozarks had attended four and eight-month-schools with high school graduates as teachers. The board reminded me to teach that the earth is flat, because the Bible states that the angels will stand on the four corners of the earth and blow their horns at the end of time. I agreed, but I did get permission to teach that there is, also, the theory of a round Earth. Most of the boys in my class were in the infantry in World War II. I assume that they learned the true facts in their travels to Normandy. Ticks were everywhere, and the first thing that each student did on reaching school was sit down and pick off the ticks, and if one hit a branch with a cluster of seed ticks, that was a task! One of the David girls in the fourth grade could spell all the words in the speller until she reached the eighth grade spelling lists, so she studied with eighth graders. She became a private secretary to a telephone company, later in life.

These "furriners" were concerned about education, and, thus, the David children, our closest neighbors, wanted to have an education, much to their father's despair. He finally allowed Crawford, the oldest boy, to walk to the bus on the highway and go to Forsyth High School, with the agreement that no books would come home, for he must do all his chores, morning and night. He graduated as salutatorian, so his brother and sister wanted to go. The same rules were set. Pauline and Byron graduated as valedictorian and salutatorian. The local papers wrote articles of praise which gave them scholarships to a Baptist College at Bolivar, Missouri.

The Davids became advocates of education after these honors. Crawford moved to Los Angeles, California. He had taken a correspondence course in engineering. In order to complete the course, he was required to go to their school. He worked for the Los Angeles Fire Department, became an elder in the RLDS church, and sent his children to Graceland. He was pastor in Los Angeles churches and, at the time of his death, was volunteering his time in developing the Hemet Congregation where his wife lives as a faithful member of the church.

In checking through the papers of Taney County, I did not find articles about the sheep, but I did find items of activities. The *Taney County Republican* of July 1934 tells of the visit of the lady who was the main preacher at Johnson Schoolhouse. To quote, "Little Claire Marie and Mrs. A. C. Stufgis have spent the week with Mrs. Ellis Minor and Oh! My, What a good times they had!" This would have been at the ranch, for after the Minors moved on Caney Creek, they became closer members of the community.[50]

One of the first surprises, when we moved down to Caney Creek, was a party to which people began to come all afternoon, until most of the community of Hilda was present by evening and everyone brought a cake or something to eat. One understood that all people of the community that wished came to a party. No invitations were sent to certain people. In November of 1935, we have a long article about a Halloween Party, "All departed at a late hour telling Mrs. Minor what a good time they had and wondering what they would do next Halloween."[51]

In September of 1935, Irah Robert, who was sixteen when he went into the Civil War, passed away from old age. Father and Mother had learned by experience that everyone goes to a funeral. Mother got on Old Nelly, who really never liked Mother for a passenger, and rode up Caney Creek, crossing the creek three times in pouring rain hoping that the creek would not be flooding by the time that they arrived at the headwaters and the Roberts cabin in a lonely spot.

As the Roberts men had been busy at their stills, some were asleep on the porch as Mother entered the house. Father stopped on the porch with some cloth to help line the casket. The scene was rather rustic, but, as Mother entered the kitchen, Aunt Lizzy began to cry and hug her, and said, "I am so glad you came, Mrs. Minor, for I feel that you are just one of us."

The Minors felt accepted. Tommy Stafford's faith had been paid, in part, for he had asked for the Roberts to wait and see if these people would be of some help to their country. The preacher was dressed as one might picture Ichabod Crane. He talked about the "sad, sad occasion." My mother was inclined to think that one hundred years of living and never missing a voting date did not add up to a sad, sad occasion.[52]

September 13, 1935, has an article about, "The best party of the year was held at the home of Mr. and Mrs. Ellis Minor in honor of their son Arthur from the School of the Ozarks, who is spending a short vacation with his parents and his sisters."[53]

During the time on the ranch, after the workers from the church had to leave, several Roberts and Maggards of Caney Creek worked a few days for Father. These families were called Caneyites, and the families who lived on the ridge near the Johnson schoolhouse were Ridgerunners, and never the twain should meet. The Ridgerunners were primarily "Hardshelled Baptist" and were bound for heavenly realms, but the Caneyites were bound for the fires of the nether world. The Caneyites came to the church and school activities, but unless the weather was cold, only came into the church to drink from the common dipper in the water bucket on a shelf at the entrance. They sometimes caused a problem, as when Ike Roberts raised his head, when sitting on a back seat on a cold night, and said of the preacher, "Oh Hell, she hasn't said one word about the Depression, yet," and stalked out.

Another time, a teacher from Hercules was preaching, "I can see Heavena, I can see Heavena," with a lot of emotion, when Rex Roberts yelled from the back, "Have you seen any of those hogs you stole from my dad last winter?" There was no answer. The people turned their pigs loose on the church land to eat the acorns and only saw them when they called them with each one's dissimilar call.

The Ridgerunners gave pie suppers and parties, but the Caneyites could not use the schoolhouse for any purpose, so Mother decided it was time for the Caneyite young people to do something to show that they had abilities, also. So she secured several copies of a play called *Aunt Jerushy on the Warpath*. As the Caney kids were our closest neighbors, they came to the house to learn their parts and actions. After sufficient time, Mother asked for the use of the schoolhouse for the play and pie supper. We were ready for the play, and the school board wanted to know if we had asked the sheriff to keep order. We knew that they had the sheriff, and we knew that they did not trust the Caneyites not to get in a fight, but, then, the Caneyites were all in the play.

We did have to get the sheriff. The play was hilarious, and the audience had many laughs, especially, when the blanket used as the front curtain fell down in the second act. The sheriff told my mother that he always wanted a personal invitation to any more of the Caneyite plays. This did break down that old separation, and one of the Caneyite Maggards married one of the Ridgerunner Davids and now live in California.

One vivid memory is that of the baptism of Lonzo Scott. He owned the ranch on which New Madden had made a down payment. He often visited one of the Roberts' stills, and we often found him deadly drunk in the middle of the road to the ranch and his faithful horse standing by. Somehow, a hard-shelled Baptist had saved him, but before his baptism, Lonzo came to our house to confess all of his sins. He came early in the afternoon and told of the many stories like the McCoys. He talked through supper and after supper. He talked until Mary Van and I went to bed, but we could hear through the thin walls. Then, Mother and Father went to bed, and he brought his chair by their bed and talked all night, always saying, "Now listen, this is not the worst. I just have to get this awful thing told and confessed." I could not tell that one was worse than the other.

The "Baptizing" as they said, was being held at that pretty meandering bend in Beaver Creek, where President Smith had so eloquently described his vision at the gathering of the Saints. Finally, by eleven o'clock, Mother and Father were able to get Lonzo to hurry to Beaver Creek where people had come in cars, wagons, horseback, or walking, to witness the baptism of this well-known hill man.[54]

In order to pay for the ranch, my Father and I cut cedar posts. Cutting cedar is a prickly, sticky, and difficult task, and I do not think that it would make one rich. Teaching at Three John paid fifty dollars a month, and, at the end of the year, I received about a one hundred dollar bonus. This was enough or more to buy groceries, and I had a little saved to return to the School of the Ozarks to work, so I could return to Warrensburg to school.

As the government was taking over the land for reforestation, I have an interesting letter that Father wrote to the forest department concerning the use of the land for grazing, which is in the appendix.

As Dr. Corlis from the Missouri Pacific had always been interested in the sheep ranch, he contacted Father for Mr. Leonard, a millionaire from Kansas City, who was interested in acquiring the sheep and buying some for a program near the School of the Ozarks. Arthur was attending the school, and I was working there, so Mother and Father decided that, perhaps, it would be a good move to get Mary Van into a good school. He was interested, as always, in developing the sheep industry.

Ozark Zionic Journey: In Realizing; Realization of Life Beyond the Taney County Zionic Journey

REALIZATION OF LIFE BEYOND THE DREAM

Bishop Olson wrote a letter, in June of 1936, asking Ellis to write to him from time to time telling of his activities. Brother Curry came as often as he could to see the family, and Apostle Clyse F. Ellis was especially helpful, for the Ellis family had Louise visit when on vacation from college, and later the Ellis family spent a summer on the Columbia River with the Minors.[55]

The move to Hollister was made in October. The Minors lived in the guest house that Mr. Leonard provided, until a house would be completed. Leonard owned a plant in Kansas City that manufactured bottle caps and were used by the State of Missouri as tokens for the sales tax.

Shortly after arrival, twelve-year-old Mary Van became very ill. The Branson doctor diagnosed it as bladder trouble, and by the time that a correct diagnosis of appendicitis was made, she was worse. Dr. Good, from the School of the Ozarks, drove her, and Mother, and Father to a Springfield Hospital, but she could not be saved. Dr. Good lost his [own] little girl when she was quite young, so he had loving compassion for the Minors. He had them live in the school hospital while the students from the school finished the house that they were building, so the Minors would not have to go to the house where Mary Van had been so ill.

The people of Hilda, near the ranch, heard by radio that Mary Van had passed away. Many came on a truck, and some were able to drive to the school. The funeral was held in the school chapel. Elder Ed Curtis, who had lived on the ranch and had gone back to Independence; Dr. Bell, the Presbyterian pastor of the school; and Dr. Crocket, the "Bishop of the Ozarks," were wonderful in their memorial.

I will never forget, as we walked along the path with Dr. Good, seeing those poor people from Hilda, students and teachers with doctor's degrees playing homage to this little girl. Ernest Maggard of

Caney Creek stopped me and gave me a knife that Mary Van had given him, for he had no other way to express his sympathy. I was working at the Taney County Court House in July of 1990, and I asked the county clerk if she remembered the Minors. She answered, "I could never forget that sweet little girl." Such a wonderful way to be remembered![56] Mary Van lies in an unmarked grave in Gobbler Knob Cemetery near Hollister, Missouri. We have not been able to find any pottery chards from the vase that marked her grave.

After Mary Van's death, I returned to Warrensburg to school. I had been in charge of the kitchen and the dining room, for the dietitian was in the hospital with what proved to be tuberculosis of the bones. She would instruct me, every day, as to the menu and work of the girls. Dr. Good asked if Mother could take my place, and she loved to work with the young people of the school. They liked working with her.

Soon, Father discovered that Leonard did not have enough grazing land nor ... did he have enough crop raising land, so they would have to sell the sheep. Mr. Leonard was also losing money, for the methods of selling milk began to change. The caps were not needed.

One family of friends were the Horines who had invented a cement pottery. Arthur became interested in making the pottery, and the Horines secured us a gift shop and lunch counter at Table Rock Inn. Mother loved meeting people, selling fits, but she especially enjoyed the fact that the Horines would take her to meetings with Rose O'Neill, the artist of the kewpie doll; Thomas Hart Benson, the Missouri artist; [and] John G. Neihardt, the poet laureate of Nebraska, but who loved the Ozarks. This was quite a different life than that in eastern Taney County.

Arthur returned to Oregon with his grandfather Minor who had, against the advice of his doctor, driven to Missouri. Arthur received the franchise for selling pottery in Oregon, so they returned to the Columbia River to make pottery, or rather sell it. They had a beautiful place at the foot of Latourelle Falls, but, with World War II, people were not able to travel up the Columbia River from Portland. Arthur had gone to the South Pacific in the army. So Dad moved into Portland and worked at the Liberty Shipyards.

Louise Murdock in 2008. From Jorgensen Collection.

Mother was very ill on the way to Oregon and finally discovered that a young Minor was on the way. Calista May was born in Hood River, Oregon, soon after arriving in the state. Calista thinks our Ozark stories are quite strange to hear.

Mother felt the hardships of living in the Ozarks were too evident, and it was a number of years before she would let me take her to her home town of Heppner. When she did, finally, go to the Memorial Day picnic, all of the persons from her high school graduation were there, and she forgot her insecurity. One was the editor of the *Portland Oregonian*.

When the war was over, the Minors developed the farm across from the Dalles, Oregon, which Mother had inherited. Father became ill with Parkinson's disease, but they had a nice home, and Mother became postmistress of the Dallesport Post Office. She always had a Sunday school in her home, but, later, the community built a building for her. She presided at PTA meetings, as well as church circles, and Klickitat County women's clubs.

At her death in 1979, she had been living eight years with Calista. Calista and Arthur decided that no one would remember her [Mother] in Klickitat County, so they sent her to be interred in Goldendale. Goldendale, Washington, was the home of the Van Vactor pioneers, and the family of Louise had lived there for twenty years. Ellis had been buried near the Van Vactors. The people of Klickitat County soon let Arthur and Calista know that they did not approve of burying Mrs. Minor without a fitting memorial. They prepared a beautiful memorial service for her in the Goldendale Methodist Church. Elder Lloyd Whiting of Richland gave a loving homily.

I think that the editorial by President Smith to my parents is a fitting tribute to their life as they mastered disappointments of the day, and remembered the vision of tomorrow, and always with the dream of Zion.

> I recently learned of the decease of the daughter of Brother and Sister Minor of Hollister, Missouri, and sent a letter of condolence.
>
> Mary Van was bright and [a] rather extraordinary studious child, one who lived with nature and delighted in converse with birds, trees, plants, and established familiarity with them, which enabled her to speak to them by their first names. Quiet of demeanor, pleasant of speech, and thoughtful of friends and loved ones. She won a place in the hearts of those who knew her which will cause her to be greatly missed. In response to a letter to Brother and Sister Minor extending my sincere sympathy, they wrote, telling a bit about her and why they would so greatly miss her.... Many of us know how much Mary Van will be missed by her parents and friends, and as fellow sufferers at the ruthless hands of death we have the feeling which makes the whole world kin and our sympathy is sent out. But there are other Mary Vans still with us, needing our guidance, our help, and our love, so we carry on as will Brother and Sister Minor in the interests of others. God bless our children.[57]

At the present, there is a pretty little RLDS church on the main street of Branson, Missouri. Mrs. Elwin Vest was pastor when I was there in 1990.

Appendix

Dear Mr. Fletcher:

I certainly favor your ideas in regard to the protection of the forests; timber, grass and wildlife.

Many times I have thought of the words of an Indian chief. He said a great deal in a few words. "An Indian builds a small fire and gets close to it. A White man builds a big fire and stands away off. Indian kill one deer, one buffalo, and a few fish to eat. White man kill many for sport or record." The forests of the Indians were filled with beaver, deer, and other wildlife; streams were abundant with fish. Mother Nature provided long waving bunch grass and other much-needed life helping materials. When the White man came, because he had no restrictions, he burned grass and forests, killed the deer, and caught the fish.

I am just enough interested in Mother Nature's ways and pioneer enough. to continue to picture in my mind the scenes of the Western Prairies, the Rockies, the frying pan on the camp fire with the smell of fresh trout and venison. I have seen this picture fade away by lack of protection and organization. We were glad when we felt the protecting service of the Forest Department. We saw them replenish the streams, limit the killing of deer and elk, and also other game, such as grouse and pheasants.

I remember a mental picture of the free range, the stockman lost, not lost, but just stealing grass and running back and forth tramping down the good grass. The next problems in mind were given allotments; no more did the stockman worry, our grass was protected and ready for us when we came to the range. There is only one suggestion that I could, let us as citizens help you to limit, and you help us by providing part of the grass in the National Forests for grazing, and at the same time charge us a small sum. We in the mountainous country depend on livestock for a living, and we must have a source of cheap pasture for the summer months. Lately, the Eastern Senators have forgotten our problems of summer pasture, and we have fought hard to have them.

My family was the first to introduce China and Golden pheasants in to Eastern Oregon Country, and now, in the valleys and tributaries of the Columbia River, there are hundreds of pheasants.

Yours for the protection of the forests.

Ellis Minor

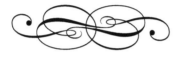

Notes to pages 235–67

1. *Holy Scriptures. Containing the Old and New Testaments. An Inspired Revision of the Authorized Version, by Joseph Smith, Junior. A New Corrected Edition* (Independence, MO: Herald Publishing House, 1947). Joseph Smith Jr., Book of Mormon (Independence, MO: Board of Publications of the Church of Jesus Christ of Latter Day Saints, 1966). Book of Doctrine and Covenants (Independence, MO: Board of Publications of the Church of Jesus Christ of Latter Day Saints, 1970).
2. Oxford American Dictionary (New York and Oxford: Oxford University Press, 1980), 811.
3. Ibid., 811.
4. *Holy Scriptures*, 1, 14.
5. Ibid., 30.
6. Doctrine and Covenants, section 6:3a, 30.
7. Ibid., section 52:1b, 133.
8. *Holy Scriptures*, 1.
9. Ibid, 2.
10. *History of the Reorganized Church of Jesus Christ of Latter Day Saints*, vol. 8 (Independence, MO: Board of Publications, 1976), 156. Hereafter cited as *Church History*.
11. Ibid., 156.
12. Ibid., 157.
13. Ibid.
14. Ibid.
15. M. H. Siegfried, Memorandum, three-page letter concerning Taney County, June 1931, [and] concerning September 22, 1928.
16. J. A. Becker, Independence, to Ellis Minor in Hermiston, Oregon, 18 January 1930.
17. J. A. Becker, Independence, to Ellis Minor in Hermiston, Oregon, 25 March 1930.
18. Grace Minor, poem, pp. 4–5, (unknown source).

19. Ibid. "We do not doubt God's plan, but many a night we lay awake thinking of our failures and how unworthy we were to be part of such a plan, but we go on praying that we may overcome human frailties and at last be of service to mankind." Chapter 4, p. 1 (unknown source).

20. *White River Leader* (Branson, Missouri), October 16, 1930.

21. *Independence Examiner* (Independence, Missouri), (1929?).

22. *Taney County Republican* (Forsyth [Rockaway Beach], Missouri), November 1930.

23. Ibid., February 30, 1931.

24. Ibid., March 5, 1931.

25. *Church History*, 182.

26. Delapp to Curry, 14 August 1931.

27. *Church History*, April 1932.

28. Ibid.

29. Delapp to Curry, August 1931.

30. Ibid., 21–26 August 1931.

31. Ibid.

32. Minor to Delapp, January 1932.

33. Letter from Vernon Reese, 6 September 1932.

34. Delapp to Curry, 13 October 1932.

35. Minor to Olson, February 1934.

36. Olson to Minor, 12 March 1934.

37. Minor to Delapp, April 1934.

38. Curry to Delapp, February 1934–June 1934. Minor, March [?].

39. *Church History*, 183.

40. F. M. Smith to Madden–Minor.

41. Ibid.

42. Minor to Bishops, September 1934.

43. Minor to Bishops, September 1934.

44. Smith to Mary Van, February 1933.

45. C. L. Olson to Minor, February 1935.

46. C. L. Olson to Curry Smith to Minor, March 1935.

47. F. M. Smith to Minor.

48. Ibid.

49. Contract-Curry Minor Ted Beck.

50. *Taney County Republican*, July 1934.

51. Ibid., November 1935.

52. Ibid.

53. Ibid., 13 September 1935.

54. Ibid.

55. Olson to Minor, June 1936.

56. "Mary Van," *Taney County Republican*, November 12, 1936. "Mary Van," *White River Leader*, October 13, 1936.

57. Fred M. Smith, editorial, *Saints' Herald* 83, no. ? (January ?, 1936): ?.

Berta Bennett Ruoff Nogel

BORN
June 15, 1920, Manila, Utah
DIED
October 4, 2010, Santa Ana, California

This is Vinnia Williams interviewing Berta Nogel on April 28, 1986. We are both members of the Lakewood [California] Congregation. Berta, first, I'd like to get a background of your family.

My ancestors, that I know anything about, were converted to the Mormon church in the 1860s, both on my father's and mother's side. Her grandparents were converted in Denmark and came to the United States, and went to Utah in the early days of the Mormon church there. My father's people were converted in England. Actually, there is a lot of the Restoration in our background, but, up to the time when I was born, I am not aware that [my] parents were especially religious. We did have a large family. There were six in my family, and I am the next to the youngest. We did not have access to church because we lived on a ranch (that was in the summertime), and it was too far. The only way we had to get there was to go by horseback, so there was not that much religion in the family.

Berta Bennett Ruoff Nogel. Used with permission of the Nogel family.

Did you have any brothers or sisters?

There were six of us. I have a sister, and there were four brothers. One of my brothers is now deceased. We had an interesting family life. Actually, we lived very much like a pioneer family. We lived on a ranch, and most of the year we lived in a small log cabin and did all the chores which go along with ranch life. A very interesting life as a matter of fact. In my early school years, I had to ride a horse six miles each way to attend elementary school—my brothers and sister did also. Rather late in the fall each year, around the first of November, my family would move into the little farming community where the school was located, and, from then until about the first of May or maybe late April the next year, we would live close to school where we could walk to school. Those were rather interesting experiences—having no way to get out of that ranch, except by horseback or by farm wagon. If we wanted to go as a family, we had to go in the farm wagon and ford the river six times in order to get to the community.

Where was this?

This was in Daggett County, Utah, at a little town named Manila. It was a very rural, frontier type of existence.

And when were you born?

I was born in 1920. I was born on that ranch.

How long did you live there?

Our home was there until I married. I did come to California to go to school in my teen years, and that was my first experience in a big city—my first experience away from home. My first trip to California was in 1934, when I was fourteen years old. I came on a bus, and I was just petrified with fear, because I knew nothing about city life. Fortunately, my sister, who had married a few years earlier, had to move to Compton, California, and she wanted me to come and stay with them and go to school, because she thought the educational opportunities were much better in California than in Manila. So I came here for several years, and stayed with her family, and attended high school. I also attended Compton College. It was while I was attending Compton College that I first became acquainted with the Reorganization.

And how did you become acquainted with it?

It was interesting that while my family was not religious, I had been baptized into the Mormon church. I considered myself a Mormon, a Latter-day Saint, and I remember that one year, when I was in the junior year of high school, our school bus would go down Olive Street (which is now Alondra Street in Compton), and I noticed there was this tremendous tent, and it had a sign on it, "Reorganized Church of Jesus Christ of Latter Day Saints." I thought, "Well, I wonder how come it's 'Reorganized.'" I really thought it was the Mormon church, and I wondered why they would have the word "Reorganized" in the title.

We traveled back and forth past that spot the whole school year, and I didn't know anything more about the church that was meeting in this tent. In the spring, when school was out, I went back to my home in Utah. The next year, my senior year of high school, I spent at home. I was seventeen. I had finished high school and had come back to Compton to go to college, and I was riding the bus in the same direction, when I noticed that the tent was gone, but there was a storefront building with the same sign. And so, it was obvious that they had moved their headquarters to this storefront building, which was just about a block from the first location. I didn't think too much about it—as I say, we hadn't been in the habit of going to church.

As I remember during my childhood, I only went to Sunday school a few times, and I didn't consider it a real fun thing to do when I did go. One day, a very close girlfriend and I were planning our weekend activities. We always went someplace and did something on the weekend. Maybe we'd go to the movies, maybe we'd go to Long Beach, or maybe we'd go to the beach. Whatever we felt like doing we would do, but she was one who usually went to church—to Sunday school—before she struck out on these other activities. So, she invited me to go to Sunday school with her, and I said I would be glad to. I had gone to Sunday school with her before, a couple of years earlier in a church that was located in Compton but was down on Long Beach Boulevard. She came by my house, and we walked to church, and what do you know—it was the Reorganized Church of Jesus Christ of Latter Day Saints. I thought this was pretty interesting because I really thought that this was the church I belonged to.

When we got inside, we went to our Sunday school class and then, after church was over, I had an opportunity to talk to the pastor, who was elder William Moyle. I told him that I was a Mormon, and he said, "Oh, yes, that church is located over in...." I've forgotten the section of Compton where all the houses were Spanish-style, white with red roofs. It was rather a nice section of Compton. I knew that church was there because I had attended it once, but not having formed the habit of going to church, had never gone back. But, on this first occasion of going to the Reorganized Church of Jesus Christ of Latter Day Saints, I found out that there was a difference between it and the regular Latter-day Saints church. I also found that the people were very, very, friendly, warm, loving and caring. I was invited back by any number of people, who took the time and effort to greet me, and to make sure that I felt comfortable, and who introduced me to the people there.

So I continued going there, both my girlfriend and I, and another girlfriend also attended. They were not members of the church, as I was not, but we attended all that winter, and it was there that I met the man who was to become my husband. He was a priest at that time. His name was Carl Ruoff, and he was the teacher of the—we called it the young people (it wasn't called the Zion's League then). But, he was the teacher of the young people's class, and I thought he was an extremely interesting man. He was very well educated and seemed to have a world of knowledge stored up in his head.

I think the thing that really kept me coming was the fact that this group of people were so warm and caring. The young people were really nice, and they always had a lot of activities going. They were a very active social group. They went on picnics, went to the beach, and did all the kinds of things that young people like to do. I had met Carl, who was to become my husband, but he was not there very long. It was only a couple of months, and he went back to attend the Theological Seminary in Chicago, so I didn't see him again until next summer, but I kept going to all the social events. Sometimes, I would think, "Well, I'm not really sure that I like church all that much," and then I wouldn't go for a few weeks.

There was this very wonderful person whom you probably would know, Vinnia—Laura Packard. She would walk seven or eight blocks down to my home, and knock on the door, and tell me what was happening—that there was this young people's party or this beach party, or an ice cream social, or whatever was going to occur, and she would invite me to come. I would usually end up going when she would invite me, because I always felt very impressed that she would walk so far, and care so much, and would invite me to come.

Through the winter months, there were more things happening, because I began to be very interested in what was said. Not only were their people kind and warm and caring, but they made me feel very welcome. I had another social group that was also very warm and caring, that I did things with, so that was not all that important to me, but, I began to listen to the things that were being said, and I began to learn the differences between the two churches. I didn't really know that much about the early history of the Latter Day Saint movement, or about Joseph Smith and his experiences, but it was through my attendance at Compton that I began to learn all these things. I found it very, very fascinating.

Was there anything in particular that caught your attention?

The experiences that Joseph Smith had really meant a lot to me—that God would speak in this day and age, and that he spoke to a young boy, who, I would say, was in my age group, and that he revealed such a marvelous work. I was very impressed by that. Then I began to learn more about such things as the ordinances. I knew about communion and that sort of thing, but I didn't know anything about administration for the sick. I went to some of the prayer services, and some of the people had such marvelous things to tell of the experiences they had had. I began to have a desire to have some experiences like this. They were very meaningful to me. I began to learn about administration to the sick, and to hear about these people who were healed when they administered to, and I thought that was a wonderful thing.

Then, I knew of a little boy, one of the Compton members' small son who got his finger caught in the hinge side of the door which was slammed shut, and his finger was completely crushed. It was flat and thin as a piece of paper. They had been visiting in the home of one of the elders at that time, and he administered to this child immediately. When I saw the child three days later, the finger looked absolutely normal. It did not have anything but a tiny red spot on it, and, to me, that seemed like a marvelous healing. I knew that fingers probably would heal from things like this, but I thought it would take a great deal longer, and that the nail would come off, and it would look very, very, bad. But his finger was completely healed.

I heard all the testimonies of these lovely people as, once in a while, I would go to prayer service. In those days, everybody knelt for prayer. They were on their knees, and I found that very difficult. I'd get so tired. I thought, "I'm never going to prayer service again; that is just too hard and just too uncomfortable," but then I'd find myself going again so I could hear these wonderful things. That's how I became acquainted with the church.

And then you mentioned the young man that was going to become your husband. Tell me about that.

The following summer I had decided to stay in California rather than go home. I had an opportunity to work for an elderly couple, and I had never spent a summer in California, and I rather wanted to be there during those months. The young people had elected me as president of the young people's organization at the congregation, and Carl had been the young people's leader prior to his going back to Chicago. He occasionally would write me a letter, because he had learned that I was the young people's leader. So, we had a correspondence going.

When he came back to Compton, he came to see me, and we started dating, and the following year we were married. It was rather an interesting courtship, because I was a nonmember, and he was a very active priesthood member. He was a very talented speaker and was invited to many congregations as a guest speaker. I always went with him on those Sundays, and I got acquainted with people all over the district (it was not a stake at that time). I found I knew people in Covina, Burbank, Ventura, Long Beach, San Diego, and Santa Ana. I found the people, wherever I went, to be very warm and loving.

There was one experience that I failed to tell you about, that occurred during that first year—that first year after I became acquainted with the church group. There was a missionary series that was conducted by Harold Velt, who was a marvelously intelligent man. He told of the America that the series was about, the people who lived on this continent prior to Columbus. It was about the Book of Mormon and the coming forth of the church. It seemed like such a marvelous thing the way it had all happened, and I was very impressed. I remember going from door-to-door distributing leaflets for this series and even got my brother to drive me. He was not at all interested in the church, but he would take me around, and I would go up one street and down another distributing leaflets. When the series was being held, people came from all over the community. There was standing room only. There were not enough seats to seat all the people who came. I found myself really being drawn into it and really believing. I was not an unwilling person, because it seemed to ring so true.

I started attending the church in 1937, and, in 1939, my husband and I were married. For quite a long time after that, in fact, probably throughout our married life, he was a frequent guest speaker in many congregations. We always went together. But, more than that, his ministry took him into many homes where I got to know people closely. He was very devoted in his ministry, in that he went so much to the shut-ins and to the sick people. I really got an opportunity to see the best things that he, and [the] people that were administered to, did every time that the person being administered to did receive a blessing. They were not only comforted, they were made to feel the closeness of God in the life of God's people. Many, many times they actually got physical blessings, as well, that helped them through their illnesses and through their times of trials. Those were very meaningful days to me.

When were you baptized?

You know, it almost seems as though I was a member, because I was involved in a lot of things. As a matter of fact, that fall after I was married, I was teaching a Sunday school class. I had about ten junior-age youngsters, both girls and boys who were ten, eleven, [and] twelve, or nine, ten, and eleven—I'm not sure. I was teaching from the old quarterlies, and most of them were about the Bible, so I was really getting an education myself learning so much that I had never known about the Bible. I don't think we had a Bible in our home as I grew up, though, we did have a Book of Mormon. But then, I think, that fall or sometime during that year, I was asked to teach the women's department class. We went through a course on the Book of John which was very revealing to me, and, to this day, because of that experience, the Book of John has great meaning to me, and I know it better than any of the books in the Bible. It has more scriptures that I can relate to than any other of the books in the Bible, and the narrative parts of it I can recall better because of that experience.

Actually, I was not baptized until July 1944, and this was about seven years after becoming acquainted with the church. Part of the reason that it was so long was that the first year that I became involved, and after Brother Velt's series, I had wanted to be baptized, but even though I was eighteen, I was still a minor, because the law hadn't changed then, so I didn't feel that I ought to do it without consulting my parents. I wrote to them and told them my wishes, and they wrote back expressing a desire for me to wait and give it more thought, and not to be baptized, because, even though they were not active Mormons, their hearts really belonged to the Mormon church, especially my mother. My dad had never been baptized, but all of his people were Mormons, and he identified with the Mormon church. After I had studied and studied, I thought, "Oh my, I am just so imperfect, I don't think I should be baptized. I'm just not a good enough person." And I kept putting it off, thinking "I'm just not worthy to be a child of God. I just don't think I'm worthy of that."

We had our first child in 1942, and a brother, a devoted, dear talented man who was a friend of my husband from his home town of St. Joseph, Missouri, came and stayed with us for a couple of days. He said, "How is it that you haven't joined the church yet? You seem like a member. You do everything as though you are a member, but you haven't been baptized." That really set me to thinking, and, then, some other dear friends talked to me and said "You know, you just can't expect to be perfect all at once. You can't be perfect before you're baptized. After you are baptized, you gain strength and greater talents for perfecting yourself."

During this period of time, the Compton Saints had been building a church. I knew that I would be baptized, but I wanted to be baptized in our own congregation. Up until that time, everyone had to go to Long Beach to be baptized, because they had a baptismal font, and we didn't. It wasn't until 1944 that we finally installed a baptismal font, and we had our first baptism. I don't remember how many people were baptized at that time, but I know I was the first one in. I think there were something like fifteen people baptized, because everyone had been waiting for this font to be built, and so it finally was an accomplished fact. We were very active. My husband, as a matter of fact, was the presiding elder at that time and was presiding elder for four years. At a later time, he was presiding elder another four years, so we were really very deeply involved in congregational life.

You mentioned your oldest child was born. How many children do you have and what are their names?

My first child was born in March of 1942 and was named for his father, Carl Frederick Ruoff Jr. My second child, Sidney Vincent, was born prematurely in February of 1943, and he lived only a few hours. In 1945, my daughter Karen Lynn was born, and in 1948, another daughter, Marcia Gaye, was born. Another son, Sherwin Lane, was born in 1951, and then, six years later, we had born to us another son, Robert Warner. Our youngest daughter, Kimberly Jean, was born in 1961.

Altogether, we had born to us seven children, six of whom survived to become adults. Most of them have not been active in the church since their adult lives or since they left home. None of them have joined other churches, but none of them are active at this time except my daughter Kimberly, who would be very active, except that she is in school and working full time. She is active when she is here. Whenever she has time and can, she makes it to church and really loves the church a lot.

I was quite impressed with the testimony that she gave on the thirtieth year anniversary on the tape that we produced.

Oh, yes, yes, she's had some wonderful experiences.

I know that Carl has passed away. When was this?

Carl died of cancer in 1976. Therein lies a rather marvelous story that indicated to me God's continuing concern over my life. There have been periods in my life when I felt very confused, and it seemed I didn't have answers. I knew that I was frustrated and confused, I was overworked, too, because I had a large family, and it seemed like there were always so many problems to be addressed. I sometime would pray on my knees asking for answers and never feeling sure that I really got answers.

I would like to go back for just a minute to an experience that occurred early in my married life. It was after I had had several children and I don't remember just what year, but I know I had several small children and this was not a time of confusion. I felt really good about life, I felt good about my membership in the church and about all that we were doing, and especially interested in my family and my role as a parent. I remember on one occasion at night that I knelt to say my prayers, it seemed as though this was the most peaceful night that I had ever experienced, that there was peace wrapped around me, if that is possible. It was dark, and I knelt to God, and I prayed to him. And as I was praying, I was thinking how often I had communicated with him, how often he had heard my prayers, and how wonderful it would be to hear from God.

As I finished my prayer, I had expressed those thoughts, though not really expecting to hear his voice, because I know that God speaks in many ways, but as I got into bed, it seemed like the quietness was so intense and I was listening. I didn't hear a voice, but I saw before me, pictures, as if they were projected onto the wall by a slide projector. Here was a scene of beautiful mountains, a scene of a lake, a scene of a brook running through a woodland, a scene of hills and meadows—just one right after another until there must have been thirty or forty of these scenes. I saw not only God's marvelous creation, but I saw cities and buildings created by man, and things that made me think it was a war-torn condition where there had been destruction like earthquakes and tornados, and such as that.

So many different pictures came, and when it was over, I lay there thinking about it. We need never ask to hear God's voice, because God is speaking to us continually in every place and in all circumstances. Those were the thoughts that came to me from this experience—that wherever you are, you can expect to realize that God is speaking out of that environment, out of those circumstances, and those surroundings.

As time went on, there were other experiences I had. I remember that one particular occasion—I think it was 19.... I can identify this one, because I remember that I was pregnant at that time with my second daughter, so it must have been late 1947 or early 1948, when I was suffering from a very severe respiratory condition. I had been ill, not bedfast, I was able to get around, but I had been ill for a least two weeks with no evidence of it lessening or becoming better, and I was afraid to go to sleep at night, because I was by myself struggling for breath. It was just a very frightening thing for me, and I felt so sick, so discouraged about it, that I found myself being very cross with my children and with my husband. My husband was a German, and if anyone was cross with him, he was cross back—even though he was a good, dear man. We would have arguments, and we would be cross with each other. I knew that I probably should be administered to, but I felt that unless I could control my temper and be kinder and less critical to my family, I really was not worthy of a blessing and would have to struggle through somehow on my own.

One night, it was in the middle of the night, I was sitting on the edge of my bed struggling to breathe and feeling totally miserable, and I said to God, "I really do need help and don't know how to get, or how to be the kind of person that really should get help." At that moment, my husband awoke, and he said, "Berta, why don't you be administered to?" And I said, "Well, I would like it, but I don't know that I'm worthy."

He then told me an experience that he had. As he was dreaming, a voice came to him and said, "Wake up and administer to your wife." He knew, of course, that I had been cross with him, and that he had been cross with me, and that is not a good condition. But he saw a hand take a bit of soap and put on his tongue, and a bit of soap on my tongue, and that was, to both of us, a testimony of God's forgiveness. My husband Carl administered to me, and, within seconds, I was breathing freely. And, to this day, I have never had a respiratory condition where I was stopped up and could not breathe.

That has been many, many years ago, and I have often felt that when God gives a healing, he gives a good one. I have had other respiratory problems, but I've never had one like that. On one occasion this occurred prior to the experience I have just related. This happened during the war when my husband was working for the Union Pacific Railroad. Sometimes he worked nights, and sometimes he worked day and night, as a lot of people did during the war. On this particular occasion, he was working at night, and I was home alone with our small child. It was cold that night, and I had put a heating pad in bed to warm up the bed for my feet, because I had a tendency to suffer from the cold. I remember that it wasn't heating fast enough, so I turned it on high and had dropped off to sleep. In the middle of the night, I heard someone shout my name "Berta!" And I woke up. I thought it was my husband—that he had forgotten his key and was unable to get in. So I went to the front door to let him in, but he wasn't there. I was very puzzled. When I went back to my bed, my sheet was beginning to scorch from the heating pad, and I knew that I had been protected, and that there was a possibility that I could have burned to death that night.

As time went on, there were many occasions when we had marvelous blessings. I remember in 1957, I was pregnant with our third son, and my husband had been laid off his job. Things were very grim for us financially, since we had no savings because, with such a large family, you live from hand-to-mouth it seems. He was on a new job and had not been able to acquire any savings or seniority at work, and no sick leave, and he was stricken with an ailment that was crippling him. Something happened to him that crippled his hip, and he was unable to walk, which meant that he could not go to work.

With my help he was able to get into the car and drive to the doctor, and I had to go along to help him into the doctor's office. At first he could get around a little bit, but it continued to get worse until he couldn't get around at all. He couldn't even get into the car to get to the doctor, and I didn't drive, and our money was about all gone. We were both greatly worried, and he was bedfast. One troubled night … all of a sudden I was awakened, and there was my husband on his feet dressed and ready to go to work. He said, "I'm going work this morning, Berta. I have been healed, and I have no pain at all."

He could walk normally, naturally, with no limp at all. He told me that during the middle of the night—this was a vision, not something that actually happened—he said that he had seen a white car drive up in front of the house and, from that car, a personage in white had gotten out and had come right through the wall into the bedroom, and had taken hold of his foot and moved it back and forth, and the pain had gone away. The personage went out the same way that she had come—it was a woman—and got into the car and drove away. He said, from that moment, he had no pain. It was gone, and it never came back.

From that day on, he was a well person. He never needed to go to the doctor until his final illness in 1976, when he did get cancer and died. He had a wonderful life and had many wonderful blessings. I realized after his passing how greatly I had been blessed, not only because of his presence, but because God had prepared me for his death in a way that I was not even aware. I have raised this family of six children and never had a day of employment, other than working for a few months for an elderly couple just helping them to take care of their house. I had never paid any of the bills or done any of the shopping, as this was all done by my husband. I had taken care of the house and the children, and had done quite a few things at the church. But other than this, I had no experience that would enable me to survive with two teenage children who were dependent on their parents.

Several years prior to the time he died, I was hired as a teacher in a children's center, and I began having money that I could work with, and that I could budget and do things with, so that I learned to handle money. Not only that, it gave me a job, so I could support myself and my children if necessary. It was not necessary at that time, but I didn't have all the experience necessary to make the home run financially. A few years after I was employed, I was promoted to directorship for a California State Children's Center where I began to get managerial experience. I had to do the budget and the whole thing for the school. I also did the buying and everything, which was a good experience for me. At the time I didn't realize how important it was going to be for me later on.

At the time my husband passed away in 1976, I was earning enough money to support myself and the children. When I look back, I can see how God has moved in my life to prepare me for this event … even though I never dreamed my husband was going to die at that time, because he had been an unusually healthy person, had never gone to doctors, and had never been ill other than a cold or something like that. It seemed to me he was so strong, that even though he was quite a few years older than I, he surely would outlive me. There was one time I dreamed that I saw my husband in death, and I thought that was a very strange dream, because I felt it was not going to happen, as I was very sure that he was going to outlive me.

But when he became ill suddenly, I remembered that dream, and I thought, perhaps, there was meaning in that dream after all, as it came to me that he had cancer. He hadn't been to a doctor and been diagnosed, yet I felt certain that he had cancer. He came from a family where there was a lot of cancer, and, when he began to tell me some of the things that were bothering him, I could see that he was really ill, even though he had gone back to work after his retirement and was working a full eight hours a day. He worked right up to within two and a half weeks of the day he died. Finally he said, "Okay, you have been begging me to go to the doctor, so I'll go."

I took him. This was just a couple of weeks before he died, although he had been ailing and not feeling well for several weeks ... the doctor took one look at him and knew he had cancer. He didn't even have to examine him. I don't know how he knew, as my husband had not wasted away. He was thinner, and he had a haggard look, but not the wasted look many other cancer patients have. A few days later, I admitted him to the hospital to undergo a series of tests, and, within a week and a half, he was gone. He passed away, and I felt that he was greatly blessed, because so many cancer patients suffer such excruciating pain.... The last three or four days of his life he did have great pain, but, up until that time, he had not had to have anything but an aspirin.

The last three days, the doctors put him under sedation, but it was a marvelous experience to me, because ... when I read back on his patriarchal blessing, it said that even the angels would hold him up and that God would turn and overturn for his sake. I have often felt that that was true, as he was spared so much of the suffering that he most likely would have gone through if it hadn't been for his great faith. Through his whole life he had been blessed so greatly.

He told me of an experience he had on his baptismal day that was indicative and that helped shape his life. His parents were very poor and lived on a farm near St. Joseph, Missouri. Carl had appendicitis and had been ill for several weeks, and the doctor had been called, because the mother was very ill, and, as you know, a large family struggling along without a mother is a very difficult situation. While the doctor was there, Carl's father asked him to look at Carl, and he found Carl's side very red and swollen and with a great deal of pain. As a matter of fact, he could hardly walk around and was lying around most of the time, because he felt so ill. The doctor said, "This child has appendicitis, and you must bring him to the hospital immediately for surgery, because if he goes much longer it will surely burst."

My husband had not been baptized at that time, and his parents were German who belonged to the Lutheran church before they joined the Reorganization. They, of course, had come out of a church which believed in infant baptism. They knew that was not right, yet, baptism to them was [the] most important thing. He had become old enough to be baptized in the church, but it hadn't been done. They hadn't gotten around to it, and his father was very worried: "What if my son should die while he's in the hospital, and he hasn't been baptized?"

Both he and his wife felt that way, so he rode into town on the spring wagon and got an elder to come out to baptize Carl in a pond that was located on the farm. After he was baptized, his father asked him, "How do you feel?" and Carl said, "I feel good, I feel fine." The swelling and redness were gone, and there was no pain left. He had received a healing on the occasion of his baptism. The next day when the doctor came to [take] him to the hospital, he saw Carl and some boys playing ball.... He rushed into the house and said, "Mr. Ruoff, your son is in very serious condition, and if his appendix breaks, then I will hold you personally responsible for this child's death."

My father-in-law smiled and said to him, "The boy is healed. He is well and doesn't have appendicitis now." The doctor wanted to know how that could be, and he told him the experience. The doctor said, "Well, God has a way of doing things the doctors cannot do." So even though he had had appendicitis at an early age, and it was very serious, he never again had an attack of appendicitis and was a very healthy man.

I realize this is an experience of your husband, but you have mentioned experiences that you have had that were very trying, and to what did you reach for your sources of strength?

There was always God. But more than that were the people of the church. They were so giving and so loving, and always rallied around you in your hours of need. In our times of trouble, they were always there to give us encouragement and strength. I went through a period of time where I felt somewhat disillusioned, very discouraged, and there were problems that I can't even discuss on this tape, but it was making an inroad on my faith.... There was a period of time that I didn't even feel like going to church, and I did stay away for quite a long time, but, during that period of time, I learned there were no other answers. I think this was why I was discouraged—because I was not getting answers to some of the problems that I had, and I felt that God was just not concerned with me, not giving me answers. During this period of time, there was an emptiness in my life that went beyond anything I can describe, and my lack of hope grew deeper and greater, and I realized there were no answers, except through God and through his plan and his way. I knew there would be times when I would not get answers to all my questions or problems, but that God was always there, and he was always concerned, and if I worked things through that, enough answers would come to help me through my times of trouble and to reassure me. That has always been true.

As I look back on it—the thing that has been the most reassuring to me—I have agonized over the fact that there were times when I felt the church was not moving ahead. We do not have the spiritual quality that we once had. I've had some misgivings and then comes the answer, "But it's the only thing that really works." War doesn't work, nor contention, arguing or fighting. The ... things that create peace and lasting tranquility, and ... answers to life's problems are the very things that Jesus outlined. The things that have always freed me from doubt and discouragement are the things of Christ, and ... the things he said: "Christ, the Son, shall make you free," and "You shall be free indeed."

Sometimes when I have thought of that scripture, I have heard the chains falling off people, the chains that have bound their minds, their thinking, their actions. It is true that he frees us from fear, from doubt and from anger—all the crippling chains that seem to bind us, and keep us little, and from experiencing greatness. If we trust him and believe in him, those chains will fall away.

I have loved that scripture, and the scripture "God so loved the world that He gave His only Son that whosoever believeth in Him shall not perish, but have everlasting life." Also, the word of Christ when he was speaking of the time that Moses lifted up the serpent on a stick while in the wilderness, and he said, "If I be lifted up, [I] will draw all men unto me." That is a wonderful promise and it has helped me when I look about and see the world in great distress because of crime and violence. Christ never gave up on anybody. He said, "I will draw all men unto me." Even those who are doing terrible things, there is still hope for them through Christ.

These scriptures are very inspiring to me. I know that I am not a perfect person, and I am a sinful person, but there is hope for me because, regardless of what I have done, he hasn't given up on me. When I found my way back to the church and became involved, that hope burn[ed] brightly again, and it's only when I disassociate myself from him and from his people that the flame flickers pretty low.

I know you've married again. Tell us about that.

After my husband's death, I was a widow for four years. I had never been alone in my life, having lived in a large family and having raised a large family, so this was a very hard thing for me to deal with … I realized that as old as I was when my husband died, the likelihood of finding a companion was rather remote, and I might not ever find a companion, but I did not want to live alone. I have children, but they have their lives. I had one or two relationships when I dated men, but they were not satisfactory experiences.

One night, I just knelt to God and prayed, "Lord, I'm not looking anymore." I was not going to subject myself to the singles scene that so many single people go through. I wasn't going to go through that, because, to me, it was a demeaning experience, and I thought, if I shall ever have a companion, the Lord would have to send someone to me, because I was not going to look any further. I thought I would be lonely, but I would not be looking.

It was maybe a week later when one of my friends called me and asked if I would like to meet a nice person who had lost his wife and who was very lonely. It was someone in the church who called me, and this was someone she knew about. I said, "Well, I'm planning a trip to Guadalajara, Mexico, and I'll be gone a couple of weeks." She wanted to get a dinner group together so we could have an opportunity to meet … a few days later [after my trip] arrangements were made for a group of us to go to a restaurant for dinner, and this was where I met my wonderful husband, Don.

We were friends at first, and I learned many things from him about his family. I got to meet his two children who are very fine people. As a matter of fact, it was his daughter who was acquainted with this church friend of mine, and, because she was concerned about her father and his loneliness, she had talked to my friend and asked her if she knew anyone that might become a friend to her father. My friend said that she didn't know anyone right then, but afterward, she remembered that I was single. It came to her that she shouldn't meddle in anyone's life, and she felt she wasn't a matchmaker and decided not to get involved. But the thought kept coming to her, to the point where she could not forget it and couldn't leave it alone, so it was then that she contacted Don's daughter and told her there was someone whom she felt her father might like to meet.

What was interesting was that, even though Don was not a member of the church, he was Christian and he believed in God. He had been praying that he would meet someone that could be a companion for him. Our relationship deepened into love, and in May of 1980, we were married. It's been a wonderful relationship. You know what they say about marriages being made in heaven—I really believe this one was, because we do get along so well, and we relate to each other, and understand each other, and are very supportive of each other.

Since that time, I've had the joy of seeing him baptized. I did take him to church with me, and we did go to classes together, but I never once suggested that he be baptized. I thought I would never pressure him to be baptized, because I had enough respect for him to feel that I could be happy with him, even if he were not a member of my church. We were married only a short time when he said, "I really need to be thinking about baptism, because we need to belong to the same church, and it will be better for us if we belong to the same church."

Since he was not active in a church at that time, it seemed very reasonable to him that he should join mine. Brother Craig Crownover came and helped him with some of the doctrinal points about our church, and the differences, and instructed him. He was baptized in October 1980, the year that we were married. In 1984, he was ordained to the Melchisedec priesthood. It's been a marvelous experience and very reassuring to me. It has helped me to realize more keenly than ever before, that God never gives up on people, that he is concerned about each of us, and regardless of what we have done that we feel is not worthy he will lead us back, if we give him a chance. He will forgive over and over again … if we keep on trying, and I honestly believe in that.

In recent years I've seen the church change. When I first joined the church, there was a great emphasis on, at least in our congregation, the differences between our church and other churches. There was also a lot of emphasis on church history—how our church came into being. I've seen the emphasis shift, and now the church is not emphasizing the differences between us, but how we relate to other Christian groups and how there are many of the samenesses. The emphasis has come to be more than a telling of the Restoration and how it came into being, into an implementation of the concepts that we have always had about Christ, and why he came into the world. I see the church now trying so hard in so many ways to implement all those things that Christ talked about—of the caring, loving concern that he had for others, actually making people free, and of people who are lonely and disadvantaged, homeless and hungry. Now our church is emphasizing that we must become a people who implement the words of Christ when he told in the synagogue that he had come to be that person and we in turn can become as Christ in the lives of others. I believe that he has no hands but our hands, and that he must rely on us to bring the love of Christ into the lives of others.

It has been wonderful interviewing you, and I have been very much impressed with your life, and hope to share it for many years.

Margaret Louise Canham

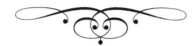

BORN
August 14, 1922/3, St. Davids, Ontario
DIED
March 30, 1995, Niagara Falls, Ontario

Interviewed by M. Galbraith and H. Sevis, on May 1, 1986,
in Niagara Falls, Ontario

Okay, Margaret, can you tell us some of your earliest memories of the church? How did you come to be a member?

Martin Ware used to come to our house, him and Gertie, and they used to come every Sunday for a visit. At that time, we had a special room in the house. The living room was always kept special for these kinds of occasions. We would go in and have a nice visit with them, every Sunday.

When we decided to be baptized, there were nine [eight] of us got baptized at once. Including my mother and father, there was thirteen of us all together [in the family]. Our two grandfathers lived with us, so it made fifteen, so we never had an even count. But eleven of us were children. Most of the family got baptized all at one time, so it was a very special occasion…. Brother Davis from Michigan came and he baptized us all. At my confirmation, Martin Ware said that it was in my confirmation that I was called to be a teacher.... Well, first of all, the day we were baptized, we, also, were confirmed that night—a real big lineup on the platform with people and priesthood taking all in [the count].

Could we have the names of your family?

That were baptized? There was my father, my mother, Gertrude, and Leonard, and Howard, and myself, and Hazel, and Ormond were all baptized at that time. And so it was a real big day for us all. I'm sure Brother Davis was quite thrilled to be baptizing so many people.

You were baptized at the falls at the church?

At the church at Niagara Falls, yes. Brother Davis came from Michigan. He was a relative on my mother's side.

How did you become interested in the church? How did Martin and Gertie Ware start coming to your house ... to talk to you about the church?

Well, my mother knew Martin and Gertie when she was young. They chummed together a lot when they were young, and they used to go down to the falls and that sort of thing. So they'd known Martin for a long time, and mother knew of the church for a long, long time.

Through your relatives?

No, through Martin and Gertie. And also the relatives. Through her sister in Michigan, and her sister's husband, which was our uncle Armand [Alma]. He was a minister in the church in Uttley, Michigan.

How do you spell your uncle's name?

Alma. A L M A.

And Brother Davis. What was his first name?

I think it was Alma, too. I'm not positive, but I think it was Alma. Anyway, it was a real moving experience to go through.

So, the following Sunday when I arrived at church, I sat in the Sunday school class waiting to be taught, and Arnold [Ware] approached me and asked me to be a Sunday school teacher. I … can still see myself sitting there, about where I sit in church today, in Sunday school today, and I can still see him leaning forward and saying to me, "Margaret, we need a Primary Sunday school teacher. Would you take that class?"

I said, "Me? I need to be taught, not to teach."

He said, "Well, you're directed to teach a class…. My dad confirmed this. In your confirmation it came through."

Sounds like preplanning.

Yeah, preplanning is right, eh? Maybe they talked this over before I joined the church. I don't know. But they never to this day have said that.

Martin Ware wouldn't do that.

No, I don't think they would. I don't think Arnold would either. Anyway, then I went downstairs, and, where the piano sits now in the lower auditorium today, that's where I had a little bench for the children. There were six of them.

Barbara and John Stoner were two of them that I had at that time. I sat on a little chair to their level. They didn't have a quarterly, and I taught from a little, wee, tiny pocket Bible. It had just some little passages out of the Bible in it. Audrey had given me this some time ago in a little card that she gave. This little Bible was in it. But, of course, I had never known that it was going to be used for this. But anyway, I based my first lesson on it.

Do you remember who else were your students?

No, I can't remember at that time. I was trying to figure out who else was around that age, but I can't just offhand tell you. I remember definitely the two of them [Stoners], whether it's because they were brother and sister that I remember it. And John, you know, with all his pocketful of toys and marbles and elastic bands. You name it, he had it. I had that handful or pocketful before I finished the class. I often thought I never got through to the class, because I was so busy collecting things to hand Doris [John's mother] after the classes. Doris never came back to me about it. I never had any problem with her. She accepted them. I don't know if she ever scolded John, but he still came with things. She would be amazed when I gave her some more the following Sunday, because she said, "I went through his pockets before he left [for] church. I don't know where he got them."

But anyway, this is one of the things that he did. I don't know whether he wanted to draw your attention or not. I thought I never, ever taught him anything, because I was always so busy taking stuff away from him that he was always playing with. But, anyway, when he grew up, he told me that I was one of his favorite teachers. He did grow up to be a very, very nice young lad. I'm sorry that the accident occurred that took his life, but he did grow up to be a very nice young man.

What accident was that?
An airplane. His first flight. He got his pilot's license, and, in his first flight, he and a friend took off, and then he crashed into some cottage or something and took both of their lives. That was a sad thing to happen.

Since then I've had many classes. Since then I've had as high as twenty-five in my class, which is quite a few people. But [at] that time, we had one hundred in attendance at our Sunday school, so we had a good attendance.

One of my favorite people during Sunday school times was Charlie VanMeer. Charlie couldn't—it's sad that he couldn't really read well. But, he knew a lot. What he did read, he learned a lot from it. He was a master at being a Sunday school superintendent. I don't think we could ever surpass Charlie VanMeer as far as a Sunday school superintendent. You'd just request something, or tell him you needed something, or that you were having a problem. He just got in there and did something about it, and he wasted no time.

We had some of the nicest Sunday school picnics we ever had with Charlie. And your Sunday school material was always there. He just was ready to give you anything and do anything to make the classes interesting for you. He always came and checked you every

Sunday to see that everything was in order, and that everybody was behaving themselves, you know.

My routine was: I used to start them out. If they acted up, they had to sit beside the teacher. Well, then, there got to be too many acting up when you got to twenty-five, you know. Then, they knew that two of them were already taken down by the teacher, so not many more could get there. So anyway, from then on, I started putting boy, girl, boy, girl. They sure didn't want to be straightened out then. That took care of that.

Another method was, the best way to get them was to keep silent. Silence is a virtue, because it really works. If a teacher isn't saying anything, what's happening? You know. Everybody looks, because the teacher isn't saying anything. That makes them be quiet. And then they begin to listen. You only have to do that a couple of times, then they learn that you're going to do it.

I was a person of my word. When I said something, I meant it. And I carried it through. I didn't say, "We'll do this if you don't behave." I carried it through. So they realized that it was pay attention or else.

Did they still have, or did they then have opening exercises sort of like we do now?

Exactly the same as we have now. Opening exercises.

Did Charlie VanMeer do them every week?

Every week. Nobody else took his place. Charlie was always there. He took the opening exercises every single week.

We had promotion Sunday, …. The way he had it systemized, it was really good, because … The adults sat on the left, and the children automatically came into Sunday school. They came in, and they came to their class. The teachers sat at the end of each pew, and the children filed in. I had two rows because with twenty-five, I had two rows. The children filed in according to the classes, and the teachers sat in the row where the children were to come in. As they came, they did not go and sit with their parents and that. They sat in the classes, as the classes were. We filed downstairs the same way—class by class. The senior classes would go out first because they were at the back, and then we'd file in that way. That's the way we did our Sunday school then—in a real orderly fashion. And Bill [Stoner] used to play a real marching piece that got you really on the march, you know. They used to file out good with that, because it made you feel like marching.

I remember that. I can hear it now in my mind, you know?

Yes, and I keep intending to ask him why he isn't playing that anymore for us. It's got a real beat to it that makes you march.

On promotion day, Charlie would call out the names and all your pupils, see, were sitting with you. And when they were promoted from the little class, they automatically came and sat with me, even though it was tight sitting for that few minutes. Or I would go up and receive them, and bring them back to sit with me. That's how it went. And then, when my class was called up, the next teacher would go up and be there to receive her or his new members. And they'd take them back and file them in with theirs. That's the way he did it, a very orderly way.

But, they all got their promotions, and they got it by filing from one class to the next. That way they knew exactly where [to go]. Like today, they say, "You're going to go with Margaret," or "You're going to go with so-and-so." And they're here, there, and everywhere, and they don't really know. When they have a new teacher, they don't really know who that new teacher is, especially the little ones. They've got to find out who that new teacher is, and that's a confusion for them. This way, they are introduced and the teacher is right there beside Charlie when he calls out the names. So, he had a real systematic way of doing things.

Charlie worked at the dairy, Rainbow Dairy, which is just over the hill from here. He ... used to get ice cream for us for our picnics. That was Charlie's big thing— to give out ice cream cones to everybody at the Sunday school picnics. You can imagine if there were a hundred of us, and then some of the parents came—we had pretty big picnics. I have some movies to show from that, because we had some really super big picnics.

The races used to be real nice races. We had lots of good races and lots of nice prizes. I have pictures of Sadie Hart at one of them, where she was helping pick up peanuts, and she bent down to help her daughter, Sandra, pick up peanuts. When she saw the movie, she decided she didn't want to be in it. She saw me doing it, and said, "Not me." And she walked out. So I said to her when she saw the movie, "It's better to be in it, because you look better than you do if you try and march out, because you've got your hands full of peanuts, and we know what you got."

We had some really good picnics, very good. Charlie was a super Sunday school superintendent. He wasn't hard to talk to at all. I think everybody liked Charlie, and we miss him dreadfully.

Somebody else that was important in my life was Brother Njeim. He was a very wonderful person, and he was one of the highlights of our —.

Why was he so special to you?

Well, not only his sermons and everything, but he made a special point of coming to see me before he left Niagara Falls. I always feel he's there with me at different times, because he picked me out special, before he got on his way from Niagara Falls—in the very last five minutes of his stay in Niagara Falls. It was special to me, because, when somebody takes that much effort—to me, it's worth a lot, and it's meant a lot to my life.

Do you remember his first name?

It probably will come to me later. He was well known.

Tell us about some of the equipment that you made for your Sunday school class.

I made a church once, on a wooden frame. My Uncle Alma from Michigan was a carpenter, so he helped me to get the proper measurements to measure the height and everything to get the right scale for the building. The roof removed from it. It was of very stiff Bristol board. The roof came off so that you could teach from that. Inside, I had [fixed it] just like our church is. I had an organ and a piano in it, and the keyboard and the stool to sit on. The hymn board was up, and the baptismal font was there. And we had the priesthood ... standing at the front. Chuck Kornman was one. I had him there. He was one of our favorites at that time, and I had him there as a missionary....

What I did was, I took pictures of these people at the church—all the members and the priesthood, all the missionaries, and anybody I could get that came to our church. I'd get a picture, and then I cut the picture out, pasted it on a form, and made a stand for it. They'd stand up in there. I had all the pews and all the people: Sister McAninch; Brother and Sister Pailing; Martin and Gertie Ware; and Flossie. I had all those in it, and all the children as well. I had quite a few pictures in there of quite a few people.

You could teach from that—the baptism and everything. Then, they got to know about the priesthood. You could tell them then, "The pastor does this," and the pastor could be an elder, you know. In this case it was. It was Martin Ware. As a result, you could tell them what positions they held and what their duties were.

Chuck Kornman was their favorite at that time. And their favorite one went to camp at Port Elgin. He used to lower our tent, and raise our tent, and scare everybody. But he also protected. Because if it rained … your tent should be slack. You have to have it a certain way. I never knew that. But he'd come and collapse it pretty well on us in the morning, and startle all of us, especially the ones on the upper bunks when it started to come down, you know.

Would you take your class to camp?

Yes, and he would have a watermelon feast with us. I have movies of him doing it—eating watermelon with all of us out in front of the tent. It was a two-room tent. But the highlight of that were Mrs. Collins and Mary Lynne. They'd come and visit us at night.

Who are Mrs. Collins and Mary Lynne?

That was Nellie Towers's sister, Sarah. They used to go to camp. Mary Lynne stayed at a cottage someplace with her grandma. So, she came and visited us at night. If they were good, they had hot chocolate. And sometimes we went for treats, for ice cream. If there was somebody that wasn't good, they didn't get the treat. They had to go, but they didn't get the treat. There was a special dairy up the street. I know that sounds hard to take, but when you say something, you mean it. So, they learned that you just don't do it. Now Myra Scott was one of them. She was supposed to help me, but she left her suitcase out in the middle of the tent floor. The tent had a floor in it. She left her suitcase out in the middle of the floor, so she had to suffer punishment, too.

She was a counselor, wasn't she?

Yes, yes. She was to really be the example. So, therefore, she had to really suffer the consequences, and she didn't get [the treat]. That made a big hit with the rest of them, because Myra was supposed to know better, and we walked in and found a suitcase. She said, "Well, I didn't mean to." In fact, I talked to her today about it, and she said, "Well, I still didn't mean to." But it was cute the way she'd, you know, walk in there. Myra is really humorous, and when she came in—she knew she was guilty as soon as she walked in, because everybody was ready for her. They let her see how her suitcase was open, none the less, out there. But we had a lot of great times out there at Port Elgin reunion.

I have pictures of Chuck Kornman playing volleyball out there. And then I have Al Pelletier and his wife and child. We had quite good times when he was there, too. I have pictures of us all standing in the lineup waiting to go into dinner. They were quite a lot of fun to go to. These pictures are interesting to look at now, to look back at. That's when you realize that they are so alive. Some of them have passed away, but they are very much alive in those pictures. And the memories are certainly beautiful.

I can remember Halloween parties were another thing that was great with Charlie VanMeer. We used to have some tremendous Halloween parties. I remember going as a scarecrow once. I stood in the corner. Hazel went down early and prepared me, and then turned all the lights off and left me there in the dark. I'm telling you, it's a good thing I didn't have to stand with my arms out, because I think I would have collapsed. Here I was standing there, and there were sticks out the ends of the sleeves, see, across my shoulders. The kids would come up, and they'd look right into your eyes, see, into the mask—right into your eyes you know. And it was hard not to blink.

Arnold realized the torture I'd be going through, so he started putting chairs across so that the kids couldn't get that close to me anymore. It's hard not to blink or move if somebody's pushing their eyes right up to your eyes, you know. They wanted to know who it was, but I was dressed and left in the dark. When they turned on the light, I was there, all the hay around me and everything—hay coming out my sleeves and up my neck, and everything.

I got first prize. I didn't have to parade, but I got first prize. I watched the parade and everything. I got first prize, but you know what it was? They didn't know if I was a girl or a boy, so I got a bag of alleys [?]. I laugh today even about that, you know. Well, they said, "We didn't know what you were, so —." Well, anyway, when I had to unmask, everybody just screamed.

I remember that Louie and Betty [Stoner] came in as a horse that time, and they paraded around like a horse, you know. Betty was the back end ... and people kept trying to get on her back. That's the worst thing you can do, because that person is bent over in a funny position to hold onto his hips, you know. It's really hard on the back if anybody gets on there. Oh, boy, you're not ready for that kind of stuff.

Some other pictures that I have—Arnold [Ware] was dressed in a skirt and stuff, and he's bouncing a ball, and putting his leg over the ball. I said to him, "I know you've got blue shorts on," because the shorts showed underneath the skirt when he put his leg up over the ball. Audrey [Ware] came as a Chinese lady. She'd just shuffle her feet along, and she had this little fan, and was fanning herself. Dennis [Ware] came as a two-headed person. I still haven't figured out quite how he did that. I talked to him this Christmas about that, that he always came in as a two-headed [person]. I said to him, "You must have the brains of two." He hasn't told me yet just how exactly he did that, but that was outstanding, too.

We had some really good costumes that time. I'm sure it must have been hard for the ones who were judging—Martin Ware, and Gertie, and them—you knew some of the people, because they didn't have false faces on, for one thing. But it must have been hard to say, "Well, this is so and so." But, you know, that line was more than once around the basement, so we had a lot of people at our Halloween parties.

Did you have a lot of church socials?

Yes, we did. We had things like that. And then we had other so-cials. I have movies of where Sadie [Hart] is serving the lunch. And (again, I speak of Sadie) she runs out of the picture all the time, and that's why I keep saying, "Sadie." She got in the camera one time, and she noticed she was serving. I don't know why she ran … I hope she got everybody served. She came in by the camera and "Not me!" she said, and she ran to the kitchen. Here's the camera showing her run-ning to the kitchen, and all you get is the backside of Sadie. So I run it backwards, and I bring her back in the picture, and she's just about kicking herself all the way back. It's really hilarious to watch a person back up in it.

[It's] the same with the races and the Sunday school picnics—when they run, and you run the movie backwards, they're kicking themselves, you know. Their legs are just kicking right up. It's really hilarious to see them. And confetti at a wedding—at Chuck Korn-man's wedding. The confetti comes down nice, but, then, when you run it backwards, it all flips up real fast. And you know it goes right back in the bag. It's just like a piece of spaghetti, you know. It goes (slurp) right up. It's fun to have all these movies now and look at them. We'll have to have a fun night at the church and show some.

Some of the other things we did—oh, yes, Christmas parties, Christmas concerts. We used to have really good Christmas concerts, too, when Charlie was there. And we had Santa Claus. I have movies of that. It is really something how these children go up and see Santa. They're so timid. They walk up so gentle. Whose daughter went up was Mona's little girl. Well, not little girl—it's her first girl. She walks up to Santa, and she goes up so gentle and so careful. He goes to speak to her, and she takes the present, and runs right back. She just didn't want to be near Santa Claus, I guess. But, it was so cute how fast she grabbed the present and ran back. She left her bag of candy, and no way, was she going back after the bag of candy. She just ran right back, and it was really something. I really enjoy some of these movies we've got.

Do you think that the church is missing something now? We don't even have the children to have those kind of things anymore, and I wonder sometimes whether —.

Well, I sometimes think we don't have the children, but ... the children [we do have] are missing something when I see these pictures, and the parties we had and everything.

They put on a real concert, you know, just like they do now. They put on a concert, but each teacher prepared her own class, or two classes together to make a skit or two ... and there was a lot of recitations. And the adults at that time took part as well. It wasn't just the children, because they were in a Sunday School class, too, see. So, this helps the young children to know that this is all the church—everybody's Christmas party. We didn't have a children's Christmas party. We had a party for everyone, so everybody was included. Now everybody didn't get the bag of candy and a present.

I remember we used to go to Komeier's in Chippewa. We [all the teachers] went one night and picked out Christmas presents for our classes. We brought them home, and we wrapped them for our own classes. Each one took care of their own class. The candy was bought and bagged by somebody in the church, but each teacher did this for herself, you know.

The races at the picnics were done the same way. The teachers would automatically get out there, and their class would be called up to do their race. The teachers would stand out there, and the children would automatically know theirs. And if there were visitors, their age was brought out, and, then, they would come in there, too.

Tell us about your work with the Skylarks now.

The Skylarks. Well, I had two groups of those. I had one up on Badger Road. It was away off of Lundy's Lane, off of Montrose Road. And I had one at the church. The church [group] I had at one o'clock, and the one out on Badger Road at three. So, I'd have to catch the bus and go out to Badger Road. I worked until noon on Saturdays, so I'd come from work to the church and have the one group, and then, I'd go on through to the other group. And then, once a month, we would [all] meet at the church.

Both groups?

Yes. Because I felt it was good for them to know each other and to have that time together. It was easier to teach them as two different groups—crafts … and, also, anything else … because, as individuals, you could get closer and do more for them—like if you had to thread a needle, or help them thread a needle. It's harder to get around a great big group than it is a few at a time.

Did you have helpers?

I never had helpers, no. Just the ones that could do it, that could thread a needle, would show them how I thread a needle to any that didn't [know how], until they got to learn to do it, you know.

But I never took "can't," because that's a favorite word of children. I don't know, probably any age. Sometimes older children, too, I guess. They don't even try it, but they say, "I can't."

You say, "Thread a needle."

"I can't."

You know, "can't" comes right out. And I'd say, "There isn't such a word as can't."

"Yes, there is."

I said, "No, not here there isn't. We don't use the words 'I can't,' because you haven't even tried. That's why we don't use it."

I said, "Have you tried?"

And they said, "No."

I said, "Then until you try, you don't say, 'I can't.' Because, you don't even know if you can do it, because you've never tried it."

So, they try it, and they learn to do it. One of the highlights is to make them know that they can do it if they really want to.

What I would do is—they'd have a lesson. Well, no, when they first arrived, everybody would play, maybe I Spy or something. Then, when everybody got there and the right time came, we would have our prayer and our lesson. And then, we would do a craft for maybe twenty minutes or so, depending on whether they were getting ready for a sale. We always had a sale of our things when we had our talent nights. Then, they would go into real active play before they went home. You know, real active games before they went home. And this is where they had their opportunity to choose the games they wanted to play.

Did you hold the one up on Badger Road in someone's home?

Yes. In my brother's house. My brother and sister-in-law would go out and leave us the house. Or else if they were not able to, then we'd meet in the basement of a neighbor's place of the girls that were in it. We used to meet in their basement. So, we always had a place within two or three doors of where we were at Badger Road. Even there, when it was nice, though, we were always outdoors with games. We never stayed in when it was nice—for any reason—because you're in all winter, and you don't need to be in all summer.

Now the winter highlight was our variety show. It was our talent night, like, and they put on this puppet show. The girls were really flexible. Verna Lynne [Ware] would run my niece, Judy, and then some others would work them. I put them on strings. They were tied at the wrists, and the ankles, and the neck, to pull the head this way— all according to the way they stepped to the music. We'd play a record. To the music they'd pull the strings and make the puppets work. Well, it was hilarious! I wish I'd have had movies of that, because they were really super, super good. And I don't think they would believe it today that they did it. You know, that way. But they were really, really super…. I had two friends that played—one played the electric guitar, and the other played the guitar. They came every year for our concert and played. And they got so many encores, to play over again and over again. I had lots of outside talent come in to sing and do different things.

So this was your own talent show for the Skylarks.

For the Skylarks to raise money for the church.

Oh, I see.

They had to learn that the church has to be provided for, because we were having meetings, and heat was to be paid for, and lights, and things like that. They used to plant a flower garden around the church, too, so that they learned to keep it nice.

Let me see, what else did we do? Oh, we went on a trip to —. Well, before I go on the trip, I'll tell you what we did in the wintertime. What we would do was, we'd go to our place on Crawford Street. Back of that, a streetcar used to go through there. There was a high bank on both sides, but right behind us was a peach orchard.

We'd go up there [to toboggan] because that was a good, safe place for them. When they'd come down the hill, they would not be running to where there were cars or anything. So, what I'd tell them was when they'd come down, if they were going to run into a tree, everybody fall off. And they only had to do that once. They knew enough what to do. They'd go … have a long [toboggan] ride, right down between the rows of the peaches. And they used to have a real ball. I really don't know how I climbed those banks now. But I used to get up there and go down with them, too. I don't know how I did it now. And then they'd come back to my place and have hot chocolate and that, you know.

But then in the summertime … we used to like to have a wiener roast in the backyard. Blanche [Canham] used to like to pile up their shoes for the shoe scramble. But she also would toss a shoe off. I don't know where she got that from, but she'd toss one of their shoes off. They'd really scramble through those. And she got a real kick out of that.

Another thing is, they'd have a peanut race. I took a movie of them with this, too. They were to toss a peanut across the grass with their nose. Well, in the movie, it shows Anne [Dalmer] picking it up with her mouth and tossing it. Anne Dalmer was doing that. So, I said to her, "You know you did a little bit of cheating."

She said, "No, I didn't."

I said, "Well, in the movie, it shows you picking it up with your mouth and tossing it."

So you see, we catch up with a few little things like that. But, they had a lot of fun on those. Every summer they had one and they had a lot of fun on that.

Another highlight was when we went down to Allegheny. Not Allegheny, but Hill Cumorah. When we went down there, we had a service. George Towers went with us. I got a picture, also, of this. I gave the girls most of their pictures over time, because I think it's important for them to all have [the pictures]. We met at Hill Cumorah, and they had a service in there. It was just beautiful. The sun shone through the trees there so beautiful.

One time when we went, it was just pouring rain outside. Pouring hard. And you couldn't take vehicles up to the grove. You had to leave them down on the roadway. So, we had to leave the bus and walk up. Well, some of them didn't want to go. So, we went up, and when we walked inside the gates, it wasn't raining. It wasn't raining at all in there. The sun came through there just beautiful. When we walked out, it was pouring. But it was not when we were in there.

When we got down to the bus and the people that were left there, they just couldn't believe that the sun could shine through there. "Because," they said, "It's been pouring ever since you left."

But it was not pouring in there. It was just beautiful. So, it's one of the real highlights of the trip to have an experience like that. I try to share that wherever I go, because it is remarkable, you know. The girls really enjoyed their trip…. Bill Burley drove us down for that trip.

Was this to the pageant?

No, no. I never took the girls to the pageant. I didn't have the Skylarks when the pageant was being put on.

This was just a trip down.

This was just a trip for them to go down and to know about what I had been teaching them, and to go through the houses and different buildings and everything, and to get the literature on it and things like that. But, we wanted to have a little service in the grove, and so I had the pictures. As I say, I gave them pretty well all their pictures now.

We also had a reunion here a while ago of some of the girls that were in the Skylarks, and they had lots of fun. We made it a pot luck, so there was no work for anyone, and we had it outdoors here. It's natural for me.

But, you know, over the years with the number of Skylarks that I've had, you know I still meet some of them. Of course, they've been married, so I don't know their names now, and it is hard to remember when you get a big list, you know. I don't have those lists any more. I'd have kept them if I had thought about it. But, they still meet me. I met one in Zeller's last summer. She came up to me and said, "Do you know who I am?"

I said, "No, I don't think so. I remember seeing you, but I don't recall."

She said, "Well, I was one of your Skylarks."

I said, "Well, that was a while ago."

She said, "Let's not mention that."

But, I thought that was really nice. She is not a member of the church or anything. I had quite a few people that weren't members of the church. But we had lots of good fun.

How I got started doing these crafts was when I was a young girl. I used to go to an auxiliary in the Stamford fire hall. At four o'clock every Wednesday afternoon, Mrs. Colstock and a couple of other women ... I think Miss Newburn was another one. She comes to the house for Ted every once in a while. [Ted is Margaret Canham's brother, who is in the plumbing and heating business.] She hasn't changed a bit. They taught us how to sew, and how to thread a needle and those things, and the different stitches of fancy work.

I always had the desire when I did these things to pass them on, and this is how I've been able to do it. I have had the chance to share it with Blanche these last few years, and it has helped her quite a bit. [Blanche is Margaret Canham's sister who has Mongolism (Down's Syndrome).] When I was talking to the doctor about it, he said, "Keep the good work up, because it is as good for you to teach it as it is for the person to receive it. So, whenever you get the chance, do that."

So you're still teaching.

I am in a way, but ... I'm not as steady with my hands as I used to be, to do a lot of things that I used to do. But I used to do them.

I had the Skylarks here just a year ago I guess it was, but we had to close down, because there was only one girl. Several had moved away out of town, and so there was only one of that age group. That made it kind of tough to have just one person, because there's no fun with one person to play games and stuff like that that are interesting. You can play quiet games, but you can't play running and real active games.

One person that was in that is ... still my gal, Mary Matheson, Netta's sister. She just really wants to go everywhere I want to go. Whenever I call and say, "Do you want to go here or there?" Mary is ready. She sheds tears, Netta tells me, if she doesn't go, because she wants to go with Margaret. So, this is a nice thing to remember, that

I cherish. Mary was a marvelous knitter. She also had the handicap of like a retardation, but she was a marvelous, marvelous knitter.

Mary was always there, always there to start on time. You never would delay on having Mary there. She still likes to come out to our church dinners, and anything that we have, I let her know. She's just so ready to come. She'll say, "Netta, can't we? Oh, can't we?" So, Netta has to give in, because she says, "I know there'll be tears if I say no." So now I have to phone Netta on the sly in order to make it so that Netta doesn't really have to change her plans, although sometimes Netta will bring Mary, drop her off, and leave her with me. Then, she'll pick her up, even if I have to bring her back here, and pick her up, which makes it nice. She says ... there's no use of Mary missing it, because she's going to leave her with somebody else anyway, and she might as well have something to do for the evening. So, she's really very considerate, I think anyway.

I've always been one that believed in administration for the sick. I have met some real instant healings.

Such as?

About a year and a half ago, I was just wreaked with pain, and I really didn't know what I was going to have to have done. But I went and asked for administration, and Bill [Stoner] and Arnold [Ware] administered to me. As soon as they put their hands on my head, I felt a real hand, like something different, just going right through my body. And that pain was just going right away. When they finished administering to me, tears were just dropping off my cheeks, but I felt like a brand new person. When I got up, I just couldn't help but tell them that ... the healing had already taken place. I felt like I was brand new, right from that minute on. I never had that feeling again, you know, like that pain or anything again. Never. It just was instant.

Were you a member of the church when you had polio? Did you have administration for that?

No. I was only seven.

Oh, that's right.

Yes, I was only seven. I was what my mother always called the "cricket of the family," because I always was acrobatic, you know. I could walk on my hands out on the lawn without [falling over], and I could stand on my head out in the middle of the lawn, and run races and beat all my brothers and everything in races. And then, just like that, overnight, it was all gone. I couldn't do nothing. I got up to walk with Mother, and I thought I was walking all right, but I wasn't. I went right to the floor. Mother just screamed, put me in bed, and called the doctor. But it was too late, I was already crippled up then.

To that doctor's dying day, Dr. McKinzie, he marveled that I ever walked again. He said, "I really didn't think you'd live, let alone walk".... Now there's not many doctors that would rush you them-selves, but he just put me and Mother in the car and took us away to Toronto himself. And he said, "You kept saying you were fine. You were dying, but you were fine." He said, "Because you have a positive outlook, that's what helped you, to pull you through."

Then, when I went to Hamilton and had a spinal surgery, I was in bed for over seven months. And I had [not] walked in three years. Every doctor that examined me said I would never walk again. But, after that surgery, I lay on a board for all that time, no pillow.... I wanted to get up. So the doctor said, "Okay, let her try." But they kept warning me that I wouldn't be able to.

It was a real new sensation, because I'd never sat up for so long. Just to put your head on a pillow was almost enough. But, they raised me up every day, and then I finally got out in a chair. Of course, as soon as I got out in a chair, then I wanted back, because I only had the bottom sheet half on. But that was enough. As I ventured out, I got so that two nurses took me walking, and I'd walk a few steps to the end of the bed, and then I'd walk a few steps around the end of the bed. And then another week, I went to the next bed, and that's the way I kept gaining and gaining, until pretty soon, I was going on my own.

So you must have had a very positive outlook on it.

Yes, I wanted to go. But all the time I was there, I rolled ban-dages for the nurses and that because my parents couldn't come to see me.... I'd seen many people come and go. Jim, the garbage man, was our favorite—my favorite then. He used to have to carry me outside to get some fresh air—on the bed, you know—and he had to keep me straight because of my back and everything, so he had to keep me flat. But he'd bump my toes on the wall going down the steps trying to keep me straight, and I'd get ingrown toenails between that and the sheets buckling down over my toes.

[I got] sties [on my eyes] from studying my books, you know, for school. But I kept my grades up. I kept up with all the girls I went to school with from the beginning. So it made it nice. I passed each year. But, I had to do it orally, of course, because I didn't have the opportunity —.

But your hands weren't affected.

Well, what it was, it hit me. I was paralyzed all down the right side. No, the left side ... and this arm is still the weakest. It shakes more if I carry groceries in it or anything. It really gets to shaking. Then, it left that side [the left] and went down my right side. So, I had it on both sides, really. That's why I had the harder time. The spinal [surgery] was to straighten my spine. I had a curvature of the spine, a bad curvature. At that time, you couldn't even move your finger and it affects your spine. You don't know that until you have some injury in your spine, and you feel it. Just moving your fingers, you say, "Ouch," [because] it hurts your spine.

Jim was really good to me. When he went away on holidays, he always sent me a nice card. I still have one.

That's the garbage man.

Yes, that's the garbage man. He was my favorite, and he always did a lot for me even though he was the garbage man.

Looking back over your life, Margaret, do you think there was a purpose to all this? Or do you think that it just happened? Or do you feel that you were really blessed through all those years, even though you were not —.

Yes, I feel it's been a blessing in more than one way. Sometimes, I think when I see the athletes today ... I think and wonder if I would have been one of those, you know, because ... I really did it, you know. When you see all these things that they do, these somersaults and these races, I often think—I wonder if I would have ever been into that sort of thing. Maybe I'd have made my way as an athlete someday, but I don't know whether I would or not.

In lots of ways, this has been a blessing, because I think I understand what pain is, and I have sympathy for people that have it. And I have sympathy for people that have a handicap, because, for a long time, when I couldn't walk, I couldn't be active in playing hide-and-go-seek, and all those kinds of things with my family and my friends. So, I'd have to be the goal. They'd have to touch me to be home free, or touch me for first base, or whatever. So, I think it made me [appreciate] the handicapped people today.... When I see somebody in a wheelchair, I think to myself, "It's nothing." Because it's not anything to be ashamed of at all, there's a lot of good comes from people. Sometimes, more good comes from people that are tied down like that than [from] people that have the whole freedom. They can do anything they want, but they don't have what these people have.

Now Blanche has a real gift of love that I wish I had.

Can you explain who Blanche is and what —.

Blanche is my sister, my youngest sister, and she is a Mongoloid. But she was baptized, her and Ted, and it was the most spiritual baptism that I've ever witnessed as of my own. She went up there with every bit of reverence that you could muster. She really did. It meant a lot to her and still does. Ted was baptized at the same time. Al Pelletier was there. Gorge Towers baptized Blanche, and she always still cherishes that. To his dying day, she always told him, "You baptized me."

A couple of Sundays ago, Brother Taylor spoke on baptism. She [Blanche] said, "I was baptized." And I said, "Yes, you were baptized." But, she has a love, that she loves all people in a way that if we all had that much love, there'd be no hate. She is just so full of love and so ready to hand it out.

But, she's just been so sick these last two years that you miss that love. You miss having her give you that big hug. But, this last week, she has got back to giving you that big hug, and she's so thankful for everything. But her church means so much to her. Oh, it means a lot. She doesn't like to miss putting in her envelope. Oh, it breaks her heart. When I went down to Independence, I bought her a carry bag that has music on the outside, for her to carry her hymnbooks in. That's what she carries every Sunday. She cherishes that book bag because that keeps her books dry in the wintertime. She knows exactly where those books are—she just has to hunt for that bag, and there are her books. So, she has those out every Sunday—her own hymnbook.

She understands more than we realize and gets out of the services more than we realize, too, because she expresses lots of things after the service—that she enjoyed this, or she enjoyed so-and-so's preaching, and so-and-so talked about this. She expresses these things, and I feel that she is touched, too.

Do you feel that the gifts are there in the church today as they were in the days past?
Well, some gifts. I have witnessed the gift of tongues in our church.

I never have.
I have.

Tell us about that. I have never seen it.
You've never seen it. See, that's something we miss now.

Not in our church [have I seen it].
In our branch, right in our branch, it's happened.

Well, how did it happen? Who was involved?
I wish I remembered the minister, but I know I was there when —.

Was it a special missionary that was there?
Yes.

Well, what form did it take?
Well, I didn't know what the language was. See, he was preaching, and then this language came out that I did not know what it was.

And then the interpretation came out—the message came out that we understood.

Who did the interpreting?

Another person that was at the foot of the rostrum.

That was on the platform?

Yes. It came through them. So, that's how it was interpreted to us.

Was it a message, like a message from God?

To us as a group. But I thought, "Oh, what a marvelous feeling that is to be —."

Why do you suppose that God feels it is necessary to speak in another tongue? What was so beneficial about this?

I think because it says in the scriptures that there'd be the gifts of the tongue and the interpretation. I just read that in the Book of Mormon. One follows the other. So, that's just filling the prophecy, I think. I just read that in the Doctrine and Covenants. Well, that was one of the things I have witnessed, and I personally have been spoken to in a service, too.

When we were in Lowbanks, Al Pelletier told me that God was very pleased with my work, that I was to continue to [?] and he would continue to bless me. He was very pleased with everything I had done, and there were others that were picked out in the service and spoken to at that time.

At Port Elgin, we've had people spoken to there, too. But the gifts of the tongues—I haven't heard that in a long time. I think we're lacking at some place that we haven't heard this, because it is one of the gifts.

Do you think that that's the thing, or do you think that maybe it's just not as necessary now? That other forms of things are taking the place of the tongues now?

Well, it could be that. There are so many nationalities now that we don't need the things interpreted, because the nationalities are all getting their own means of worship, aren't they? Missionaries now are going into the world more now than they did then ... therefore they are getting their own ministry. And so, maybe there isn't the need to fill this anymore, because in their own interpretation (language) they're getting it. Where if they gave it to us, and there wasn't anybody in our congregation that needed it that way —.

You don't feel it's a lack of spirituality in the church? Or, you did say you think perhaps something's lacking, didn't you?

Well, it could be. I realize that we're very slim on priesthood in our congregation, and I know we have a lot of outside ministry, mind you, but our own priesthood—we don't have very many. At the time when I joined the church, there was a lot of ministry.

Do you suppose that this is the reason that God has given us section 156, because of the lack of male priesthood?

I really feel that way, because it seems that there is such a few. They say we'll get somebody from outside, but that only takes from another church someplace, if we do that. So, as a result, if they don't start calling women, then who are they going to get? Even in our own branch, we don't have very many young men to call, or even men—period—to call in our own branch when you think about it.

How would you feel about a female elder, though? Would you be reluctant to come to her with your problems or talk things over with a woman?

No, I don't think so, because I think ... like, I could talk to you. So, do you think that I couldn't talk to somebody [female] that was an elder in our church? If I could talk to [?], now Vera is Ross's wife, Vera Wood. I have every bit of confidence in Vera, and Ross is our pastor. But, I have confidence in Vera, that I could talk to Vera, and feel just as confident as [when] I talk to Ross. So, why wouldn't I feel like that when I talk to any woman?

What about a sermon, though, from a woman?

I've heard some very good talks—we call them talks now. And, I have said at the time when I've heard these people, that that's as good as any sermon. But, you have to call them talks when they're not in the priesthood. You can't call them sermons. I mean, you feel that they're that good, but you can't call them that, because they're not really priesthood. So they can't title it something it isn't.

Would you feel strange taking the communion from a woman?

No. No, I couldn't say that I would. If I have confidence in them, just like I've said— like in Vera, and that I have in Ross—why would I shun anything that a Christian —?

So, you believe that if a woman was really called of God, then —.

As much as anyone else, yes. I think there are a lot of good, very good, qualities in women. And I don't think God would call women if there weren't the good qualities in women to be used. Now, women today are getting lots of good study, and they are knowledgeable. So, I'm sure that God wants that knowledge used in the proper sources. In lots of cases, women get more time to study than men, to actually study the scriptures, than men. So, I actually think that this is why you create the confidence in them.

They're saying that we don't emphasize the Book of Mormon enough in the church today. What do you think about that?

Well, I have felt this way for a long time, because I went to that study [session?] that you provided here for us a while ago. Do you not remember when we had it in the lower auditorium? I took tapes on it.

Yes, Della Smith taught it.

Right, and you know the church could have been filled more. As we said tonight, sometimes the time, when it's called out, is not appropriate for everybody ... It was booked on a Saturday, which, true, it has to be sometimes booked that way. But there are people who are busy. Their work calls them and, you know, there's something they can't do [attend]. They can't take that time out. And so therefore, I was very happy to have that course. I took tapes and passed them around. I just got them back, so I'm going to restudy that all over again, even though I'm almost finished reading the Book of Mormon.

They kept saying, you know, everybody should read it. Well, I was like Ross. I used to read a paragraph and have to start back up at the top again and go down. Somehow or other, you just read so much, and then your mind doesn't grasp. So then you start back up and down. This is the way I was reading. I don't know whether I was doing it wrong or not, but it just seemed like I couldn't grasp for a long time. Now I'm beginning to be able to read it like a story book. I realize it just seems like there are wars and wars and fighting and fighting and everything. But there's a lot of good scripture in there, too, and I think we need to learn what all it's about, so those kinds of things don't happen again. We'll have this peace on earth that we want and that God promises us. But, I think it would be a very good idea to study it more. I think we need to study our own books. We need to know where this all comes from.

I know people who'd like to study it [the Book of Mormon], but they want to have a study time. At one time, we used to have what they called Religio, and we used to study all the church material. So, these are things that are good, and I think that we will profit by it.

I remember Audrey and Arnold [Ware] saying, when they went to Florida, they stopped in to Kirtland to see June [Garrett], and they had the tour [of the Kirtland Temple]. They talked all the way to Florida that that's the thing we've got to be studying. And they told them in no uncertain words, that we've got to get involved in that Book of Mormon, or we're going to be a lost people

The church has in recent years, I feel, more or less just come to dwell on the idea that we have got to live God's word, and that is what the church is. Now, maybe, they feel that we have to get back to the Book or Mormon in order to —. Well, we do have a unique church and a calling, and maybe we've got to get back to that.

The reason I think we have to is, because a lot of us don't really know all the Book of Mormon. And I'll bet there are lots that haven't yet read it all. Even if you've read it all, there's a lot of depth in there that I know it doesn't register [the first time]. The problem I have with reading it is to remember the names, because the names are so different than the names today, that it's hard to remember the name that conflicted with this name, and who was the good and the bad. You know, to pick these out and remember them.

That's where the study would help.

Where the study would help is to hold these names within your mind, because I think it's important. I think that study would be very, very interesting, and I know a lot of them in the church that would.

That's the way Audrey came back—very concerned. And she has told me this several times. She thought that June would bring it back to us really hot and heavy when she returned, but I didn't hear [from] June. I haven't heard her yet, except last Sunday, I think it was. She said that we should be studying the Book of Mormon. Audrey was sure that she would really tell us to get with it and get studying, because of the things that she had learned there [at Kirtland] and the pressures they had put to bear. It isn't too often that Audrey and Arnold come away concerned about things. When they go, they get a lot from it, but they were very concerned. She said they never hesitated a minute all the way to Florida to talk about the things like that. So these are very important.

One experience I didn't tell you was when I went to Independence. That was the first trip that I had ever made. When I used to babysit for Audrey and Arnold, when they went there, they always said, "I'll take you on a trip to Independence one day, to the world headquarters." Of course, you always think that's just, you know, here-nor-there. But, anyway, their family grew up, and it was about four years ago they took me there.

When I went to their house, just shortly after Christmas, they gave me a Christmas present, but when I went, of course they were going to go to Independence. Whenever they were going to go to Independence, they always invited me for supper.... Let's see, it was a Saturday, and they were leaving the [following] Wednesday. So they called me in for supper, and they gave me this parcel, and I opened it. It was the *Hymns of the Saints*. And, oh, I was just so thrilled with that. I just was so thrilled, because I could never afford to buy that, and I really wanted it, but I never could afford it. Audrey said, "Well, that's not all. Are you going to tell her, Arnold, or shall I?" And he said, "You." She told me that they were going to take me down to Independence. Well, I just couldn't say anything. I was just plugged right up. I just couldn't believe what I was hearing. They said, "We're

leaving Wednesday, and we want you to go with us." I didn't say anything. I just couldn't say anything.

So … I was talking to Ted [Canham] the next day. He said, "Why
didn't you say, yes?" And I said I couldn't say anything. I was tongue
tied. He said, "Well, why don't you phone them and say yes? …You've
got nothing to stay home for." Because they said they would pay
everything—my Blue Cross and everything. All I had to have was
some spending money. So spending money came from every direction. I went to my craft meetings on Monday, and my leader gave
me twenty dollars. I went someplace else, and they gave me twenty
dollars. Everybody said, "Go, go, go," you know. And they're all giving
me American money. I didn't have to gather money. Money was just
coming into my hands, just from people that were just so happy to
see me get there.

Anyway, I phoned them and told them, and I had to be ready by
Wednesday. So, Wednesday morning Arnold pulled up out here and
picked me up. We went back to his house, had a word of prayer, and
we were on our way. It took us till Saturday. We pulled in Saturday
afternoon, because Arnold can only drive during the day.

It was just so thrilling, so thrilling. I wish I could have had all of
you with me. I just wished I could have. It was just such a delightful,
delightful thing. I can still see the auditorium when we stepped out
of that trailer that night—the lights on it. Oh, it was just the most
gorgeous —.

Was the auditorium the way you pictured it?

It was just more beautiful than what I ever pictured it even. Well,
this was the remarkable thing. This was the outstanding thing. We
parked in the [camp]grounds, is it that the church owns? Just up a
bit from the church. We got to the end, and you have to go down a
bank. Well, you know if I had gone down that bank, I'd have been on
my head. When I saw some of them go, [I thought] "There's no way I
can put on my brakes. When I'm going down a steep hill like that, I'd
be rolling more than I'd be walking, I'm afraid. I'm sure I would." So,
my gosh! When we got there, there were steps with a railing! Audrey
said, "Margaret, this is a miracle." And Arnold said, "I can't believe it
either."

He said, "I've always had to help Audrey down the bank and back up." And he thought he was going to have to go down with Audrey and come back up and get me, because he knew I'd never make it if she can't make it. He said, "I can't believe it." Vera told me last year, there were no steps there—there were no steps. Now, believe it or not, [there are steps]. And there was a railing. And that was a miracle. When I said to Vera, "Did you go down the steps?" she said, "Where are the steps?"

I said, "The steps down there. When I went, the steps were there." Isn't that amazing, how those steps were there? And that railing? It was a piece of pipe, but there was a railing.

And so Audrey said, "You can go at your freedom." And I said, "Fine." So, I packed a lunch. They went whenever they got up. And I got up, and I went…. So, I got up, and I went over, because Saturday there wasn't much doing, but I wanted to see it. We went over, and we listened to some of the services, and I had my lunch downstairs in the lobby. Then, when we came back at night, Audrey said to me while we were eating supper, "You feel free to do what you want. You are on your own. If you want to be with us, it's fine."

Well, we sat with each other most of the time during the services, especially at the afternoon meetings—you know, the business meetings. But, I mostly stayed over there. I found a secret hiding place for a little snooze, and I stayed for the day. The meals for two dollars and two-fifty were just scrumptious, I'm telling you. So, I just stayed and had my meals over there; and the spending money I used was for my meals. They were good.

Saturday night, we met all the apostles and their wives. They were downstairs in the downstairs lobby. We came down the ramp (It's all ramps, you know), and … we'd meet the apostles and their wives, and then we'd have lunch after.

Then, starting Sunday morning, I couldn't sit with Audrey and Arnold. They were over here, and there was one seat over here. So I had to sit someplace else. I've never walked into a place that was so full so fast. I found I was better to walk on my own, because there was quite a hill to climb, and Audrey and Arnold are more used to walking, and so they could walk a little faster. I did everything on my own. I just stayed over there for the whole thing. I saw Audrey and

Arnold just in the evenings, and I didn't see much of them for eating or anything.

It was just a thrill of a lifetime. It's something you always dream about, but you never think you'd ever make it. But, oh, if I could have had you all under my arm, I would have had you there in a minute.... You know everything is just immaculate, how it's done.

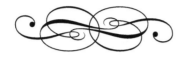

RLDS Women's Lives: Summary & Conclusion

BY LINDA KING NEWELL

The lives of the ten women represented in this volume may be little known, but they are historically important. Each represents a different view into the larger landscape of women's lives as shaped by their belief in the gospel of Jesus Christ and, in particular, the Reorganization. This collection is unusual in several ways. There are few accounts of women—either published or archived—that are available within the framework of the Reorganization, particularly before women were ordained to the priesthood and began taking a more public role in the church.

Eight of the accounts in this volume are part of a more extensive, unpublished project called "Oral Histories of Women Serving in the RLDS Church in the Twentieth Century," housed at the Community of Christ Archives in Independence, Missouri. When Danny Jorgensen came across this collection, he recognized an unexplored treasure of information. His dogged determination to give at least some of these voices a public audience is commendable. He rounded out the selection here by adding the narratives of two women who are related to him, although somewhat distantly: Emma Locine Whiting Anderson (1853–1922), a sister to his great-grandmother, and Louise Minor Murdock (1916–2009), wife of his mother's brother. These two accounts further enrich the offerings in this book.

Emma Anderson's account is written in 1915 as a letter to her children seven years before she died, and is one of the more detailed in this collection. The historical value of her narrative is enhanced by the inclusion of her parents' and grandparents' stories. The latter came in contact with the Mormon church in the 1830s in Ohio, endured the persecutions in Missouri, the martyrdom and expulsion from Illinois, and (as followers of Alpheus Cutler) exile to the rolling hills of Iowa, where Emma was born.

Louise Murdock's reminiscence spans a little-known era of Restoration history when a group of church members interested in *Zionic concepts* or the "stewardship plan" moved from Oregon to the Ozarks in eastern Taney County, Missouri, in 1928. They, and a few other families, settled as sheep farmers on ten thousand acres of church-owned land. Louise's account begs for a more detailed study of the Ozarks Zionic experiment, as well as similar endeavors supported by then church president Frederick Madison Smith.

The remaining narratives are interviews conducted between 1986 and 1988, late in the lives of the players. Many focus, almost exclusively, on the subject's church service, thus narrowing the scope and, in some cases, insights into the women's lives by simply not asking the right questions. By being unprepared for their task, several interviewers missed opportunities to place these women's stories in a broader context. Of course, there are exceptions and Beatrice Noel Deaver Darling (1910–1991) is one. Her account began with an interview, but she insisted on editing it before turning it over to the archives. This allowed her to look up dates and names, and to give a more detailed and accurate report of her life. Unfortunately, others who were interviewed did not take an opportunity to clarify and expand their stories. The reader longs to know more about their families, their vocations, their day-to-day struggles, and their aspirations—all of which add richness and diversity to any history.

The majority of the stories here are not unlike many others that could be told of or written by RLDS/CofC women. Taken together, however, some patterns begin to emerge, perhaps giving a broader interpretation to the book, and a more varied look into the everyday workings of the Reorganization.

While all of the women lived in the twentieth century, only Emma Anderson was born in the nineteenth century. Her life spanned nearly seventy years of early church history, from 1853 to 1922. There is no indication that any of the women in this volume knew each other. Eight of them did overlap in time with Emma Anderson, albeit briefly. Elsie F. Andes Doig Townsend (1908–1994) was fourteen when Emma died in June 1922. Seven others were between two and twelve years old at that time. The ninth woman, Margaret Louise Canham (1922–95), was born on August 4, 1922, just two months after Emma's death. Of the ten women, Emma died the youngest at age sixty-nine. Four lived into their eighties and three were over ninety. The oldest of this last group, Enid Irene Stubbart DeBarthe (1912–2005), lived just four months longer than Louise Murdock. The last to die of those interviewed was Berta Ruoff Nogel (1920–2010). In all, the lives of these ten women spanned 159 years.

Three of the women featured were converts and two had husbands who were converts. Emma Anderson, whose family had been followers of Alpheus Cutler, was eleven when Cutler died and set them adrift. In 1884, missionaries from the Reorganization found Emma and her husband, Edwin Anderson (they had married when she was sixteen), living in northern Minnesota. On March fifth of that year she and Edward were baptized in East Battle Lake in a hole cut in the ice. Berta Nogle had been born into an LDS family near the tiny town of Manila in the northeast corner of Utah. She joined the Reorganization while living with her sister in Southern California as a young adult. Margaret Canham was baptized at the church in Niagara Falls with her entire family—her parents, brothers, sisters, and two grandfathers—fifteen in all. Margaret, the only one of the women in this volume who remained single and the only African American, found her niche teaching young people in her congregation. Her account is sprinkled with spritely stories of parties, activities, trips to the Hill Cumorah pageant, and teaching crafts in tandem with the gospel to her classes. She also taught her Down's syndrome sister to sew and delighted in the telling of it all.

These narrations are also unusual because of their far-flung geographical settings spanning thirteen states and two Canadian provinces, and adding glimpses into the workings of the Reorganization in

places other than the traditional Independence and Lamoni locales.
That said, around half of the women did spend at least part of their
lives in one or both of those areas, but mostly in spurts. For example,
Emma Anderson and her family lived in Independence a year and
a half from fall 1887 to spring 1889. Elsie Townsend left Montana to
attend Graceland College for two years before returning to Montana.
She later resided in Independence with her second husband.

For the most part, the women lived in or near small towns, often
far from other church members or congregations. They often traveled
long distances to attend church meetings, bringing with them a variety
of talents and enriching their congregations, as well as their families.
Emma Anderson lived on the Iowa frontier, northern Minnesota, and
Montana in the latter half of the nineteenth century, eventually settling near Saskatoon, Saskatchewan, Canada. She and her husband,
Edwin, homesteaded adjacent to their grown son, Victor, and his
family. Three weeks after their arrival in Canada, they began a Sunday school and, within a year, a branch had been formed with Edwin
as the presiding elder. Their home became the place where the missionaries stayed when they proselyted in the area. Emma commented,
"We tried to make all the missionaries at home at our house.... They
were always welcome." Missionaries frequently found lodging with
members in these far-flung locations. The arrival of church leaders,
however, became an event, particularly if the women had a personal
experience with that leader. For example, during Alexander Smith's
visit with Emma's family, he gave her, Edward, and their daughter,
Alice, their patriarchal blessings. Likewise, Beatrice Darling recalled
receiving a similar blessing from visiting church patriarch F. A. Smith.

Beatrice was born in Webb City, Missouri, and attended Graceland College, but she also lived in Kansas and Wisconsin before her
convert husband took a church assignment in Independence as associate director of religious education. From that time on, as the wife
of an appointee, Beatrice's life was at the mercy of his assignments, as
they left Independence for Alabama on church assignment. Beatrice
would pack up all her household goods six more times before they
retired to Resthaven Nursing Home in Independence.

Elsie Townsend spent her growing up years (1910–1930) on a
homestead in northeastern Montana, remaining in the area after

her marriage to James Stuart Doig. Like several of the women, Elsie gives us glimpses into previous generations. One marvels at her midwife mother who delivered ninety-eight babies, sometimes traveling unplowed roads in subzero temperatures. As a child, Elsie remembered attending church services in places as unlikely as her father's blacksmith shop before there were enough members to build a small church across the street from where they lived. Elsie savored the memory of her father presiding over meetings where the congregation was warmed by a small coal-burning stove and illuminated by a kerosene lamp. She also remembered him leading the singing while holding one of his small children in his arms.

Dorothy Harriet Elkins Wixom (1912–1991) lived most of her life in California, except for the few years that her husband, Harold, attended Kansas State College, and they lived in Manhattan, Kansas. What her early life lacked in physical comforts (her family was poor, and her father went from job to job to support her and her mother), it certainly made up in adventure—riding horseback with her Cherokee grandfather, learning to shoot a gun, and eating what she called an "offbeat" diet of "mule meat, horse meat, buffalo, antelope, ground squirrels, jack rabbit, elk, quail, pheasant, crows, and rattlesnakes." Gypsies and circuses were, also, part of her colorful growing up years.

Although interesting stories emerge from these pages, they do have some limitations. For example, although Elsie Townsend's story is one of the more compelling, only once does she mention the name of her first husband, James Stuart Doig, and she gives no hint of what snuffed out his life at the young age of thirty-one. He left Elsie with four daughters and a son between the ages of three years and three months, including two sets of twins. Her only son was one of the younger twins and had cerebral palsy. Her moving account, however, of trying to keep her family together as a young widow while pumping gas at the station attached to her home, and going back to school to become a teacher, provided the material for her first book, *None to Give Away*.

Attitudes toward what women could do or not do in the church in the era when Elsie and her cohorts were mainstays in RLDS congregations across the country, will seem quaint and even ridiculous to younger generations, for example: Enid DeBarthe's expulsion from

Graceland College when she became pregnant—even though she
was married; or women not being allowed to have their own organization or even hold a prayer meeting without a man present. Frustrated with the *status quo*, Enid did her own research and discovered
a letter from Joseph Smith III, in reply to his daughter's (Adentia
Smith Anderson) complaints about this same issue. His reply was
forceful, "You go ahead and have your meeting and don't let a man say
a peep. If you do go down, go down with your flags flying, everybody
at the helm; but don't let an elder or the son of an elder have a thing
to do with it from A to Izzard." Entrenched beliefs don't die easily,
however. As late as 1985, Enid was still dealing with this subjugation
of women in church circles.

 Although nine of the ten women represented in this volume lived
to see the ordination of women, there are only a couple of brief reac-
tions to that historic event. Dorothy Wixom said, "I think ordination
of women is o.k. I think we, the members of the church, have been
coasting along … and forgetting the mission that has been before us
for over 150 years: to get out and follow Christ into the world. I'm
all for it!" Enid DeBarthe, who attended the conference where the
ordination of women was announced, provides a moving account of
the experience, one that will prove important to future historians as
they write more complete histories of women of the Reorganization.

 Reports of healing and other spiritual manifestations are not un-
common on these pages. Half the women cited occurrences of healing
after priesthood administrations—naming at least a dozen separate
incidents. Two told of more than one healing: Emma Anderson reported six and Berta Nogel four. Examples include Emma Anderson's
story of being healed of a debilitating earache at age six, of her aunt
being healed of tuberculosis, and of the local elders healing her son,
Victor—once from pneumonia and pleurisy when he was seventeen
and several years later of an unnamed ailment. After the doctor had
given up hope for baby Enid, whose little body was weakened by infection, her mother called the elders in to bless her, and she revived.
Elsie Townsend, however, offers a different perspective on blessings
after having been administered to. "I have learned many things," she
wrote, "many mornings I play on my organ and sing 'Have thine own
way Lord, have thine own way.' And I receive a blessing of peace."

One unusual event recorded in Elsie's recollection happened at a reunion in Missouri. She heard a member of the priesthood speak in tongues. "I will never forget it—how it enlarged our knowledge of God's commandments—His purpose for us," she said. It was her first and last experience with this phenomenon. Although glossolalia was common in the early years of the church, it had faded from practice by the 1930s and 40s.

The Three Nephites are alive and well, and performing good deeds in several accounts. Who was the man with kindly brown eyes who reached out and comforted that same shy, sickly Enid? She had been bullied in school and did not want to live. He told her that God loved her and wanted her to be happy. "Remember, you have work to do." Her mother had not seen the man and told Enid she had been day-dreaming, but when her grandfather heard the story, he said, "Bless you, child, you've been visited by one of the Three Nephites."

Who were the two men who suddenly appeared on each side of Beatrice Darling's husband, John, as he walked on a dark street with two ruffians approaching? All fear left John as the thugs passed by. After they were gone, his protectors also disappeared in the darkness without a word. John believed two Nephites had kept him from harm's way.

When Elsie Townsend, her two sets of twins and five-year-old daughter were stuck in deep snow on a steep mountain pass in Montana, did one of the Three Nephites come out of nowhere to shovel her car out and push to get it started up the slope? Her friends thought so after hearing her account. This story, however, is reminiscent of one that Paul Edward's told of helping a stranded motorist with a flat tire, then, later that day, hearing a member of the congregation he was visiting tell of one of the Three Nephites changing the tire on her car that morning, enabling her to get to church in time to fulfill her assignments. Paul recognized the woman as the one he had assisted, but rather than saying anything, he delighted in his elevated status.

The hardships some of the women endured are not atypical of lives lived on the frontier or during hard economic times, but are nonetheless wrenching. Elsie Townsend's experience of being left a widow with five small children, as mentioned earlier, is a case in point. During World War I, Elsie's father was forced to sell his store and house, and the family of nine took residence in the barn with "we kids sleeping in the hayloft," she wrote. "My parents slept in the granary room. Our cookstove stood outside—right out in the open air whether it was raining or not and we ate at a table that was set up in a cow stall." Fortunately, they were able to rent a house, as it turned cold in the late fall.

Emma Anderson gave birth to ten children, including twins. Two of her children died as infants—a daughter from measles at eight months and a son at seven months. Like many early settlers who had no dental care, she suffered from aching, rotting teeth until she had them all pulled. She saw her new false teeth as a blessing. Her house burned to the ground twice, the flames taking all she owned.

Enid DeBarthe's facial disfigurement led to a childhood of rejection, physical pain, and bullying so intense that she did not want to continue living. Other difficulties recorded in these stories remind us how precarious life can be in any age.

These interviews and reminiscences are a beginning. The ten women whose lives are chronicled here are all worth knowing. Some of their stories are courageous, some inspiring, some entertaining, but in very different ways and to different degrees. All are worth examining in further detail. Much more can be gleaned by supplementing these accounts with additional research in archives, public documents, genealogy records, and family attics and closets.

As Danny Jorgensen suggests in his introduction, the stories here are a beginning. Many women whose lives continue beyond the ones in this volume deserve a place in the history of the Community of Christ Church. For some, the window of mortality is closing and the opportunity to record their life stories will be lost. Perhaps the effort to preserve stories in this volume will be the catalyst leading to a new and expanded project of oral histories, using skilled interviewers who are trained to encourage depth and details in the stories they will hear. By doing so, fuller accounts of women in the Restoration will emerge to help fill in blanks in the institutional history and inform church members in ways that will enrich their own lives.

Index

About the Editors

Danny L. Jorgensen is the son of Matie Murdock Jorgensen, a Community of Christ elder; the grandson of Cora Jensen Murdock, an RLDS member; and the great grandson of (Sylvia) Cordelia (Cordie) Whiting Murdock who converted to the Reorganization, having been born a Cutlerite to a family that included some of the earliest members of the new American religion founded by Joseph Smith Jr. Danny graduated from Catalina High School in Tucson, Arizona, in 1969, earned a BS in sociology from Northern Arizona University in 1972, an MA in sociology from Western Kentucky University in 1974, and a PhD in sociology from The Ohio State University in 1979. He has been employed by the University of South Florida (USF) since 1978 where he is a professor of religious studies, and a former chairperson of that department. Over the past thirty-some years Jorgensen has published extensively on participant observation and other issues in the methodology of the social sciences as well as the sociology of religion, especially new American religions, including Neopaganism, occultism, and witchcraft, Scientology, Anabaptists, and the Latter Day Saints. He is the father of five adult children, four grandchildren, and one great grandchild. Danny currently spends one semester a annually at the University of South Florida in Tampa, teaching and writing, while residing much of the year on a farm near Lebanon, Missouri, with his spouse, June Hanson Jorgensen, while teaching internet courses, writing, and conducting field research.

Joni Wilson worked for Community of Christ from 1991–2004. She was a Temple School curriculum specialist, also providing editorial work for *Restoration Studies* and the *JWHA Journal*. She attended

Graceland College, earning a nursing degree, and later completed a master of arts degree in religion from Park College, and a master of liberal arts degree from Baker University. She has published articles on women of the RLDS church, including Emma Smith Bidamon, Marietta Walker, Alice Smith Edwards, and Carolyn Brock.

Made in the USA
Columbia, SC
15 May 2018